D0706946

Mothers of Heroes, Mothers of Martyrs

Mothers of Heroes
Mothers of Martyrs

World War I and the Politics of Grief

S U Z A N N E   E V A N S

McGILL-QUEEN'S UNIVERSITY PRESS
Montreal & Kingston • London • Ithaca

© McGill-Queen's University Press 2007

ISBN 978-0-7735-3188-8

Legal deposit first quarter 2007
Bibliothèque nationale du Québec

Printed in Canada on acid-free paper.

This book has been published with the help of a grant from the Canadian Federation for the Humanities and Social Sciences, through the Aid to Scholarly Publications Programme, using funds provided by the Social Sciences and Humanities Research Council of Canada.

McGill-Queen's University Press acknowledges the support of the Canada Council for the Arts for our publishing program. We also acknowledge the financial support of the Government of Canada through the Book Publishing Industry Development Program (BPIDP) for our publishing activities.

The author gratefully acknowledges the permission granted by the Canadian War Museum to reproduce Francis Derwent Wood's *Canada's Golgotha* (AN 19710261-0797) and Charles Sims' *Sacrifice* (AN 19710262-0662). Every effort has been made to trace copyright holders and to obtain their permission for the use of copyrighted material.

Library and Archives Canada Cataloguing in Publication

Evans, Suzanne, 1957–
Mothers of martyrs, mothers of heroes : World War One and the politics of grief /
Suzanne Evans.

Includes bibliographical references and index.
ISBN 978-0-7735-3188-8

1. Mothers of soldiers—Canada—Attitudes—History—20th century.
2. Mothers of war casualties—Canada—Attitudes—History—20th century.
3. World War, 1914–1918—Casualties. 4. Mother and child—Political
aspects—Canada—History—20th century. 5. Mothers of martyrs—
Attitudes—History. 6. Mother and child—Religious aspects—History.
I. Title.

JZ6405.W66E92 2007   303.6'6   C2006-904113-X

This book was designed and typeset by studio oneonone in Sabon 10.3/14

CONTENTS

CONTENTS

ILLUSTRATIONS

PREFACE

I remember as a young mother looking at a picture of a Palestinian woman who had just lost her child to martyrdom but was smiling with a serene pride. This was the first time I had come across the phrases "mother of martyr," or "Intifada smile." How could a woman show joy over the death of her child? I could not get the question out of my mind. I later discovered that stories of women who publicly rejoice in the death of a child in support of their community have been told for centuries in the Jewish, Christian, Islamic, and Sikh traditions. There was a depth and complexity to the image of a mother of a martyr that required much more than a passing glance to be understood.

Does the image of a mother rejoicing in her child's sacrifice fit into Canadian culture? Surely not. Yet I noticed the Silver Cross mothers who, on Remembrance Day, lay a wreath on the National War Memorial on behalf of all Canadian mothers who have lost children in Canada's wars and peacekeeping missions. Who were these silent mothers, I wondered, and what history was behind their public act? They seemed pale in comparison to the mothers of the Intifada. But the Silver Cross originated in World War I. Did the mothers of my great-grandmother's generation look more like the Palestinian mothers, albeit through a different cultural lens?

As the Great War of 1914 to 1918 raged, it was often described in the religious language of sacrifice. Canadian mothers were depicted as offering the sacrifice of their sons for the sake of civilization, justice, freedom, and God. After the war they were honoured in their bereavement with the Silver Cross medal. Like the mothers of martyrs of the past, the image of the war-supportive mother had a powerful influence over public opinion and was able to draw supporters to the cause.

In this book I examine the role of mothers of martyrs in various religious traditions and compare it with the position of the mothers of Canadian soldiers during World War I. Across cultures and historical eras, in times of great stress, societies will channel all resources, even maternal love, for a common cause. The traces of this extraordinary phenomenon are now largely forgotten (or taken for granted) in Canadian society.

Whatever the mix of public pressure, opinion, and religious values, and whatever the directives of their own hearts, many people were faced with agonizing choices. Yet the focus of this study is the mothers of the fallen and how their stories have been used and modified in different historical contexts to create a martyrology. These stories, used by master propagandists to unite society in the waging of war, still maintain their grip. They retain their power to shock, appall and compel – which is precisely what all martyrologists are aiming for.

ACKNOWLEDGMENTS

Many people have helped me in the writing of this manuscript – with humour, wit, wisdom, patience, knowledge, and encouragement. I am most appreciative of these gifts, which came from many sources. This book began as a doctoral thesis under the gentle guidance of Dr Reinhard Pummer, who provided a secure and steady hand with the lightest of directional touches. I am thankful to Dr Peter Beyer, who would push and pull my ideas around and send me back to the books with more questions. Dr Eugene Rothman provided me with "Rothman's Ruthless Routine" – a plan designed to assist one through the muddy terrain of writing a book, so that in the end there is still some poise and balance in one's step. I am also most grateful to my copyeditor, Anne Marie Todkill, who has a keen eye and a sure touch.

Kathy Bergquist, Dave Murray, Mark Wilson, Dr Jonathan Vance, Dr Eric Ormsby, and Dr Laura Brandon all gave generously of their time to read, comment, and work through the logic and the concepts with me. And to all my other friends who were patient enough to listen to the subject of martyrdom for so many years, I am indebted. Gurinder Singh Mann was generous in his support for my studies in India, and I thank Bruce Cherry for sharing his expertise of every memorial and every nook, hollow, and trench of the Western Front. It has been a luxury to have had this time to study and to have had the patience of my children, Anna and Gwenlyn, to keep me focused and let me know it was all worthwhile.

The financial support that provided me with the opportunity to carry out my studies came from the University of Ottawa, the Ontario Graduate Scholarship program, the Sikh Educational Foundation of Santa Barbara, California, and the Social Sciences and Humanities Research Council Fellowship program. This support allowed me to gain experiences ranging from drinking the syrup of martyrdom in Punjab – without having to lay down my life – to gazing up at All-ward's figure of "The Spirit of Canada" dominating the Vimy memorial in France. The latter view was shared with my husband, novelist Alan Cumyn, whose research on the Great War helped produce the novel *The Sojourn*, while my perspective of similar terrain has highlighted a different story. I owe Alan my greatest thanks for his guidance and encouragement.

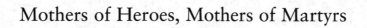

Mothers of Heroes, Mothers of Martyrs

Introduction

Heroes and Martyrs

In the 1996 Irish film *Some Mother's Son* the role of the mother of a martyr is depicted in modern terms, making realistic and compelling a mother's decision to sacrifice her son. The film tells the tale of two educated middle-class women whose sons are involved in the Irish Republican Army (IRA). The young men are imprisoned for their actions and end up going on a hunger strike with the IRA martyr Bobby Sands, with the aim of achieving "political prisoner" status for incarcerated members of the IRA.

One mother, played by Helen Mirren, decides to keep her son alive, while the other chooses to let her son die. The title of the film, from a 1969 Kinks' song about a mother's son killed in the trenches of World War I, broadens the perspective of war and points to the sad reality that the choice these mothers face is one that mothers have dealt with through more than the "troubles" of Ireland or the horrors of World War I, but in fact during times of conflict for thousands of years. This is the image of the mother of martyrs, sometimes silent and other times vocal, but in the end supporting the decision of their children to risk death in the fight for a cause held dear.

This book shines a spotlight on the role of the mother of the sacrificed within communities in conflict. Here, through their side-by-side placement, the stories of the mothers from different times, places, conflicts, and religious traditions can be seen for the first time as falling into a pattern. Mothers bereaved in times of conflict have been remembered and honoured by their communities and their leaders in proportion to the perceived need to support and develop a sense of patriotism and, if necessary, militarism. Commonly, this remembrance is kept in isolation from the stories of mothers of martyrs from other cultures and faiths. This isolation helps to promote a sense of the uniqueness of mothers who are willing to make such a sacrifice. Yet a comparative analysis dispels the notion of uniqueness: whether we remember them or not, and whether we are impressed or appalled by their stories, women in a wide variety of cultures, including Canadian culture, have commonly been called upon to accept the sacrifice of their children when their society understands itself to be in extreme danger.

Previous studies analysing the role of the mother of martyrs are few and primarily concern Palestinian mothers. In 2001–2, Nahed Habiballah, a woman's studies scholar interviewed sixteen Palestinian mothers of martyrs in Jerusalem and wrote an article on the reactions that these women had in common. Social anthropologist Julie Peteet mentions briefly the power emanating from the public role of bereaved mothers in modern-day Palestinian society in her 1993 study. The year before, Najjar and Warnock conducted an interview with the mother of the first female martyr of the Intifada (1987–91), and while Philippa Strum was conducting studies in Palestinian refugee camps during this period, she recorded a conversation she had with a mother of a martyr. Within the Canadian context, historian Jonathan Vance discusses the importance of the role of the soldier's mother in Canada's memory of World War I. According to Vance, the two characteristics that stand out in the image of the Canadian soldier of World War I are "his youth and his attachment to a mother figure."[1] He tells us that the Mother Britain school of Canadian literature was an important element in the development of the prevailing myth of the war, which emphasized Canada's devotion and fidelity to the memory of its founders. This stress on the fidelity of the son, coupled with the appeal to Canadian mothers to act as "recruitment officers" for the cause, helped to maintain enlistment. Considering the importance of the role of the mother to the war effort, it is surprising to find such a paucity of analyses of Canadian war mothers, as well as of the mothers of martyrs from other times and traditions. This book aims to begin filling that gap.

There are many stories of modern-day martyrs from around the world. Palestinians, Israelis, Iranians, Salvadorans, Sikhs, and many others have been presented as willing to die for a homeland and political rights. Since the attacks of 11 September 2001 and the subsequent wars in Afghanistan and Iraq, our media have been filled with stories of suicide bombers and martyrs. There seems to be an endless supply of young *shahid* longing for death. This is an attitude many Canadians find difficult to understand, and from the dominant perspective these would-be martyrs are just as Lucian viewed the early Christians: "A fanatical species enamored of death who ran to the cruelest tortures as to a feast."[2]

Part of the reason we find it so challenging to understand a desire for martyrdom is that we have a difficult time producing heroes, let alone martyrs, in Canada. In a recent book entitled *Great Questions of Canada*, Charlotte Gray and Peter Newman answer the question, "Where have all the heroes gone?" Their responses deal with both the emotional and the geographical makeup of Canadian society. Newman quips, "If God had meant us to be heroic, he wouldn't have made us Canadians."[3] He backs up this statement with a fact that says as much about Canadian self-deprecation as it does about how Canadians view their heroes: "Ottawa has actually struck three Canadian medals for bravery – our own versions of the Victoria Cross, the Star of Military Valour and the Medal of Military Valour," but, he adds dryly, "none has ever been awarded."[4] These medals, although more than a decade old, are awarded only during wartime. Thus, the lack of recipients says nothing of Canadian bravery and everything of the state of relative peace in which Canadians live.

Charlotte Gray explains that it is not just that we have "no idol industry here."[5] The reason "we do heroes badly" is that we have a stronger understanding of our regions than of our nation. But, for much of English Canada, World War I reconfigured our sense of regions and made us look more toward the nation for our heroes. During that period we, too, exhibited a kind of fervour – some might call it madness or fanaticism – that parallels the structure and intensity of the stories of martyrs who have died for causes in other lands. Alan Young, writing of the mythology of heroic sacrifice during World War I in Canada, compares the "high diction," or, as Bertrand Russell called it, "the foul literature of glory" with "the rhetoric of martyrdom and sacrifice employed by Muslim fundamentalists in the war between Iran and Iraq."[6] The sentiment is widespread within Canada today that when Muslims (or almost any explicitly religious group) speak of martyrs and sacrifice, the actors are "fundamentalists." Just as for the Romans viewing the early Christians, it is the *other*, willing to die for a cause, who is touched with fanaticism. But the literature of World War I is full of examples of supportive stories of noble Canadian mothers willing to sacrifice their heroic sons for an Empire and its Motherland.

Much of this literature, as well as the mood of the time, has been forgotten – but traces remain. In the main lobby of the House of Commons in Ottawa, for example, are two quotations carved into the walls on either side of a statue of Lieutenant-Colonel Baker, the only member of parliament to be killed in World War I. One quotation is well known and is repeated annually in a ritual of remembrance:

> To you from failing hands we throw
> The torch; be yours to hold it high.
> If ye break faith with us who die
> We shall not sleep, though poppies blow
> In Flanders fields.

These words, written by the Canadian soldier-poet John McCrae, have gained fame far beyond Canada's borders and have done a great deal to shape the remembrance of the war. The other quotation comes from a much older source, 2 Maccabees 6:31: "And thus this man died, leaving his death for an example of a noble courage, and a memorial of virtue, not only unto young men, but unto all the nation."

6

The man referred to is Eleazar, who was not a typical soldier-hero, for he was old and feeble. His heroism lay in the strength and loyalty of his faith to his God and his community. In the many stories of the Maccabean martyrs, Eleazar is portrayed as the first to be killed. His example of steadfastness and willingness to die for a cause was followed by another, involving a family of seven brothers whose mother has long been known as "the Maccabean mother." She encouraged her seven sons to stand firm in their belief in the face of certain death and watched as each one was slowly tortured to death. The word "macabre," from the medieval expression *danse Macabré*, in turn a corruption of Maccabaeus, indicates how the horror of this story has been kept alive in language.

Since this depiction of the Maccabean mother, many other mother-of-martyr figures have been included in martyrologies and are remembered for their sacrifice. In the case of Iranian mothers during the Iran – Iraq war and of Palestinian mothers of martyrs of the Intifada, this remembrance has taken the form of official recognition and remuneration. Canadian women, also, are offered governmental recognition for their maternal sacrifice. The Memorial Cross, better known as the Silver Cross, was first struck on 1 December 1919 as a "memento of personal loss and sacrifice on the part of the mother and widow of a sailor or soldier of Canada or Newfoundland who laid down his life for his country during World War One."[7] Although, officially, widows are eligible for this award, it is the bereaved mothers who are its most famous recipients. This is especially evident each year on 11 November when the "Silver Cross Mother" lays a wreath at the National War Memorial in Ottawa in the name of all Canadian women who have lost children in war, and more recently, in efforts for peace.

Yet, despite the similarly heroic status of the Maccabean mother and the Silver Cross mother, it seems quite a stretch to equate these two roles. After all, we are a country that produces soldiers, not martyrs, to fight in our wars. Nevertheless, the parallel is closer than we might first imagine. Both mothers of martyrs and Silver Cross mothers share an essential characteristic in their acceptance of the necessity to offer their children for sacrifice. This acceptance is the truly compelling and powerful aspect of the story, for if the mother, of all people, can support the giving of her child's life to a cause, then not only must that cause be of ultimate worth, but it would be shameful for anyone else to give less. This trait of acceptance reaches its pinnacle in her manner of mourning – for she must accept her son's death quietly when it comes – whether during the war so as not to damage the morale of others, or after the war so as not to damage the peace or amnesty that the state then supports.

The ability of the mother to influence and recruit others to her cause rests heavily on a particular understanding of the strength of a mother's love for her child. The nature of parental love as expressed in different cultures and historical periods has provided fertile ground for debate. Historical examples of child sacrifice and abandonment have been taken as indicating that the feeling, be it called "mother love," "nature," or "instinct," is in fact a product of culture and historical accident. However, Shari Thurer argues in *The Myths of Motherhood: How Culture Reinvents the Good Mother* that those examples of child neglect or infanticide point to societal misogyny as their cause rather than a lack of caring.[8] She believes that mother love is a "stubborn, hardy emotion," for "attachment to one's children is usual in ordinary, decent circumstances. Any human being in his or her right mind, when presented with a helpless infant, will tend to provide for its care rather than kill it, eat it, or ignore it. Mother love, though it is vulnerable to environmental manipulation, seems to be a fact."[9]

As the title of Thurer's book suggests, different cultures at different times can augment or diminish the "fact" of mother love. The image we now have of the mother in much of the Western world bloomed in the modern era. With the Industrial Revolution, sex roles became exaggerated as men moved from home-based industries into factories and women remained at home. The idea of the "noble" mother presiding over the hearth and doting over her children as the centre and meaning of her life reached a high point during the Victorian era and held sway into the early twentieth century and World War I. Many "how-to" books of conduct, for instance, were published during the Victorian era, designed to teach women how to accomplish the task of being a noble mother. The mothers of soldiers would have been brought up with these ideas. An often reprinted (1833–55) and popular example was *The Mother at Home: or, The Principles of Maternal Duty* by Rev. John S.C. Abbott. This book, like others of its kind, attempted to reconcile Christian doctrine with the everyday life of a mother. Another book, by Rev. Charles B. Hadduck, took this task even more seriously and attempted, as its title suggests, to educate mothers on how to prepare their children for life in heaven: *Christian Education: Containing Valuable Practical Suggestions in the Training of Children for Usefulness and Heaven* (n.d.).

Another book, H.M. Wodson's *Private Warwick: Musings of a Canuck in Khaki*, although written in Canada as war propaganda, provides an image of an English mother who reflects a popular role model of the time. Hoping to instil a sense of honour and bravery, she brings up her son with stories of how her father had fought and died for England in the Crimean War.

American literature also had a strong influence on Canadian popular culture, and books dealing with the Civil War were no exception. Dr L.P. Brockett, a medical doctor who tended the wounded during the war, collected stories from the people he met and published them in what became well-known books. His first, *The Camp, the Battlefield and the Hospital* (1866) was dedicated in part to the women who freely gave their male relatives to preserve their nation. He included a story of a "Spartan mother," Rachel Somers, who after seeing her husband and two older sons die, offered her youngest, sixteen year-old Tom, saying "I'd give all – all I've got." Brockett's next book, *Women's Work in the Civil War: A Record of the Heroism, Patriotism and Patience of Women in the Civil War* (1867) carried on with the Spartan mother's theme of showing just how much a woman could give.

The platform that history provided the mothers of World War I ensured that their stories of sacrifice would be told often and widely. Although war exaggerates the differences between the spheres of men and women, the passion for this kind of tale would eventually wane as the gap between the roles of mothers and fathers lessened. Yet, as I write, two American mothers of fallen soldiers of the Iraq war are publicly trying to influence their country's conduct: Cindy Sheehan by protesting American involvement in Iraq and Linda Ryan by supporting it – both in the name of their fallen sons.

The Canadian sources I have used to elucidate the image of the mothers in World War I and the mood of their times include newspapers and journals such as the *Winnipeg Free Press*, the *Evening Tribune* (Winnipeg), the *Ottawa Citizen*, the *Globe* (Toronto), *Saturday Night* (Toronto) and *Everywoman's World* (Toronto), a journal geared toward educated, middle-class women. English speakers were most supportive of the war because of their close ties to England. From the beginning of the war in August 1914, the Canadian press presented it as a battle for the British Empire. Most of the first battalion to be raised in Canada, the Princess Patricia's Canadian Light Infantry, was made up of men born in England. It is not surprising that supportive stories in English of noble mothers willing to sacrifice their heroic sons for an imperial "mother" land were prevalent at the time.

Long before Canada was even part of the Empire, stories of mothers of martyrs were being created in other parts of the world. Chapter I presents a selection of archetypal tales from Jewish, Christian, Islamic, and Sikh traditions: that of the Maccabean mother of seven sons; Mary, mother of Jesus; Fatima, mother of Husayn; and Mata Gujari, grandmother of Zorawar Singh and Fateh Singh. It is necessary to clarify the archetypal character of the mother of the sacrificed in order to see, in chapter 3, how the Silver Cross mother can be described in terms of this image. The first chapter also examines how stories of sacrificing mothers were reused in their own traditions, serving to shape the attitudes of future generations of mothers, martyrs, and their audiences. As well, chapter 1 shows how more recent communities compensated mothers of martyrs not only by publicly honouring them and repeating their tales, but also through financial support.

Chapter 2 examines images of sacrifice in World War I and how they provided a way for the public to understand the value of the war. Even though the term "martyr" was not commonly applied, some influential figures such as the Bishop of London, Arthur Foley Winnington-Ingram, referred to the soldiers this way. The idea of the soldier as sacrificial offering was presented in other forms as well. I take the "language" of sacrifice as being expressed in the Canadian War Memorial Fund Art Collection, the cartoons of Louis Raemaekers, newspaper articles, and the propaganda of the time – notably in the martyrology of Edith Cavell and the tale of the crucified Canadian. The atrocity stories of the war functioned, as in older martyrologies, to compel individuals to support the weak and victimized not only by uniting in fear for their own lives, but also by presenting the enemy in terms of ultimate evil. When the depravity of the enemy is construed as equal to that of the devil, the tenor of a conflict changes. It becomes a cosmic battle of good against evil, a story of war and propaganda over which a religious veil has been draped.

After setting the stage of the times in chapter 2, I present the stories of mothers of soldiers in chapter 3. Like the mothers of martyrs, the supportive mothers of World War I held the position of honorary recruitment officers. Although no one has previously analysed the role of these mothers, I will draw on the ideas of Nicoletta Gullace (1997), who has examined the recruitment actions of the White Feather campaigners during the war. She discusses the tactics of the White Feather women in trying to shame men into joining the army. Notions of honour and of shame are also embedded in the stories of mothers' relationships with their sons in both the martyrologies discussed in chapter 1 and in the wartime tales. Like mothers of martyrs, mothers of soldiers received forms of compensation such as the Silver Cross medal, which served both to honour them and recognize their loss as well to help them to maintain their connection to and support for the state.

The final chapters examine how the mothers of the sacrificed have been depicted and remembered since the Great War. Chapter 4 looks at how the role of the mother in the war was commemorated in monuments and rituals. One of the most impressive images of a mourning mother is that of "The Spirit of Canada" or, as she is also known, "Mother Canada,"[10] the largest statue of the Vimy Ridge Memorial. This chapter analyses not only the artwork of the Vimy Ridge Memorial but also that of the Memorial Chapel of the Peace Tower on Parliament Hill in Ottawa. As well, it includes a discussion of the Vimy Pilgrimage in 1936 and the development of the rituals of Remembrance Day.

The final chapter looks at the traditional role of the mourning mother in relation to the burial of the dead and how that role was affected by the institution of the Imperial War Graves Commission

(IWGC), which was responsible for the design and maintenance of the graves of over one million Commonwealth soldiers. It also examines the evolution of the Silver Cross mother from the mother of a wartime soldier to the mother of a peacekeeper.

An important principle that guided the actions of the IWGC was that the structures and words used in war cemeteries would promote peace among nations. The atrocity stories that had such currency during the war, together with the feelings of revenge that they incited, were to be silenced in the name of amnesty and peace. Nicole Loraux's work (1998) on the Amnesty of Athens in 403 BCE describes amnesty as a ban on the recollection of misfortune to be used as an exit from the endless cycle of retaliation for past wrongs. Her theory of the control in ancient Athens over the mothers' mourning of their slain sons provides guidance for an analysis of the IWGC and the mothers of peacekeepers. No character more poignantly recalls sacrifice than the mother. How she fulfills her role reflects how a society balances conflicting desires for memory – honouring the slain –and for amnesty – safeguarding the future.

Those mothers of wartime who willingly sacrificed their sons for the cause presented a difficult image in the aftermath of World War I, when "the war to end all war" was understood with an irony and cynicism that persists to this day. They appear, to use the expression of the battlefield, "over the top." Although this phrase has come to mean "excessive" or "crazy," during the war it signified an act of war that all who fought in the trenches knew. To make an attack, the troops, with utmost bravery, had to hoist themselves over the wall of sandbags at the front of the trenches, often to face a murderous barrage of machine-gun fire. Gradually for the soldiers, and subsequently for the mothers and others back home, the consistent horror of this kind of warfare became clear. The phrase that had started off as "over the top and the best of luck" was shortened in the obvious absence of luck and the growing appearance of insanity. But what now looks extreme was once seen as a duty to secure a free and just civilization. The stories of mothers willing to sacrifice their sons challenge us to understand the thinking of many of our predecessors in Canada, as well as of those from other cultures and times, and their reasons for going "over the top." This book thus offers a challenge to remember our own history so that we might better understand what moves us and others to war. But remembrance is a two-edged sword, and sometimes the path to peace requires a willingness to forget.

Chapter 1

The Seeds of the Martyrs
Stories of Jewish, Christian, Islamic,
and Sikh Mothers of Martyrs

S tories of martyrs have changed considerably through the centuries, to the point where nowadays suicide or homicide bombers
are called martyrs by some. Such cases raise questions about the
line between suicide, an act generally unacceptable in religious traditions, and martyrdom; between desiring to kill others and accepting
death for oneself; and between dying for land and dying for God.
Daniel Boyarin, in his book *Dying for God,* "propose[s] that we think
of martyrdom as a 'discourse,' as a practice of dying for God and of
talking about it, a discourse that changes and develops over time."[1]
Like scholars before him, he looks to the origins of the concept of martyrdom in order to arrive at a satisfactory definition.

Boyarin's interest lies with the Jewish and Christian traditions, as
does that of W.H.C. Frend, who, since the publication of his classic,
Martyrdom and Persecution in the Early Church in 1965 has been a
voice to contend with on this topic. Frend argues that martyrdom
began with Judaism, which provided a prototype of the concept later
developed in Christianity.[2] Writing thirty years after Frend, Glen Bowersock locates the origins of martyrdom within the Roman cultural
heritage of early Christianity.[3] Boyarin agrees that martyrdom began

during this period, but within Judaism and Christianity. The defining characteristic of true martyrs is, for Boyarin, that they will "suffer torture and death because they are passionately in love with God."[4] Although most martyrologies draw on the power of the divine to ground the validity of their cause, not all have God written into them. Bobby Sands, for example, the imprisoned Irish republican who died on hunger strike in 1981 in The Maze, was a political martyr. Other scholars of martyrdom have referred to the quality Boyarin is concerned with as "conviction" and oppose it to "compromise," that attribute held dear in liberal democracies – which do not provide the ground upon which martyrs grow. It is difficult to find agreement on the essential characteristics of a martyr, but Boyarin's description of martyrdom as a discourse that changes through time puts the interpretive stress on the story and the storyteller. If a tale of a hero is taken up by a community, repeated, and embellished, and its protagonist is given the status and label of "martyr," it becomes a martyrology to those people and to the teller of the tale, the martyrologist.

It may be that some heroes were not granted martyr status until long after their death, when for whatever reason the power of their stories was needed to strengthen community pride and cement religious loyalties. Civic leaders now as in the past recognize the usefulness of martyrs in the promotion of causes. Similarly, martyrologists find ways of adapting the ancient format to new scenarios and redrawing lines around issues such as suicide and homicide. For the purpose of this book I take as martyrologies stories of those individuals who are *called* martyrs by their followers. These stories are meant to influence the way people think. In this respect I understand them to be a form of propaganda, for they are designed not only to make believers of their audiences, but also to inspire them to support and promote the cause with all their resources, including their lives. Tertullian, the third-century Christian, was explicit about this function of a martyrology when he famously stated that the blood of martyrs is the "seed" of Christianity.

From ancient times in Israel the Maccabean martyrs were written about and their stories given dramatic readings, transcribed, and adapted to new situations. The story of the Christian martyrs of Lyon of 177 CE was incorporated into letters and sent to far-away lands. Posters produced from photographs of Palestinian martyrs of the Intifadas are pasted on the buildings of refugee camps, and videos record their last words. Paintings of renowned Sikh martyrs undergoing torture adorn gurdwaras around the world.

It is evident in the early martyrologies that the desire to communicate with God is an important part of the tale. The act of proving one's worth to God, to die in his name, was based on the belief that God was watching, listening, and being sustained by the martyr's love.[5] In more recent martyrologies, however, few words are directed to the attention of the divine. The story is meant to propagate the message, for the benefit of friends and foes alike, that the martyr's cause is that of truth and justice.

In cases where the tale includes the figure of the mother of a martyr, she is at times the one who bears witness to her child's convictions. At other times she is a silent but prominent character. Either way, her presence heightens the poignancy of the story, making it an even more compelling tale to spread far and wide. But how does the mother-of-martyr story work in various religious traditions? What sort of propaganda techniques have martyrologists used over the ages? Why do so many of these stories involve atrocities? Why are so many extremely similar in detail and tone? What is their role in ensuring that messages from history are kept alive, and that old boundaries of gender and nationality are remembered and, in some cases, strengthened?

All of the stories of mothers of martyrs come from patriarchal societies in which women were or are viewed as needing protection. Their message is in large part directed at those members of society who would defend the "weakest" in the group. It is aimed at jolting the audience out of complacency by the unexpected example of a heroic woman. In *Propaganda and Persuasion*,[6] Jowett and O'Donnell note the necessity of knowing the target audience of propaganda, that group of people who will be most useful if they respond favourably to the message. In this case the target group is the men whose masculinity is challenged by the courage shown by women.

The poignancy of the mother-of-martyr figure lies in the bond between mother and child, which through time and across cultures has often been depicted as the strongest form of human love. L.M. Montgomery, whose journals are a great source of information about life and attitudes in Canada during the early twentieth century, speaks to this bond as she reconsiders stories of martyrs after the birth of her first son in 1912:

> Motherhood is a revelation from God. In reading tales of
> the martyrs I have shuddered with horror – and been lost in
> wonder. How, for instance, could any human being face
> the prospect of death at the stake for his religion? I knew I
> could never do it. I would recant anything in the face of
> such a hideous threat. *Nothing*, I thought, could fortify me
> to endure it. And now – I know that for the sake of my child
> I could and would undergo the most dreadful suffering which
> one human being could inflict on another. To save my child's
> life I would go to the stake a hundred times over.[7]

The mother-of-martyr image turns this view of motherhood on its head. Therein lies its power to shock and, the martyrologist hopes, to force the question, "What is this cause that could make a mother agree to give over her child?" The image of a parent sacrificing a child is so powerful that it is not surprising it should become a touchstone, a measure of love and devotion to a cause and to the divine.

Stories of child sacrifice have a long history. Through many times and cultures and during episodes of great duress people have offered their gods their most valuable possessions, assuming that the divine beings will agree with their assessment of value and reply with gifts of equal significance. Joyce Salisbury gives a summary of child sacrifice in the ancient Mediterranean world. Biblical descriptions dating from the ninth century BCE tell of the battle between the Moabites and the Israelites. When the king of Moab saw that he was losing the battle, "he took his firstborn son who was to succeed him, and offered him as a burnt-offering on the wall" (2 Kings 3:27). Salisbury describes a site near Carthage where archaeologists found a cemetery containing approximately 20,000 urns holding the remains of children and ani-mals who had been sacrificed to the gods. "This still sad space, which is filled with layers of rubble, vividly expresses the fears of ancient par-ents who responded to their deep anxiety about the future by sacrific-ing their children."[8] Many, including Eusebius, Tertullian, Augustine and Plutarch, have written about this infamous sacrificial ground. Plutarch described how those who had no children would buy them from poor people to be sacrificed. The mothers were not allowed to "utter a single moan or let fall a single tear."[9] Grief was taken to be a bad omen that destroyed the positive effect of the sacrifice. Plutarch explains that tears would cause forfeiture of the money paid for the child, and that the child would be sacrificed nevertheless.

This analysis of martyrologies begins with the Abrahamic tradi-tions, within which the touchstone case of child sacrifice is that of Abraham and his son Isaac. In the Genesis story Abraham does not say a word to object to the divine request to make a burnt offering of his son. For his unquestioning obedience he, who had such trouble fathering children, is granted the blessing of offspring "as numerous as the stars of heaven and as the sand that is on the seashore" (Gen. 22:17). In the Koranic version of this story, Abraham tells his son Ish-mael that he had a dream that he was sacrificing him and asks for his son's thoughts on the matter. The boy responds, with a calmness not found in most children, that Abraham should do as God wills and that he hoped his father would be strong. In this version of the story both father and son go through the initial stages of the sacrificial rite with full knowledge of who the intended victim is. As in the Bible, obedi-ence is rewarded.

Following in the footsteps of Abraham is the Maccabean mother of seven sons. The oldest surviving version of her story is in 2 Maccabees. When exactly the book was written is unknown, but it is thought to have been sometime during the late first to early second century BCE. The mother and her seven sons were arrested and brought in front of King Antiochus, who demanded that they eat pork. Upon their refusal, the mother was forced to witness the killing of all her sons. Her first son had his tongue cut out, was scalped, mutilated, and roasted. The second was scalped and tortured. The third, fourth, fifth, and sixth were tortured in ways not told and the youngest underwent tortures described only as worse than the others. The mother watched all of this and, in the end, died.

The tortures that the boys endured were horrific, but the fact that their mother was forced to watch makes it all the worse. The details of what the boys went through are meant to be telling of the character of the pagans and the Jews. The king and, by extension, those who follow him are evil and no better than butchers; worse, they are weak for they cannot even control unarmed boys. In contrast, the boys and their mother are strong and loyal to their God. When it came time for the youngest of the Maccabeans to step up, the king offered him not only life but riches if he renounced "the ways of his ancestors" (2 Macc. 7:24). The mother counselled him not to accept the offer, relying on her influence as his mother and the respect that he owed her to convince him to die for his God.

The mother's story was repeated with variations many times after this, notably in 4 Maccabees, the Pesiqta Rabbati (43), Babylonian Talmud (b. Git. 57b), and the Midrash Lamentations (1:16). In the last two of these the mother's plight is compared with that of Abraham. This comparison would likely have been drawn by the story's audience anyway, but by making it explicit the authors provide a historical frame that gives the mother's story greater value. Abraham's sacrifice was the epitome of tales depicting the passion a parent has for a child and the willingness of the parent to override that passion in the name of God. Hence the allusion to Abraham is a potent one. But the Maccabean mother achieves an even greater pathos from the comparison: she loses not just one son, but seven; there is no last-minute reprieve; and the strength she needs does not come naturally, for she is not a man.[10]

For these reasons it is not surprising that the stunning image of the sacrificing mother endured in future stories. But other features of the story have added to its popularity and influence. The author of 2 Maccabees did his best stylistically to ensure a long life and a wide audience for his book. He shortened the original story and eliminated the "flood of statistics" (2 Macc. 2:24) from a five-volume text to make his book accessible and entertaining. He saw himself not as the master builder of this history but as the decorator, aiming for brevity. In another metaphor, appealing to those who know the labour of cooking, he confessed the sweat and loss of sleep he endured in the task of preparing this "banquet" for the benefit of others.

2 Maccabees is categorized by some as a "pathetic" history that evokes feeling through sensational language and by presenting women, appreciated for their emotional natures, in starring roles.[11] It has also been called a "tragic history," a common genre in the Greek world that blurred the distinction between the truth of history and the fabulous nature of tragedy.[12] As Robert Doran points out in *Temple Propaganda*, Aristotle's separation of history and tragedy was an "aberration, not the norm."[13] Even the historians Herodotus and Thucydides relied on being able to draw on their audience's emotions, although they seldom admitted as much. The appeal to emotion had a moral purpose. Both histories and tragedies created their version of events to move the audience in directions believed to be worthy.

⸺⸺

Just as Abraham's story had lent historic and mythical status to that of the Maccabean mother, so too did reference to her courage augment the significance of future stories. Over time the Maccabean mother became known as the "joyful mother of children," and it was this reference to her joy that was repeated in the story of the Hebrew chronicles of Solomon bar Simson from the First Crusade.[14]

One of the most dramatic scenes from Solomon bar Simson's chronicle is that of Rachel and her children. When the Christian Crusaders were approaching her city of Mainz to rid it of Jews through either murder or conversion, this young mother killed her four children in a manner that would make it clear that they had been sacrificed, not murdered. She caught the blood of her eldest, Isaac, in her sleeve "according to the practice in the ancient Temple sacrificial rite" and ensured that the knife she used to slit the throats of her two daughters, Bella and Madrona, had no nicks in it that would have invalidated the sacrifice.[15] Her youngest, Aaron, seeing what was happening, begged his mother not to kill him and hid from her. She found him, "drew him out by his feet from under the box where he had hidden and slaughtered him before the Exalted and Lofty God."[16] Rachel was afterwards killed by the Crusaders. "Thus she died together with her four children, just as did that other righteous woman with her seven sons, and about them it is written: 'The mother of the sons rejoices.'"[17]

It is difficult to believe that joy could be associated in any way with these stories. But, as we have seen, the boundary between history and tragedy is permeable. The authors are trying to sway our reason by way of our emotions, to a moral end. By adding "joy" to the story, they instruct us on how we should feel, just as the parents in Plutarch's account are taught not to shed a tear. Having said this, it is also possible to see joy in Rachel's relief that, even if she is not able to provide a faithful Jewish life for her children, she is at least able to control their death and save them from an unknown fate at the hands of the marauding Christians.[18] More than this, she is able to give their death a purpose just as the Maccabean mother had done.

——⊷∘⊶——

I have followed Abraham's story as it was remembered in 2 Maccabees and then considered how the Maccabean mother was invoked in the story of Rachel during the Crusades. Now I will trace the influence of the Maccabean martyrology in Christianity. The Books of the Maccabees were carried to Palestine by the Christians.[19] The early Christians were clearly impressed by the martyrs in these stories, and some Christian narratives, such as that of the Martyrs of Lyon, include characters modelled after the Maccabean martyrs. For example, like Razis in 2 Maccabees, Vettius Epagathus, one of the Christian martyrs of Lyon (177 CE), defied the rule of the tyrant: the martyrs in both stories disregard the pain of torture and in so doing are able to defeat the strength of the tyrant. W.H.C. Frend takes these similarities as evidence that the earlier book is a source for the Christian martyrology. Versions of the Maccabean martyrology are included in the work of many Christian authors, including John Chrysostom, Origen, Cyprian, Augustine, and Gregory of Nazianzus.[20]

The Church Father, Origen (ca. 185–ca. 254) provides an interesting example of a Christian reference to the Maccabeans. In his *Prayer and Exhortation to Martyrdom*, written in 235 CE to two friends awaiting death in prison, he used the story of Eleazar and the seven brothers to exemplify the ultimate models of martyrdom. He never acknowledged a difference of religious traditions, but in summation said merely: "What dead person could be more deserving of praise than he who of his own choice elected to die for his religion?"[21] The historical details of the religion of the martyrs may have been left aside, but the story of the martyrs lived on. The ancient image provided a way to understand the bitter days. If a story is repeated often enough, people will begin to believe it; what is more important, they will believe it provides an admirable model to follow.

Although the image of the Maccabean mother lived on in Christianity, the most famous mother of a martyr in that tradition, Mary, did not carry joyfulness in her role. In this she was like Fatima, the mother of Husayn and daughter of the Prophet Mohammad.

Both Fatima and Mary stand in contrast to the Maccabean mother with respect to the position they hold in their traditions. Mary, "The Queen of Heaven," and Fatima, "The Shining One," are the immaculate female members of a holy family. They differ from the Maccabean mother in another fundamental way: they are mothers who express an intense and timeless sorrow at the death of their sons.[22] Mary is called "The Mother of Sorrows," while Fatima lives in the "House of Sorrows" in Paradise, continuously weeping until the Day of Judgment, when her son's murderers will come to justice. Devastating sadness envelops their characters to such an extent that the joy written into the story of the Maccabean mother is for the most part overshadowed. In both Christianity and Islam a sense of joy is instead attributed directly to the martyrs. The strength of Mary and Fatima is expressed not with a defiant joy but in their acceptance of the responsibility of raising a child who will be sacrificed. Living through this experience gives them the status for which they are respected as emotional confidantes and intercessors.

Before the Middle Ages, Mary did not have a significant inspirational role in Christianity. For this reason I will move quickly through the early centuries of the tradition, examining Mary's image as the mother of the sacrificed before discussing her later dramatization. In Christian scriptures, Mary is quiet on the subject of her son's death. She provides a model of gentle acceptance, not revolutionary zeal. John's is the only Gospel in which Mary is present at the Cross while Jesus is dying. She does not speak, but is spoken to by Jesus, who entrusts her to John the Baptist's care, and John to her care. Even though she is silent, her presence implies her acceptance of the sacrifice of her son. It is in this aspect that she gains fame in the Middle Ages as the Mater Dolorosa and is visualized as the *pietà*.

Mary was part of a new cult that set out to reconfigure family relationships. Unlike the Jewish mother of martyrs, in early Christianity Mary's status was not guaranteed simply because she was Jesus' mother. The new Christian family was made up of philosophical brothers and sisters. The story of the Martyrs of Lyon, for example, stressed the brotherhood between the martyrs. A reference to the Maccabean mother was included, however, indicating that Christian authors knew this story would still have the power to influence their audience by virtue of its personal intensity. The story was well known and would have provided the Christian martyrology with both a narrative structure and an historical precedent, thus lending greater authority to the cause.

The Virgin Mother also appears in the story of the Martyrs of Lyon, likely as a reference to both Mary and the Church. She has the role of a mother who had lost her children and then found them again. These lost or "stillborn"[23] children are those who had been members of the Church but then shied away from declaring their faith when the Christians were captured. Unlike the Maccabean mother, the Virgin Mother is not responsible for encouraging these people to return to her and their faith. That role is taken by the martyrs, who are inspired by the "infinite mercy of Christ"[24] during their imprisonment in the summer of 177 CE.

Joyce Salisbury argues that by the time of Perpetua's martyrdom in 202 CE, the Christian ideal of philosophical kinship had been embraced by the community to the extent that "the time of the

Maccabean mother was over; martyrdom was a matter of private conscience, not family ties."[25] Yet, as we know, the importance of family rebounded; the image of mother Mary became increasingly popular, and her status as the mother of the sacrificed son grew.

It was not until the end of the eleventh century that the legendary Mary adopted the role of Mater Dolorosa in Italy, France, England, the Netherlands, and Spain. She gained a following among the cloistered Christians in the twelfth century. The *pietà* or "Image of Pity" was introduced in early fourteenth century sculpture and in paintings of the fifteenth century.[26] Another very significant presentation of Mary by this time was as an intercessor. Alongside her son she was seen to appeal to God on behalf of petitioners. Jesus attains this position through the offering of his blood, while Mary achieves her status as intercessor through the offering of the milk from her breast – a sign of the sacrifice she has made for the Christian community.[27]

By the end of the Middle Ages, Mary had been talked about, dramatized, painted, and sculpted so often and so widely that she had taken hold in the imaginations of those who lived beyond the cloisters.[28] During the years of the Crusades, warriors and pilgrims travelled to the birthplace of Christianity and returned to European countries with an invigorated faith informed by Mediterranean influences, including expressive mourning practices.[29] It was at this time that the cult of the Mater Dolorosa started to spread through Europe. The cult was promoted by the Franciscans, who by adding drama and image to the Passion story circumvented the problem of appealing to audiences who did not speak Latin, the language of the Church. Seeing an enactment of the Passion must have been an intense experience for those who could not afford the trip to the Holy Land. The techniques used in the presentation of the dramas were borrowed from existing forms of dramatic entertainment. As William Tydeman writes in his essay on medieval English theatre, "dialogue [was] racy, earthy and often declamatory, comedy [was] prominent and often scabrous."[30] In this broadly appealing manner the plays were able to bring home the Christian teachings. Warner puts it in modern terms: "The Stations of the Cross were a cycle of meditations that operated as satellite television of some great international event does now: it reported the drama of Christ's sufferings at first hand."[31] The mother–son relationship came to be highlighted, for "The Virgin was the instrument mediating bafflement at the mystery of the Redemption into emotional understanding. She made the sacrifice on Golgotha seem real, for she focused human feeling in a comprehensible and accessible way."[32]

The earliest liturgical drama extant comes from Britain, although it probably originated on the Continent.[33] The plays were sponsored and acted by guilds, each of which was responsible for specific episodes.[34] The medieval dramas have been described as "Corpus Christi or craft cycles, moralities and moral interludes, saint plays, miracle plays," but Tydeman argues that these classifications are arbitrary and should not obscure what the plays have in common: their "evangelizing purpose."[35] He describes the authors' primary intent as "to instruct the populace in those truths essential for their salvation by rendering them accessible, and to alert men and women to the cosmic battles being waged over the fate of their own immortal and individual souls."[36] In carrying out their aim, the authors of these plays exhibited what Tydeman views as a great "understanding of what popular taste will accept," even for those who did not have much faith in Christian doctrine.[37]

Elizabeth Witt's comprehensive study, *Contrary Marys in Medieval English and French Drama*, summarizes the presentation of Mary's character at the points where she enters the stories in the English cycle dramas and the French Passion plays. In the English plays there is a section in the Annunciation and Incarnation scene where Mary obediently accepts the will of God.[38] Mary's biggest scene is at the foot of the Cross, although she is less vocal in this scene than in the French versions of the drama.[39] In all versions she is disconsolate, wishing that she would die before her son, for she cannot stand the pain of seeing his beautiful body tortured on the Cross. In Christ's death and burial scene in the York Cycle, Mary cries "Allas, sone, sorowe and site, / That me were closed in clay! / A swerde of sorowe me smite, / To dede I were done this day!"[40] Mary's speech here, as in much of the poetry of the time, can be described as a form of complaint literature of the laments of bereaved mothers.[41] Both Jesus and John in the York cycle admonish Mary to stop crying, for it will not change anything.

In spite of the tears of the Mater Dolorosa role and the pathos inspired by the *pietà* image, some of the joy of the Maccabean mother is written into Mary's character in medieval drama. In the resurrection and ascension scenes, Mary perceives that her pain has been worth while and finds happiness in Jesus' ascent to heaven.[42] But the sorrow of Mary's character is tempered less by this joy, which is to be shared by all people, than by the strength of her acceptance of Christ's role in history. This strength, however, does not translate into power within the Holy Family or function as a model of strength for women. Witt argues that the power that Mary's character took on in popular culture, evidenced by the large number of miracles attributed to her, was undermined in the English plays, which exclude all those stories in which Mary acts on her own volition.[43] Witt believes that "by manipulating the image of the Virgin Mary, the primary official role model prescribed for women, the church and by extension the dramatists could effectively marginalize women."[44] At the same time, Mary held sway outside the Church.

Mary has gone through many character changes through the years in the places she has been known. In Victorian England she presented an appealing image to many women from different faiths and classes. This coming together in respect for Mary was possible "because the age itself venerated motherhood."[45] Paul Fussell, a noted World War I historian, argues that the canonization of motherhood during Queen Victoria's reign was tied to a rejuvenation of courtly ideals, which held that "one's attitude towards one's mother should be conspicuously chivalric, if not reverential."[46] This sentimentality grew in opposition to the "utilitarianism, industrialization, materialism, agnosticism and socialism" of the times.[47] It was during Victoria's "reign that it became popular to domesticate Britannia, formerly imagined as a rather threatening classical warrior, by designating her 'Mother Britain.'"[48] It was of course in defence of Mother Britain and all of civilization that Canadian soldiers would, before long, be called to sacrifice their lives.

Just as Mary has provided a model for many Christians, Fatima has done the same for many Muslims. In this section I will focus on the legends, dramatizations, and developments of Fatima's story through the Middle Ages and, much later, in the war between Iran and Iraq.

Fatima, as in some of the medieval stories of Mary, had foreknowledge of her son's death. In a story written in the tenth century by Ibn Qawlawayh, the angel Gabriel was sent by God to tell the Prophet Mohammed that his daughter Fatima would have a child who would be killed by the community after the Prophet had died.[49] The Prophet repeated twice that he had no need of such a child, until Gabriel told him that the leadership of the community would remain with the progeny of that child. The Prophet then accepted the news and told Fatima, who responded just as her father had done.[50] Thus she had to live with the painful anticipation of her son's death, even before his birth.

One of the many ways in Islamic legend in which Fatima has been compared with Mary concerns the birth of their sons. While Fatima gave birth through her left thigh, Mary did the same through her right thigh.[51] There are many such delightful tales of Fatima, which, as in Mary's case, give colour to the sparse historical information available. One such tale concerns Fatima's legendary sadness over her father's death. She was said to have cried so much that she disturbed her neighbours and was asked to go to the graveyard at night so that her weeping would not keep people awake.[52] Her strong association with her father is alluded to in one of her names, Umm Abiha, "mother of her father." There are a few possible explanations for this title, most of which deal with the close association between the cults of Mary and Fatima; thus it may be a counterpart to Mary's title, "Mother of God."[53] She is also called al-Muhaddatha because, like Mary, the angels told her she was chosen among women and purified by God.[54]

Unlike any other grieving mother of a martyr, Fatima was already dead when her son died. Husayn was beheaded at Karbala in 680 CE by the caliph Yazid. Fatima's mourning for her son in Paradise extends beyond the boundaries of time, reflecting the sorrow that pervades the earth and carries universal meaning. As Mahmoud Ayoub puts it in his book on suffering in Islam, "All things weep in emulation of her tears, and the tears of the faithful here on earth are but a way of sharing in her sorrows and a means of bringing consolation to her broken heart."[55]

Erika Friedl writes in her essay "Ideal Womanhood in Post Revolutionary Iran" that as a modern model of behaviour "Fatima is remembered and invoked when a mother mourns her son, when she cries for her family's troubles, for her own sorrows, because Fatima knows what a woman's suffering is all about."[56] Her role as a model is reflected in the fact that her name is one of the most common names for girls in Iran, and her image is present in posters and murals on the streets.[57]

Similarly, Fatima is an important figure in the Muslim counterpart to the Christian passion play, the ta'ziyeh.[58] In 1879, Lewis Pelly, a member of the British Legation in Persia, observed, "If the success of a drama is to be measured by the effects which it produces upon the people for whom it is composed, or upon the audiences before whom it is represented, no play has ever surpassed the tragedy known in the Mussulman world as that of Hasan and Husain."[59]

Pelly was so impressed by the impassioned grief caused by the ta'ziyeh that he asked a friend who taught actors to transcribe the stories for him. In 1879, he published thirty-seven of the fifty-two scenes that he had collected.[60] The first volume contains many of the sad tales of the Muslims, including the deaths of Ibrahim, the son of Mohammed, of Mohammed himself, his daughter Fatima, and his grandsons Hasan and Husayn.[61] Pelly believed it important to present to the Western world a translation of what he considered a singular drama. Its uniqueness stemmed from "its intolerable length … its marvellous effects upon a Mussulman audience, both male and female … and in the circumstance that the so-called unities of time and space are not only ignored, but abolished."[62] He was impressed by the fact that Mohammed and his family are central figures in stories that extended from Joseph and his brothers to the Day of Judgment. Thus, like God, they seem to be universally present.

The core of the tragedy takes place at Karbala, where Husayn and his family and followers meet an Umayyad force and are defeated. The colour and poignancy of the tale come with pious details added over time. Pelly's version tells how Husayn, on the morning of the battle, prepared himself by washing and anointing himself with musk.[63]

When questioned about his actions he gives a reply that reveals his expectation of death: "Alas! There is nothing between us and the black-eyed girls of Paradise but that these troopers come down upon us and slay us!"[64] Speaking to the cruelty of the enemy, legends have developed about an infant boy who was killed with an arrow through the neck while he was held in Husayn's arms during the battle. Husayn caught the child's blood in his hand and threw it up to heaven, and not a drop came down.[65] This was not the only story of a young life lost. Husayn's nephew was also killed at his side. After Husayn himself was killed, his head was cut off and sent to the caliph, Yazid.

In considering the role Fatima plays in the *ta'ziyeh* it is important to understand how this drama shaped people's attitudes. The central stories tell of the siege at Karbala of Husayn and his followers by Yazid the Sunni caliph. It began on the first day of the month of Muharram and ended on the tenth day, called Ashura, in 680 CE. Soon afterward the battlefields and tombs at Karbala became pilgrimage sites for Shi'ites.[66] Right from its origins the *ta'ziyeh* commemorated the battle for political power of the caliphate and was used to represent and intensify the present struggles. An early example of this occurred in 962 CE when the caliph Mu'awiyah ibn Abu Sufyan in Syria was accused by Mu'izz al-Dawla of being an oppressor of the Prophet's family. Mu'izz al-Dawla condemned the caliph publicly by putting up manifestos on the mosques of Baghdad.[67] The next year he instituted mourning ceremonies, which Mayel Baktash argues in his essay on the philosophy of the *ta'ziyeh* "were allegorical affairs, redolent of revolution and designed to obtain psychological control by means of the parallels they drew to stories of oppression and misfortune."[68] During the Shi'ite dynasty of the Buyids in northern Iran (932–1055 CE) the *ta'ziyeh* ceremonies were focused on the goal of opposing Sunni power. The re-enactments of the battle scenes were so passionate that they resulted in deaths.[69] Through the years audience participation has not always been so dramatic, but the *ta'ziyeh* is still known for its active audiences. Under the Iranian Safavid dynasty in the sixteenth century the Muharram ceremonies received official support.

Fatima's death scene is incorporated into Pelly's *ta'ziyeh* collection, which presents much of the legend of the daughter of Mohammed.

Her attitude toward being the mother of a martyr is shown in her conversation with her daughter Zainab. She asks Zainab to bring her a collection of small boxes. The last one causes Zainab to cry tears of blood when she sees that it contains the torn shirt in which her brother will die. Fatima, knowing she herself will be dead when Husayn goes into battle, asks her daughter to kiss his throat and remember her when he prepares for battle.[70] She tells her daughter that Husayn's body will not be washed or covered in the powder of lotus leaves or camphor when he dies. "His camphor shall be the dust of Karbala."[71]

This small scene confirms Pelly's comment that the *ta'ziyeh* seems to take place in a universal time and place. Fatima is able to show her daughter the shirt Husayn will be wearing when he dies, with the evidence of battle already on it. Thus she has already experienced the death of her son. The fact that she knows that his dead body will not be washed indicates that she is aware of his future (or timeless-present) status as a martyr, for Islamic martyrs took their bloodied clothes to Paradise as a sign of their status. Her request that her daughter kiss Husayn's throat is a gentle reminder of her maternal feelings for her son. Not only is this a vulnerable part of the body that one would expose only to someone trusted and loved, but it is where he lost his life when his head was cut off.

By the time Pelly was viewing the *ta'ziyeh* in southern Iran, the dramas had absorbed secular details from folklore. These details close to home helped the audience to perceive their own suffering in the characters represented. "For women especially, they served as a wound-healing agent, for the point was always made that all suffering was slight when compared to that of the victims of Karbala."[72]

In the *ta'ziyeh* the holy family is traditionally portrayed as having to deal with poverty and hunger. This not only added to the picture of a suffering family, but it was easy for many of the viewers to identify with. Fatima fulfills the maternal role of nurturer when, through her faith in God, she helps her family in a time of great hunger. One story tells of the day Mohammed comes to Fatima asking for something to eat, and she admits she has nothing. Just then, a neighbour arrives with a dish of food. When Mohammed asks her where it came from, she says, "From God," and he compares her with Mary, whom he believes was also able to produce food when it was needed most.[73] This story is based on Sura 3:37 of the Koran, where Mary explains that her constant supply of food is from God, "Who gives without stint to whom He will."

Of course, hunger and poverty are nothing compared with the suffering Fatima experiences in her bereavement. The closeness of mother and son is apparent in the following poem of lamentation written for the *ta'ziyeh* celebrations from Fatima's perspective. It tells of her pain when contemplating Husayn's death.

> How great is my grief for you, O my child, you who are the
>   one lost to friends and family.
> Again I say how great is my sorrow, O my child, for after you
>   I shall desert sleep and even sleeplessness.
> Woe is me, who took care of his shrouding, who beheld his
>   face, throat and eyes,
> Woe, woe is me, who did wash him and walk behind his bier.
> Woe, woe is me, who did pray over him and lay him in his
>   grave.[74]

It is clear from the beginning of this passage that, although Husayn dies in middle age, Fatima still thinks of him as her child. This implies an intimacy that his adulthood cannot eradicate; nor is that intimacy dissolved by the fact that she has already been dead for some time. Fatima speaks as any bereaved mother would in tending to the body of her dead child. She does not speak as a mother of a martyr–for she has washed his body, and martyrs traditionally remain unwashed, purified by their blood.

Both the Corpus Christi plays in Christian medieval drama and the *ta'ziyeh* were popular dramatic reminders of a religious world order that drew attentive audiences each year. Part of their story focuses on how mothers of brave sons who were willing to sacrifice themselves should behave. Fatima's tale was invoked during the Iran – Iraq war to instil the appropriate sentiments and behaviour in Iranian mothers. In the days of the Iranian Revolution, Ayatollah Khomeini appointed women as the pillars of the nation; their most important task in this role was to raise "brave and enlightened men and meek and united women."[75] The role of the mother was made sacred by those who offered their sons as martyrs to the cause. Khomeini encouraged women to follow the example of Fatima, for as one scholar stated during the war "it is by their ability to raise martyrs, and educate them to be believers and dedicated soldiers for the cause that women become invaluable to Khomeini."[76]

Khomeini was not the only prominent leader to set up Fatima as the epitome of role models for women. Ali Shariati, who was the Shah of Iran's political prisoner in the 1960s and 1970s, wrote a famous essay entitled "Fatima is Fatima." A scholar of sociology and religion who, some argue, was more influential than Khomeini, Shariati saw Fatima as providing an alternative model of womanhood from either the Western commercialized woman or the conservative Islamic type.[77]

Although there are stories from the Iran–Iraq war of strident mothers claiming they are sad not to have had more sons to offer into martyrdom, more common are the images of mothers of martyrs that combined the attributes of joy and sorrow. During the war the newspaper *Kayhan International* carried a daily feature claiming to be the last will and testament of martyrs. Yossef Ibrahim included a section of one of these wills in a *Wall Street Journal* article. He quoted one *basiij*, a young wartime volunteer likely destined for martyrdom, who wrote to his mother, "I know it is hard for a mother to lose a child but dear mother rejoice that your son has chosen the only road leading to God and to perfection from among so many materialistic and worthless ways."[78] This letter asks the mother to follow Fatima's model and look patiently beyond the things of this world to the purity of the Hereafter.

The parents of martyrs often announced their sons' deaths as they would a wedding or birth. They showed great pride in giving their sons to their country, and those who had lost three or four sons had their stories placed on the front page, asking their compatriots to "share their joy and sorrow."[79]

The sorrow of Fatima, rather than any joy, is present in the huge graveyard in Tehran, Behesht-e-Zahra, built by the Iranian government for martyrs. With 27,000 graves it is perhaps the largest such cemetery in the world. Mothers would come to the graveyard once famous for its fountain, which flowed red for the martyrs buried there. In 1993, the government turned off the "blood" as part of an effort to develop friendlier relations with Iraq. This made no difference to one mother of a martyr who, for thirteen years, lived in a shack constructed over her son's grave until her poor health forced her to reduce her overnight stays to once a week.[80] This mother was a living reminder of Fatima, Umm Abiha, weeping each night over her father's grave and grieving for her son for all time.

There is one last Islamic mother of a martyr whose story needs to be mentioned. Al-Khansa, a seventh-century CE poet and convert to Islam, brings a different emotional response to her bereavement than does Fatima. Her behaviour is closer to that of the Maccabean mother and, ironically, it is she who has been invoked as a model in the Palestinian resistance, initially against the British Mandate and, more recently, during the Intifada. It is noteworthy in these times of friction between Muslim and Christian worlds that the woman who raised the image of al-Khansa in the 1930s, Matiel Mogannam, was herself a Christian. Mogannam wrote of the early days of the women's movement in Palestine. In her book, *The Arab Woman and the Palestine Problem* (1937), she prefaced her discussion on the political role of women during the 1920s and 30s with a review of the social contributions of early Muslim women, including al-Khansa. Al-Khansa's life spanned the origins of Islam at a time when loyalty to one's tribe was a way of life. She wrote of her deep sorrow following the death of her two brothers in tribal warfare. Although little is known of her life, the traditional stories from her tribe, the Banu Sulaym, state that not long after the death of her brothers she headed a delegation to Medina (ca. 629 CE) to convert to Islam.[81] If there is any truth to this story it does encourage one to think that she saw the new religion and political philosophy as a means to overcoming the constant tribal warfare that had taken the lives of her brothers.

According to the tradition, al-Khansa exhibited her full support for Islam the night before the battle of al-Qadisiyya, when she counselled her four sons to fight for the faith and, if necessary, to die for it. She claimed her right to be heard and obeyed by them on the basis of her status as a mother who had suffered pain for them, and as a woman of purity. She assured them: "I have never betrayed your father, nor cast any reflection upon your dignity of honour."[82] This same argument for the mother's power over her sons on the basis of her purity was made by the Maccabean mother. She notes, "I was a pure virgin and did not go outside my father's house; but I guarded the rib from which woman was made. No seducer corrupted me on a desert plain, nor did the destroyer, the deceitful serpent, defile the purity of my virginity. In the time of my maturity I remained with my husband." (4 Macc. 18:7–9). When al-Khansa heard that all four sons had died, she remarked, "I consider it an honour that they died for the sake of Islam. I ask only that God allow me to meet them in Paradise."[83]

Al-Khansa's story can now be found on a variety of Internet sites, all of which show respect for her as a great poet, and many of which view her as a political model for women. An elegy to her sons is often repeated on these sites: "My sons I bore you with pain and brought you up with care; You have fallen today for the cause of Islam. Who says you are dead; You are very much alive, and alive with honour. I feel proud to be the mother of martyrs."[84] Not all Arab women are impressed by the pervasive image of al-Khansa. Author Terri DeYoung quotes the feminist scholar Nuha Samara, who was writing at the time of the Gulf War (1991). Samara rejected al-Khansa's image as "crowned in black ... her voice and her opinions circumscribed, unable to say how the war might benefit her and how it might harm her."[85] Speaking directly to al-Khansa's role as a mother of martyrs, she asks, "Is the Khansa of the past also the Khansa of the present? Have the roles of Arab women changed since the time of Khansa? Or do they still come and go in her place? Shouting jubilation when one of their children suffers martyrdom, ululating with their hearts black as night ... Is she the geography that mothers heroes?"[86]

Clearly, for many, al-Khansa is still the prototype for mothers of heroes. Her image was brought to life again during the Intifada of the late 1980s and in subsequent years. There is an overabundance of stories that show how popular she is in this role. One example was reported in the *Chicago Tribune* on 2 February 1996. It concerned a three-year-old boy, Eyad, from the Palestinian refugee camp of Jabaliya.

His mother, named after the other famous Islamic mother of a martyr, Fatima, said that she "deliberately conceived Eyad during the Intifada to replace a brother of the same name who was killed ... a martyr to the cause of Palestine."[87] In parts of the Middle East it is still common for a later child to be given the name of a dead sibling, or a name showing that the young one is a replacement for the earlier child.[88] Thus asserting the power of the mothers, Umm Eyad (mother of Eyad) said, "The mothers of the martyrs are very fertile and fruitful. If you plant one martyr, you will get 500 more."[89] The truth of this statement is often expressed in the media reports of the second Intifada, which began in 2000, where martyrs of the suicide-bomber type and their supportive mothers are the subjects of frequent headlines.

The recognition of the spreading influence of a martyr's story had been expressed in the language of growth and fecundity before. There is an interesting link here with the etymological origins of the word "propaganda," which carries the sense of "to propagate" or "to sow." In a letter to Roman officials warning them of the cost of their injustices toward the Christians, the Christian, Tertullian (ca. 155–ca. 222), wrote: "The oftener we are mown down by you, the more in number we grow: the blood of the Christians is seed."[90]

The wisdom of Tertullian and of Umm Eyad is also known in Sikhism, the final religious tradition to be examined here for its stories of martyrdom and bereavement. As in the other religions discussed, there are stories of heroic Sikh mothers from the early days of this monotheistic faith. They were repeated and embellished from the seventeenth to the twentieth centuries whenever the community found itself in times of conflict.

From its beginnings in the fifteenth century the community faced powerful enemies. It was initially led by a succession of ten gurus, two of whom were martyred (Arjan in 1606 and Tegh Bahadur in 1675) under Mogul emperors. In one of the popular cartoon booklets sold in Punjab today, which present these and subsequent Sikh heroes, there is a piece of doggerel expressing Tertullian's sentiment that fallen

35

heroes propagate the faith. Referring to later martyrdoms at the hand of another Muslim leader it states: "Mir Mannu is our Sickle / We the Fodder for him to mow, / The more he reaps / The more we grow."[91]

Muin-ul Mulk, known by the Sikhs as Mir Mannu, the sickle, was the governor of Lahore (1748–53). According to Sikh tradition Mir Mannu captured and tortured Sikh mothers and their children in his continued efforts to kill the Sikhs. In a version of this story written by Amar Singh in 1906, these mothers were said to have taken comfort in remembering the fortitude of Mata Gujari, the mother of the tenth and last guru, Gobind Singh, and grandmother of his martyred sons. Mata Gujari planted the first "seed" in the Sikh tradition of the stories of mothers of martyrs. Her version of this tale differs from the variants in other religious traditions in that she was a grandmother of martyrs. Her status as both mother and grandmother adds to the poignancy of the story. She loved and cared for her grandsons like a mother, but her age made her even more vulnerable than a woman in her prime, thus pulling on the reader's heartstrings all the more. Her emotional and physical fortitude is unexpected on account of both her gender and her years.

Her first personal acquaintance with martyrdom came when her husband, the ninth guru, Tegh Bahadur, was martyred in 1675. Her next taste came in 1704, precipitated by the trickery of the emperor Aurangzeb, who after encouraging the Sikhs to leave the fort at Anandpur by promising them safe passage, attacked them. In the ensuing battle the members of Mata Gujari's family became separated. Her son, Gobind Singh, and his two eldest sons went on to fight. These two young teenagers were killed. Mata Gujari and her two younger grandsons, Zorawar and Fateh Singh escaped together. Although they finally found a safe haven, they were betrayed by a servant and eventually imprisoned.[92] Zorawar and Fateh refused to renounce their faith and were sentenced to be bricked-up alive. Before the wall was built past their heads they were beheaded; soon after, their grandmother also died.

In the section entitled "Perseverance of Sikh Women" in the martyrologist Amar Singh's *Anecdotes From Sikh History* (1906), the mothers captured by Mir Mannu are said to have remembered Mata

Gujari in order to gain the strength to face the tortures ahead. Like the Hebrew chronicler, Soloman bar Simson, Amar Singh makes use of a previous story of a famous mother to augment the impact of his tale and give it a classical frame. There are other ways in which the Sikh martyrologists made their stories more compelling. Lou Fenech, a Canadian scholar who has studied and written on Sikh martyrdom in depth, outlines some of these techniques. His intent in tracking changes in the details of these stories is to show that the bravery of mothers of martyrs was deliberately amplified in response to the political environment of the time. He argues that the heroic mother icon "was largely constructed and perpetuated through the tireless campaigns of the principal Sikh reform movement of the period (end 19th beginning 20th century), the Singh Sabha."[93] In the development of the story of the mothers captured by Mir Mannu, Fenech pinpoints a change with the publication of Giani Gian Singh's *Panth Prakash* in 1887. This version of the story of the captured mothers and children, as well as that of Amar Singh, expanded the presence of the mothers and increased their bravery in comparison with an earlier, pre-Singh Sabha, version published in 1841. In Amar Singh's telling, three hundred captured women were offered the opportunity to convert to Islam and thereby save themselves and their children and gain a life of riches. Upon their refusal they were starved and forced to do hard labour. When this did not break the mothers, Mir Mannu ordered that the babies be killed with swords. "Their gory corpses were thrown into the laps of the [mothers] or suspended from their necks."[94] In Gian Singh's version, also written during the time of the Singh Sabha, the details are even more vivid: "Several [of the children] were caught on spears as they came down [and afterwards hacked into pieces. Their severed limbs were subsequently] threaded through to form garlands [which were placed around each respective mother's neck]. Those young innocents (lit. 'milk-drinkers')[who were impaled][95] writhed and wriggled as they died."[96] In contrast, the atrocities in the pre-Singh Sabha version are minimal. In fact, the 1841 version makes no mention of killing the children; rather, one child is jailed, and the mothers' reaction is to weep.

In the versions of Giani Gian Singh (1880) and Amar Singh (1906), the youth of the children is stressed through their description as suckling babies. This exact emphasis is made in versions of the Maccabean tale (b. Git. 57b and Lam. 1:16) that came after the earliest version still in existence, 2 Maccabees. Doran notes that in the case of the Jewish story this emphasis on youth "only underlines the miraculous character of the resistance."[97] The resistance Doran is speaking about is that of the youngest son; however, a similarly miraculous resistance is also exhibited by the mother who could watch her innocent baby being killed without giving in to the temptation of conversion. So, too, in the story of the Sikh mothers, the miracle of religious conviction is found in the mothers who watch their children being killed without submitting to Islam. In fact, they are presented as doing more than merely resisting temptation, they are thankful, in a manner reminiscent of the Maccabean mother's joy, for their children's fate. The mothers thanked God that "their children had no chance of ever being called unworthy, and had tasted of the cup of martyrdom in their very infancy."[98]

Not only were the babies to be congratulated on their purity, but so were the mothers as well. This question of honour arose in the introduction to "The Perseverance of Sikh Women": "Our mothers, who could outrival even their Spartan sisters, gave us no cause for shame ... not once did they do aught calculated to bring shame on the people to whom they belonged."[99] Just as in the stories of al-Khansa, the Maccabean mother, and, of course, the Virgin Mary, the Sikh martyrologists felt it was important to clarify that these women were not only brave, but were also pure.

One would expect that a tale as compelling as this would be remembered and repeated, particularly in times of political conflict – and so it was. Cynthia Mahmood interviewed Sikh militants in the United States and wrote about these encounters in her book *Fighting for Faith and Nation: Dialogues with Sikh Militants* (1996). She included an interview with a Sikh soldier and his wife concerning their reaction to Operation Blue Star, the Indian Army's storming of the Golden Temple in Amritsar in 1984. In this context the woman repeated the story of what the mothers and babies of Lahore had suffered, prefaced by a statement of her willingness to sacrifice her own sons. "As for my sons, I'll feel proud if they get killed for a holy cause. Everybody has to die, but those who die for honour never die, for they are immortal."[100] The question of honour was just as important to this woman as it was to the mothers of the past, regardless of their culture.

The wife of the Sikh soldier summed up the bravery of the eighteenth-century women, saying, in much the same way as Amar Singh had done, "With folded hands they thanked God that their children had stood the test of their faith and had died bravely."[101] In this case, though, the children gained a sense of agency they had not had in the older story, for here our story-teller says that they had withstood the test of their faith.

Fenech makes reference to this modern Sikh woman's story in *Martyrdom in the Sikh Tradition*. He argues that it is likely that her understanding of Sikh history, specifically the episode of the slaughtered children, was influenced more by Kirpal Singh's painting of this event, *Sacrificing Family before Faith*, than by any written version of the story. If so, she would not be alone in having her views structured more by image than by the written word. "So influential are these paintings [of martyrs] that many Sikhs often describe eighteenth-century Sikh struggles by unknowingly alluding to the scenes depicted in them (particularly those episodes depicted in the paintings of Kirpal Singh) rather than to historical texts."[102]

Paintings of martyrs by Kirpal Singh and others in his style are easily accessible for viewing, from the museum within the precincts of the Golden Temple (Harimandir Sahib) in Amritsar to the Internet, and are widely reproduced and available for purchase in the form of posters and comic books. Much like Christian art and the Passion plays of the Christian and Shi'ite traditions, the accessible and graphic images of Sikh martyrs will help ensure their influence over the future; as martyrologists would say, they will plant the seeds of more martyrs.

In 1998 the American scholar Mark Juergensmeyer interviewed the family of the young militant Kanwarjit Singh, a member of the Khalistan Commando Force, whose aim had been the creation of a homeland, Khalistan, "land of the pure." In 1982 Kanwarjit had been inspired by the words of Jarnail Singh Bhindranwale, the militant leader who was later killed in 1984 during the Indian attack on the Golden Temple and is widely hailed in the Sikh community as a martyr. Kanwarjit was eventually caught by the police in 1989 and took

Illustration of Sikh mothers with their infants' bodies hanging around their necks, by Devinder Singh. (In Satbir Singh, *Illustrated Martyrdom Tradition*, 1983.)

his own life by ingesting a cyanide pill. His family considered him a martyr, as was evidenced by a shrine dedicated to him on the living room wall and another "more intimate" one in the bedroom of Kanwarjit's mother.[103] Although the family may have been proud of their martyr-son, Juergensmeyer describes an "aura of sadness" surrounding the household.

Though plentiful, the assertions of pride and joyfulness attached to these stories of martyrs are not meant to overlook how saturated the tales were and are with this aura. The pain is understood to be an essential part of the tale. We are meant to assume that no matter how defiant the supporters and family are (and, in particular, the mother of the martyr), that sadness is present. In these Sikh stories, to actually speak of the heartache of losing a child would undermine the power of the tale in the same way that in ancient Carthage the mother's tears would have nullified the sacrifice of her child.

These many stories of mothers who accepted the sacrifice of their children are not the only ones to be found in the pages of history, yet they are enough to allow us to see the common characterisitics of the mothers. Their emotional reaction ranged from a show of joy to a sadness that penetrated all of time. Nonetheless, all of them were presented as accepting the necessity of the sacrifice. That message of acceptance was reinvigorated through the centuries. The Maccabean mother's story was so powerful that it was often repeated by both Jews and Christians to fire the spirit of those facing persecution and unite their forces. The *danse macabre* enacted by the seven sons as they were tortured set a standard for gruesome deaths suffered by young children while their mothers watched. But martyrologists have found ways to increase the poignancy of their tales, for example by decreasing the age of the children who are sacrificed. In the repetitions of the story of the mothers of Lahore, the atrocities suffered by the children increase in inverse proportion to the children's age. Although Mary and Fatima are not tearless mothers of martyrs, the message of their acceptance of their sons' deaths was clearly portrayed, and with particular efficacy, through dramatic representation. Unlike all the other tales, al-Khansa's story did not rely on the details of atrocities to make it memorable, but all who heard her story understood that her sons died the painful death of the battlefield. Like all the other mothers in the end, she did not question the need to sacrifice her sons.

During the late nineteenth and early twentieth centuries, the veneration of motherhood held sway over the imaginations of many in the British Empire. This sentiment arose in reaction to industrialization, which was seen by many as causing the disintegration of society. The mammoth three-volume anthropological work, *The Mothers*, written by World War I veteran Robert Briffault and published in 1927, still bears the mark of the Victorian age, as he concludes with a deep bow to the powers of mothers.[104] "Social organization itself – the associated group to which humanity owes its mere existence – was the expression of feminine functions. Those social sentiments, without which no aggregate of individuals can constitute a society, were the immediate derivatives of the feelings which bind the mother and her offspring, and consisted originally of these, and of these alone. Upon them the superstructure of humanity, and the powers and possibilities of its development, ultimately rest."[105]

It would be difficult to assign a greater power to the sentiments of the maternal relationship. But, as seen earlier in this chapter, when the devoted nurturer of the son agrees to his sacrifice, the strength of the mother–child bond is highlighted with an intensity sufficient to affect the emotions of a great number of people. During the monumental conflict of 1914–18, extraordinary numbers of mothers were suddenly being asked to support the sacrifice of their sons to a larger cause, variously named as the defence of country, of Empire, of civilization, and of God. Like martyrologists of many different cultures and times, the recruiters and propagandists in this new industrial war realized the power of the role of the mother both to sanctify what might otherwise be a paralyzing loss and to encourage even greater effort in the battle against the foe.

Chapter 2

The Language of Sacrifice
The Voice of Preachers and Artists in World War I

It was no coincidence that the shot that killed Archduke Franz Ferdinand and precipitated the series of events leading to World War I was fired on 28 June 1914. That summer day marked the anniversary of the Battle of Kosovo in 1389, believed to embody a heroic Serbian nationalism. The assassin, Gavrilo Princep, knew of the fourteenth-century battle through ballads composed by Serbian monks of the Eastern Orthodox Church. The version of history sung through the centuries in these epic poems told of the sacrifice of warriors who stood against the invading Turks. The leader of the heroes, Prince Lazar, knew he would lose yet preferred the kingdom of heaven to life in this world as a slave. His was not the only martyr's tale to be told. Alongside him his nine brothers-in-law rode into battle, the sons of Mother Yugovich. The ballads tell of the strength this mother exhibited in supporting the cause for which all of her sons died. Her image lived on, and five centuries later was embedded in the nationalist spirit that inspired Princep.

The legacy of World War I soldiers is one of bravery but not, generally, one of martyrdom, despite the fact that at the time the war was overtly described and pictured in religious terms. It may be that, had the war not been enveloped in an ironic understanding from the late 1920s onward, the concept of martyrdom would have been more closely associated with the soldiers. Even so, the nature of the battlefield was not conducive to the creation of martyrs. The colossally stagnant and mechanized theatre of war provided few opportunities for a hero to act in a courageous manner that would distinguish him from others and become the stuff of legend. Yet some influential people, such as the Bishop of London, Arthur Foley Winnington-Ingram, did refer to the soldiers as martyrs,[1] and others attributed martyr-like qualities to soldiers without using the actual term. Soldiers were presented as Christ-like figures in sermons, newspaper reports, novels, poetry, paintings, cartoons, and music. They were often described as filling Christ's shoes and being more truly Christian than either those at home or the chaplains who served at home or in the war. T.A. Patterson, who served with the Canadian chaplaincy service and was critical of himself and his fellow officer-chaplains, nevertheless felt that he spoke for those who had served overseas when he said, "We have had our Gethsemanes and Golgothas. Most of us who went to 'the place of the skull,' sounded to the depths the sternest relations between Life and Death, and have had mental and spiritual visions of the things of Time and Eternity impossible to those who stayed home ... I saw more genuine Christianity in my two years' stay 'over there' than I have among ministerial place-seekers in my life-time as a clergyman."[2]

Not only were soldiers taken as exemplars of Christian sacrifice, they were also often depicted as peace-loving men forced into action by the aggressor. This quality of pacifism is reminiscent of a more traditional understanding of martyrs as gentle souls who do not want to hurt anyone. As with martyrs, the self-sacrificing and peace-loving nature attributed to soldiers helped to promote the cause for which they fought. This view of soldiers was, as many historians have stated, a great asset to the Entente, for "the Germans were never able to efface the initial impression that they were aggressors."[3]

That we have forgotten the language of sacrifice used to describe the war is apparent in the fact that the story of a highly influential martyr of the time has all but disappeared from common knowledge. Edith Cavell, a British nurse executed on 12 October 1915 by the Germans for helping British prisoners escape from occupied Belgium, was widely hailed as a martyr. Nurse Cavell's martyrology has many traditional features. Being a woman, she was considered physically weak; this was contrasted with her strength of spirit, which gave her the courage to help those in need even though it put her in danger. The last letter she wrote to her mother before going to prison indicates that she knew she was in danger of being arrested.[4] After her death the power of her tale to shape peoples' attitudes toward the enemy was quickly recognized. One of her biographers, Rowland Ryder, explains the speed at which her story spread as the work of the propagandists who "seized upon the affair: here was a splendid opportunity to build up this nurse ... as a saint and a martyr."[5]

On Trafalgar Day, just nine days after Cavell's death, Bishop Winnington-Ingram "pointed out that Britain had now no need for a recruiting campaign, the execution of Edith Cavell was enough."[6] Interestingly, soon after Cavell was shot, the French executed two German nurses for similar activities, but the Germans failed to seize this opportunity to propagandize. According to Harold Lasswell, the Germans took a narrow view of military protocol, which they believed gave the French the right to kill the nurses.[7]

For the British, Cavell's martyrdom turned into an enlistment boom. In the eight weeks before the announcement of her execution, voluntary enlistments in the Territorial Force averaged 5,000 per week. For the same length of time after her death, enlistments averaged 10,000 per week.[8] By December, the numbers had subsided to the previous level, but Ryder concludes from his analysis of the enlistment figures that her death added "40,000 extra recruits to the army alone."[9]

Canadian enlistments show an increase as well, beginning in November and steadily going up through early 1916.[10] Enlistment was affected by many factors, such as battle casualties, requests from Prime Minister Borden for more support, recruitment posters, and propaganda. Yet it is safe to say that Cavell's execution would have added to the language of sacrifice that described the war as a battle against evil requiring men to enlist and fight for "good."

Apparently, Cavell's mother accepted the news of her daughter's death with stoic dignity. But the British propaganda office did not make use of her show of strength to create a mother-of-martyr legend. Through the efforts of the Bishop of Norwich she received some financial support from the government, but did not live to see the end of the war.

Although the propagandists made much of Cavell's death, they did not create a martyr out of nothing. The daughter of an Anglican minister, Cavell was a faithful Christian. The evidence from her friends and from trial records shows that, like courageous martyrs of the past, she was calm during the period before her arrest, during her imprisonment, and even when the verdict was announced. She spent a good deal of time with her copy of the fifteenth-century devotional prayers of Thomas à Kempis, *The Imitation of Christ*, marking passages to help keep up her courage. Although generally the prayers ask the reader to turn toward a spiritual life, one seems particularly apt for a woman awaiting news of her possible execution: "Without a combat thou canst not attain unto the crown of patience. If thou are unwilling to suffer, thou refusest to be crowned. But if thou desire to be crowned, fight manfully, endure patiently."[11] In traditional martyr fashion Cavell did not seek the crown of the martyr, for this would border on suicide, but she did nothing to avoid it.

A small postscript to her recognition as a martyr concerns the state of preservation of her body when it was exhumed on 17 March 1919, three and a half years after her death. A Reuters correspondent wrote that "the body was well preserved and the features perfectly recognizable."[12] This comment places Cavell in a long tradition within Christianity of martyrs whose bodies do not decay. This notion is also found in Islam, where the everlasting nature of the martyr's body is indicative of holiness.

The English chaplain Stirling Gahan gave Cavell Holy Communion the evening before she was killed and was the last person to visit her. A statement she made to him became famous for a time and has had an interesting history of its own. "This I would say," she considered, "standing as I do in view of God and Eternity, I realize that patriotism is not enough. I must have no hatred or bitterness towards anyone."[13] One would expect to hear words of this nature, which stress an early-

Christian attitude of love, from a martyr, but it is easy to see that they would be a stumbling block to a war propagandist.

George Bernard Shaw commented cynically on the use of Edith Cavell's name by the British propaganda system in the preface to his play, *St Joan*, published in 1923. He called Edith Cavell an arch-heretic like Joan of Arc because of her critique of patriotism in the middle of war. She was a nurse to wounded soldiers from both sides, "acknowledging no distinction before Christ between Tommy and Jerry and Pitou the Poilu." When she was shot, "her countrymen, seeing in this a good opportunity for lecturing the enemy on his intolerance, put up a statue to her, but took particular care not to inscribe on the pedestal 'Patriotism is not enough,' for which omission, and the lie it implies, they will need Edith's intercession when they are themselves brought to judgment."[14]

The monument to which Shaw refers stands near Trafalgar Square in London and now carries her famous statement, along with the words "Humanity, Fortitude, Devotion, and Sacrifice." Her words were added in 1924, soon after the publication of Shaw's play. A Canadian memorial to Cavell, begun in 1919 by sculptor Florence Wyle, stands on the grounds of the Toronto General Hospital. This bronze relief depicts Cavell supporting two wounded soldiers.[15] The earliest Canadian "monument" to Edith Cavell is a mountain in Jasper National Park named in March 1916, at the suggestion of the premier of British Columbia, just five months after Cavell's death. The naming occurred officially in 1921 with an Anglican dedication service; a memorial service is still held annually in the Jasper Anglican church. Even Cavell's defence lawyer, Gaston de Leval, has a mountain named after him in Banff National Park.

Although Edith Cavell's martyrdom gave a boost to enlistment, recruitment officers needed more tales of this nature to ensure that men would continue to sign up. Thus, war propaganda, like martyrologies, came to rely on atrocity stories. Details of physical torture were frequently included in martyrologies as the genre developed. To describe in terms of blood and gore just what evils an enemy is capable of helps to startle the public out of complacency into hatred. If the enemy can commit ultimate evil, it follows that only an act of supreme sacrifice is powerful enough to defeat them and achieve ultimate justice. This was the reasoning Pope Urban II had used in 1095 when he presented tales of Muslims invading Christian churches, raping women, and defiling altars to incite men to take part in the first Crusade. During World War I, Dr Samuel Dwight Chown, general superintendent of the Methodist church in Canada, similarly combined images of violated women and religious icons to urge men to enlist: "For myself it is enough to know that Christ, as I perceive Him, would not stand with limp hands if a ruthless soldier should attempt to outrage His holy mother as the women of Belgium were violated. To him all motherhood is sacred; nor would He retreat and give place to the armed burglar, breaking with murderous intent into His home; nor would He witness, without any effort to prevent it, the destruction of the civil and religious liberty which His teaching has enthroned in our British Empire."[16]

The Committee on Alleged German Outrages presided over by Viscount James Bryce, formerly the British Ambassador to Washington, published a report on the conduct of the German troops in Belgium in 1915. The report was based on a volume entitled *Evidence and Documents Laid Before the Committee on Alleged German Outrages*. Both books were made available in Canada by the Ottawa Government Printing Bureau in 1916. The shorter *Report of the Committee on Alleged German Outrages* (17 May 1916) included an insert stating that the Dominion Government wished this "official" document to be "circulated widely and read with care." Moreover, "the recipient should read and pass it on to a friend, with a request to do the same." The Report claimed to give evidence according to the provisions of the Hague Convention of 1907, to which both Germany and England were signatories. Part I concerned the "Conduct of German Troops in Belgium"; Part II dealt with "Breaches of Rules and Usages of War and Acts of Inhumanity in Invaded Territories." The latter included the killing of noncombatants, the mistreatment of women and children, the use of civilians as screens, the killing of prisoners, firing on hospitals, and the abuse of the Red Cross and white flag.

Peter Buitenhuis, writing on the propaganda of World War I, describes the sources of the Report as "unnamed witnesses, second hand eyewitness reports and imagination."[17] Yet Lasswell tells us that a good propagandist does not stray too far from the truth. In *The Guns of August*, historian Barbara Tuchman describes "the usual orgy of permitted looting" that seems to be the fate of most if not all civilians during warfare.[18] She then goes on to detail the mass murders the Germans committed in Dinant, Belgium, where 612 bodies were identified and buried. Just after this massacre came the burning of Louvain, including its world-famous library, on 26 and 27 August 1914, an act that was broadcast to the world.[19] In a more recent study, Horne and Kramer add other massacres to this list and point out the brutality that occurred in Belgium was not committed by a few renegade German soldiers but by many regiments.[20]

The stories of atrocities committed against women and children held great poignancy for their audience and were transformed into potent images on recruitment posters. Lasswell describes the Bryce Report as "the magnum opus of the War on this front."[21] The Report follows what Lasswell describes as "a handy rule for arousing hate ... if at first they do not enrage, use an atrocity."[22]

The effectiveness of this rule was explained by the British author Mrs Peel in a very down-to-earth way in her book about domestic life in England during the war. "Because the state of tense excitement in which we existed upset our judgment and made any event seem possible, and also because if people must go to war and continue to be at war they must be made to hate each other and to go on hating each other, war stories were a feature of our life."[23]

The two stories that Mrs Peel mentions as having caused "unnecessary distress" were those of the babies whose hands had been cut off and of the crucifixion of a Canadian.[24] Lasswell comments on the importance, for the propagandist, of what Mrs Peel referred to as "tense excitement": "the propagandist who deals with a community when its tension level is high, finds that a reservoir of explosive energy can be touched off by the same small match which would normally ignite a bonfire."[25]

The impossibility of escaping the power of atrocity stories and the hatred they engender is poetically expressed in *Why Stay We Here* (1930), George Godwin's novel about a young Canadian officer in the war. The character Piers states: "Only a saint or a sage could escape the mass emotions of a nation at war."[26] The atrocity stories to which Godwin refers in his novel were all well known during the war and included the boiling of dead bodies by the Germans to extract chemicals from them and the crucifixion of a Canadian soldier. He presents the stories as part of a training lecture that causes one young Canadian soldier to "quiver with rage."

One of the most gruesome atrocities depicted in the Bryce Report, and certainly an equivalent to the tortures committed on the Maccabean boys as told in 4 Maccabees, was provided by an unnamed eye witness in Belgium who described an event that allegedly took place on 23 August 1916 outside Malines. A German soldier shot a Belgian peasant for taking too long to answer the door. The peasant's wife then came out with a "little suckling child." She put the child down and attacked the Germans like a "lioness" – an act for which she, too, was killed. Another soldier "took his bayonet and fixed it and thrust it through the child. He then put his rifle on his shoulder with the child up it, its little arms stretched out once or twice."[27] The inclusion of the adjective "suckling" is reminiscent of the stories of the Sikh and Maccabean mothers whose children were similarly described in later versions of their tales. More recently, the apocryphal story of Iraqi soldiers taking Kuwati babies out of their incubators at the beginning of the Gulf War was pivotal in raising support for the war against Saddam Hussein.[28] Thus, across cultures and times, the younger the victims of terror and torture, the greater the impact of the story. This repetition speaks to an important characteristic of atrocity stories that Lasswell notes: their lack of originality. These tales of atrocity were spread widely, just as the publishers of the Bryce Report had requested they be. From the number of times the raping of Belgian women and killing of the children are mentioned in the media, cartoons, and fiction we can assume that the Report had a large impact on the Canadian public, however far removed they were from the events that were being described.

For example, the reception of the Bryce Report in Canada is mentioned in Ralph Connor's 1917 novel *The Major*. Connor, the most widely read Canadian author of his day, has his protagonist Larry speak of a change that came "over the heart of Canada and over his own heart. The tales of Belgian atrocities, at first rejected as impossible, but afterwards confirmed by the Bryce Commission and by many private letters, kindled in Canadian hearts a passion of furious longing to wipe from the face of the earth a system that produced such horrors."[29]

The soldiers, on the other hand, tended to be more skeptical. There was a distinct lack of respect among the men for printed information. As Marc Bloch writes in *The Historian's Craft*, "the prevailing opinion in the trenches was that anything might be true, except what was printed."[30] This did not mean, however, that the soldiers were immune to rumour. Bloch explains that, given a lack of confidence in written forms of communication, there was "a prodigious renewal of oral tradition, the ancient mother of myths and legends."[31] An expression used at the time, "latrine rumour," referred to "wild and unsubstantial stories and prophecies."[32] The latrines were one of the few places where the men were away from the officers and could talk freely. Brophy says the British latrines were not quite the open and chatty places described in the first chapter of *All Quiet on the Western Front*. This novel, by Erich Maria Remarque, gives a wonderful picture of these "regimental gossip-shops and common-rooms."[33]

Bloch argues that the rumours did not start at the Front, where the soldiers were isolated from one another, but with those who brought food to the Front from the field kitchens. He explains that the soldiers would not have been as skeptical of the stories brought by these men because, just as in the Middle Ages, "we have faith in that narrator who, at rare intervals, brings us distant rumors over a difficult road."[34] Thus, even those most likely to question the authenticity of rumours could still be susceptible to their power.

Francis Derwent Wood, *Canada's Golgotha*, 1918,
83.0 cm × 63.5 cm. (Canadian War Museum artifact
number 19710261-0797.)

One of the most repeated and widely recorded atrocity stories of
World War I was that of the crucified Canadian; it gripped the imagination of many story-tellers and writers and found notable visual representation in the 1918 bronze statue, *Canada's Golgotha*, by Francis
Derwent Wood. The story presented the death of a soldier in the religious framework common to a majority of the fighting men. There
were many versions. Some said it was one man who was crucified, an
American or a Canadian; others claimed three or six. The Germans

said the Belgians had crucified German soldiers. But most accounts said it was a Canadian who was killed, near St Julien, the site of the first German gas attack on 22 April 1915 during the Second Battle of Ypres. Much research has been undertaken over the years to determine the truth of this story. Attempts to discover its origins began during the war, continued right after, and have carried on since.

An early reference to the crucified Canadian was published in the Toronto *Globe* from a Canadian Press dispatch on Thursday, 6 May 1915. Under the headline "Canadian Crucified by the Germans?" it began: "*The Morning Post* says that a Lieut.-Col. writing on April 29th says: 'The Canadians have done splendidly. But they are mad with rage because they say that they have found one of their men crucified. This is not mere camp gossip: a General vouches for the fact.'"[35]

Thus the article, entitled with a question, draws on the status of "a" lieutenant-colonel and "a" general to guarantee its truth. Not only are the sources unnamed, but these senior officers would probably not have been in the field themselves to witness the alleged crucifixion and so would have depended on the word of others. The need to draw on the word of an officer as a presumed expert – a common technique used by propagandists – and the denial that this was a piece of gossip presents the information in a defensive way, as if assuming that some would not believe it. But, through its repetition over the months and years in news, novels, and films, it grew into fact in the public mind.

The Canadian chief censor, Colonel Ernest J. Chambers, in charge of the Canadian Information Service, began to investigate the story early in 1915. He received a letter from Rudyard Kipling on 18 June 1915 attesting to the truth of the story.[36] This famous author was another individual with a great deal of status but who was not likely to have seen the sight himself. Although Kipling had been a journalist for a short time, he was not a war "expert" in the manner of the other witnesses, the general, and the lieutenant-colonel. Still, he was appealed to as a reliable witness because of his status as an author – albeit of fiction.

Chambers searched for eyewitnesses. He found a private who swore under affidavit to have seen three Canadian soldiers bayonetted to a barn door three miles from St Julien. The Canadian general Sir

Arthur Currie also investigated the story but concluded it was not true. In late 1917, the story made its way into the *Daily British Whig* in Kingston, Ontario, via the American media and featuring an American protagonist. At this time, Chambers felt that although the story might have been useful for recruitment in the United States, it should be "soft-pedal[led]" in Canada, which meant not reprinted. His reasoning was that it might be used by "certain sections of politicians actively engaged in encouraging certain sections of the community to avoid military duty."[37] Canadians were involved in an intense conscription debate in the lead-up to the election of December 1917 in which pacifists risked censorship to speak out against this platform of the government. At the same time that the story could be used for recruitment purposes in one context, in another it could be used to scare people away from enlisting.

In fact, "crucifixion" was used during the war to intimidate and punish soldiers. It was more formally called Field Punishment Number One and was described by George Coppard, a private in the British Army.[38] The punishment consisted of lashing the offender to a gun wheel or cross in public view. This form of punishment continued until 1917, when protests in Parliament forced the war minister to end it.

The war cartoonist, Louis Raemaekers, flips the horror of this British punishment onto the Germans in his cartoon, "Prussianism and Civilisation," published in 1915, which shows the female figure of Europe tied to the wheel of a field gun. G.K. Chesterton, who wrote an accompanying commentary when the cartoon was republished in 1916 under the caption "Europe," compared the present torture of Europe with the ancient form of torture for martyrs. He said that the despair of the war was far worse; in the past, those who were tortured for their beliefs could accept conversion, but in the Great War "even the terms of surrender are unknowable; and she [Europe] can only ask 'Am I civilized?'"[39] Another comparison with an ancient form of torture for martyrs is visible in the cartoon. Europe's hand hangs over a small fire that has turned it black, as if she were being burned at the stake.

The story of the crucified Canadian next came to the attention of Canadian government officials just after the Armistice, during the

"MIGHT IS THE SUPREME RIGHT, AND THE DISPUTE AS TO WHAT IS RIGHT IS DECIDED BY THE ARBITRAMENT OF WAR." *BERNHARDI.*

Louis Raemaekers, "Prussianism and Civilisation." The quotation from General Friedrich von Bernhardi reads, "Might is the supreme right, and the dispute as to what is right is decided by the arbitrament of war." (In *Raemaekers Cartoons*, 1915.)

exhibition of the Canadian War Memorials Fund collection, which included Francis Derwent Wood's sculpture, *Canada's Golgotha*. This collection came into existence as part of the Canadian War Records Office in London, begun by Sir Max Aiken. Originally from New Brunswick, Aiken became Lord Beaverbrook in 1917. He was a successful businessman whose chief concerns were newspapers. As a supporter of the war, he had wanted to have a record of Canada's involvement in the war and firmly believed in the power of photography and film to capture images of the front that could be helpful to the war effort. Although not originally interested in paintings to document war, Aiken later decided that they provided "the most permanent and vital form in which the great deeds and sacrifices of the Canadian Nation in the war could be enshrined for posterity."[40]

Canada's Golgotha, a 32-inch high bronze sculpture, was well publicized before the exhibit opened. It depicted a soldier nailed to a barn door surrounded by German soldiers jeering at him. The publicity package sent out by the Canadian War Records Office included a photo of the statue. The *Daily Mail* published the picture of the sculpture with the comment, "Canada's sternest memorial to her sons' sufferings in the war."[41] The show of war art at Burlington House, London, was scheduled to open in January 1919, just before the signing of the Paris Peace Treaty. Clearly, the *Golgotha* sculpture was going to be troublesome for those who wanted to arrive at a peaceful solution at the Versailles conference. One of those people was the Canadian prime minister, Sir Robert Borden. Borden requested further investigation into the veracity of the story. Two more sworn statements were presented. One of these, from a Victoria Cross recipient, seemed to count for a great deal and finally attached a name to the victim: Sergeant Brant. Just at this time the German government formally requested that the Canadian government publicly acknowledge that the story of the crucified soldier was untrue, or else provide evidence of it.

The first official Canadian response to the Germans was that they had enough evidence to believe the story was true, but when the Germans demanded a role in the investigation the sculpture was withdrawn from the exhibition. It was not shown again until the 1990s.[42]

As Lister Sinclair commented in a CBC Radio *Ideas* documentary on "Canada's Golgotha," aired on Remembrance Day 1987, the Canadian government must have felt intense embarrassment at the prospect of being investigated by the losers of the war.[43] In insisting on Canada's place at the conference as an entity separate from Britain, Borden was hoping to gain an international reputation for Canada at the peace table. In fact, Germany's efforts to gain some control over the power of the story eventually came to greater fruition when the Nazis used it as an example of the horror of British propaganda lies.

Even though the sculpture was withdrawn from the exhibition in 1919, the Canadian government continued to look into the story but could never prove that the incident had occurred.

In the 1920s and 1930s, when not only disbelief but cynicism and irony coloured the reception of atrocity stories, the story of the crucified Canadian was dismissed. A clear example of this was Sir Arthur Ponsonby's *Falsehood in War-Time*, subtitled, *An amazing collection of carefully documented lies circulated in Great Britain, France, Germany, Italy and America during the Great War* (1928). Ponsonby quotes two articles from the London *Times*, published May 10 and 15, 1915, which wrote of the "ghastly" deed, followed by two excerpts from House of Commons debates of May 12 and 15, 1915, which referred to the "vile" act. He then confidently disproves the story.[44] In 1930 the acting deputy minister of militia and defence, H.W. Brown, asked to have the sculpture put into permanent storage "so that the government may be protected against the embarrassment of its being exhibited or photographed at any further time as the portrayal of an event."[45] Desmond Morton sums up this change of mind in his book on Canadian prisoners of war, *Silent Battle*. "From avid credulity, the public mind had swung to a resolute skepticism about 'atrocity stories,' which, for many, would last until the gates of Belsen were opened in 1945."[46] Yet the government ban on exhibiting or photographing the sculpture was still in effect in 1989, when Maria Tippett's request to include a photograph of it in an exhibition was denied. Such was the potential of *Canada's Golgotha* to incite powerful emotions.

When the historian Seth Feldman was researching the 1987 *Ideas* program,[47] he found in the National Gallery's records of the sculpture the name "Harry Band" given as the identity of the victim – a name interestingly close to "Sergeant Brant," who had been identified as the victim in 1919. In 1991, the *Vancouver Sun* ran an article entitled "Kin of Crucified Soldier want Depiction Shown." The article briefly went through the history of the story and of the sculpture, culminating with the comment by the great-nephew of Harry Band that he found it "interesting that people professed to be shocked by such an occurrence. Especially in today's climate. It's happening all over the world."[48]

Thus through its history the story's presentation has shifted along the continuum of fact and fiction in accordance with the politics of the times. Most recently, British historian Iain Overton has investigated this story as well as other myths of World War I in his doctoral dissertation and developed them into a television documentary. He asserts that the story of the crucified Canadian is true.

But, perhaps more instructive for a wider discussion is Feldman's summation of the story, which goes beyond questions of truth. "It's a story the sacrificial lambs tell to the people who thrive on sacrifice. But what really matters more is that they were all crucified – the soldiers, the civilians, all the story tellers, all the people who believed them."[49]

This story presented the Canadian public with an image of one of their own sons reliving Christ's sacrifice. The Christian imagery was so strong that it overshadowed the fact that this was a soldier who was, more or less, trained to kill. Instead, the audience during the war was left with the idea that this man, like Edith Cavell or any other Christian martyr, should live in memory not because of his mere physical strength but for his spirit of sacrifice to the cause and for his bravery in facing death.

The crucified Canadian as depicted in the sculpture *Canada's Golgotha* was not the only image of crucifixion included in the Canadian War Memorials Fund Collection. Charles Sims' large painting, *Sacrifice* (ca. 1918), shows Christ on the cross overlooking representatives of the Canadian population. This was the most explicitly religious and

Charles Sims, *Sacrifice*, ca. 1918, 416 cm × 409 cm.
(Canadian War Museum artifact number 19710262-0662.)

nationalistic of the paintings and the most important in the collection.
It was also to be the last image to greet the viewer in the planned war
memorial art gallery in Ottawa. (It was never built.[50]) The painting
has the crests of the nine provinces then in Confederation across the
top, just above the horizontal bar of a crucifix. The Jesus-figure hangs
on the other side of the cross, facing away from the viewer and toward
scenes of the wounded and dying on the battlefield and those left on
the home front. In the snowy scene of Canada at the bottom of the

picture are the bereaved, the old, the very young, and women. One mother in black holds her infant in a white christening gown above her. The child has just become a new member of the Christian religion, and of the country involved in this great sacrifice. Looking back through the lens of time we can see this infant as next in the line of those who will be sacrificed in the coming war, but at the time the child represented the innocence and promise of the future for whom the battle was being fought.

The scene at the bottom of *Sacrifice* is reminiscent of the grieving figures in another very popular painting in the Canadian War Memorials Fund collection, *The Flag* by Byam Shaw. Grieving women, children and old men stand around the bottom of the monument, where a dead Canadian soldier lies. The soldier, holding the Canadian flag, rests between the hand-like paws of the monumental lion of Britain. There is one woman, perhaps the mother of the dead soldier, dressed in black with her arms stretched up above her. Unlike in *Sacrifice*, the woman with her arms raised up holds no infant. The caption for this painting in the book published to accompany the show in 1919 reads: "A memorial to those Canadians who willingly gave their most beloved for the honour of The Flag and the upholding of Freedom, Justice, and Right."[51]

These and other works of art in the Canadian War Memorials Fund collection, created during the war, connect ideas of Canada, the nation-state, and horrific sacrifice, but most were not viewed until after the war. More widely available images that commented on participation in the war could be found in the cartoons of the day.[52]

The most powerful cartoons linking the ideals of Christian sacrifice with the Allied war effort were those of the Dutch artist Louis Raemaekers. This cartoonist's work, readily available in Canada during the war, had initially become known in Europe soon after the war began. Because their political content threatened Holland's neutrality, Raemaekers was forced to emigrate. He went to England and began publishing in the London *Times*. Collections of his works were published by Hodder and Stoughton in London, New York, and Toronto. The publishers announced that they were "anxious to obtain the widest possible distribution for these Cartoons,"[53] likely with the same intent as that of the Canadian government regarding the dissemination of the Bryce Report. Francis Stopford, the editor, states in his introduction to one volume of cartoons that Raemaekers was "one of the supreme figures which the Great War has called into being," and that the type of Christianity he expressed was "not perhaps of the theologian, but of the honest and kindly man of the world."[54] The power of his propaganda, published on both sides of the Atlantic, is summed up by Stopford as "worth at least two Army Corps to the Allies."[55] Today, scholars John Horne and Alan Kramer concur with Stopford on the importance of Raemaekers' work, stating – in less metaphorical language – that the cartoonist "became the single most influential figure projecting the Allied vision of the German enemy to home audiences and to the rest of the world."[56]

Probably the most accessible medium for Raemaekers' cartoons was a set of cigarette cards or "stiffeners." Before World War I, cigars, pipes, chewing tobacco, and snuff were preferred by men (who made up the majority of smokers) to cigarettes, but these were found to be less manageable at the battlefront than cigarettes. Tobacco companies promoted their product during the war by giving away cigarettes, and although women did not smoke very much, those at home were encouraged to supply the soldiers with cigarettes. Grace Craig mentions in her memoir, *But This Is Our War*, how she gave away cartons of cigarettes to soldiers on a train in Pembroke, Ontario, so as to "improve the men's spirits."[57] Under these conditions cigarette production began to increase substantially through the second decade of the century.

The stiffeners were initially just part of the packaging inserted into the paper wrap to help prevent the cigarettes from getting damaged, but marketers soon came to see their advertising and propaganda potential. Companies produced the cards in sets and, like baseball cards, they were collected. The set of "Raemaekers War Cartoons" was large, consisting of 140 cards. They were issued in 1916 in Canada with Black Cat cigarettes, manufactured by Carreras Ltd (London and Montreal). One side showed a colour cartoon while the reverse presented,

"HIM WHO OPPOSES ME I SHALL CRUSH TO PIECES."

THE KAISER.

Louis Raemaekers, "Kultur and Calvary." The quotation attributed to
the German Kaiser reads, "Him who opposes me I shall crush to pieces."
(In *Raemaekers Cartoons*, 1915.)

under the title of "Lest We Forget," a paragraph of explanation further emphasizing the visual message. These cartoons were consistent in their style and message with those published in book form.

A religious influence in the cartoons printed in books or on cigarette cards was clear and often repeated. One striking example, entitled "Kultur and Calvary," pictures Christ on the Cross with a faceless, fully armoured, Teutonic warrior chopping down the Cross from behind. Even the crows are shown fleeing from this scene.[58]

An example of a cartoon much like *Canada's Golgotha* is entitled "Easter 1915" and depicts Christ surrounded by laughing German soldiers, one of whom is placing a German helmet on Christ's head.[59] This cartoon is dated close to the time when the Canadian was said to have been crucified, just after the first German gas attack. Another cartoon originally published in 1916 is called "Thrown to the Swine: The Martyred Nurse." Here the dead and bound body of Edith Cavell is shown surrounded by drooling pigs wearing German helmets. Nowhere on the cartoon nor in the commentary by the Dean of St Paul's is the name of Edith Cavell mentioned. Her death was so well known that mention of her name would have been superfluous. Instead, the Dean states: "though not the worst of their misdeeds, this has probably been the stupidest. It gained us almost as many recruits as the sinking of the Lusitania."[60]

After the publication of the Bryce Report, Raemaekers produced cartoons illustrating some of its stories. One cartoon, "Germany's Victims," shows a man cradling a tiny casket in his arms with the inscription below, "We find many well-established cases of the slaughter of … quite small children." This is signed, "Report of Lord Bryce's committee on German Atrocities."[61] Another, without specifically mentioning the Bryce Report, refers to the same killings. In "The Massacre of the Innocents," a crowned and robed man holds his hands to his face in fear as he is surrounded by disembodied faces of crying children.[62]

Raemaekers certainly did not have a monopoly on illustrating the atrocities described in the Bryce Report. On the subject of the use of civilians as shields, Bernard Partridge published a cartoon in *Punch* in which a German soldier stands behind a woman and two tiny children,

THE MASSACRE OF THE INNOCENTS.

HEROD: "ARE THEY CRYING 'MOTHER'—OR 'MURDER'?"

Louis Raemaekers, "The Massacre of the Innocents." The caption connects German acts of atrocity as told by the Bryce Report with a biblical villain: "Herod: 'Are they crying 'mother' – or 'murder'?" (In *Raemaekers Cartoons*, 1915: 29.)

raising his hand and eyes upward while he pokes them in the back with his sword. The caption reads, "God (and the women) Our Shield"; below this is the explanation, "Study of a German Gentleman going into Action."[63]

Taking another Christian image and tying it to German atrocities, the Raemaekers cartoon "The Stones Cry Out" depicts a cringing German soldier accusingly pointed at by two stone figures of saints come to life in front of a burning cathedral.[64] Bernard Vaughan wrote the commentary on this image in 1916. He collected together most of the atrocities of which the Germans had been accused and packaged them as a sin against Christianity: "Not content to crucify Canadians, murder priests, violate nuns, mishandle women, and bayonet children, the enemy torpedoes civilian-carrying liners, and bombs Red Cross hospitals. More, sinning against posterity as well as antiquity, Germans stand charged before man and God with reducing to ashes some of the finest artistic output of Christian civilization."[65]

Through his powerful cartoons Raemaekers depicted the war as a religious battle between good and evil. Thus his work provided a platform upon which an image could be created of mothers of dead soldiers as mothers of the sacrificed.

———— ·>●<· ————

Raemaekers was not alone in his vision of the war. Chaplains, whether at the front or at home, conferred Divine support upon their side in the war. This support was also written into much of the fiction and poetry of the time, complementing messages of the nobility of the battle that the public received through stories of atrocities and martyrs.

Winnington-Ingram, the Bishop of London, fully recognized the propaganda value of the death of Edith Cavell, as we have seen, and in a sermon preached in Westminster Abbey on 28 November 1915 and later published as "A Word of Cheer" in the *Christian World Pulpit* on 8 December 1915, he made use of the story of the crucified Canadian. "To save the freedom of the world, to save liberty, to save the honour of women and the innocence of children, every one … is banded in a great crusade – we cannot deny it – to kill Germans, to

"THOU ART THE MAN."

Louis Raemaekers, "The Stones Cry Out." The accusatory caption reads, "Thou art the man." (In *Raemaekers Cartoons*, 1915.)

kill them not for the sake of killing, but to save the world, to kill the good as well as the bad, to kill the young men as well as the old, to kill those who have shown kindness to our wounded as well as those fiends who crucified the Canadian sergeant."[66]

Thus the Bishop ties together the Belgian[67] atrocities, mentioning the honour and innocence of women and children, with the story of the crucified Canadian to raise the ire of his audience to the point where they are willing to kill all Germans. Further on in the sermon he quotes a Scottish preacher's description of this war for "purity" and "freedom" as a "war of the nailed hand against the mailed fist." Where many would leave it at that, Winnington-Ingram goes further, to make it explicit that he "look[s] upon everyone who fights in this war as a hero, and upon every one who dies in it as a martyr."

Winnington-Ingram was not alone in this rhetoric. Captain J.H. MacDonald, Headquarters Staff, Canadian Chaplain Service, was quoted in the *Times* as saying, "After my experience at the front ... I should like to say that who fights for England fights for God, and who dies for England dies for God."[68] Even by the end of the war there were still chaplains who were able to repeat this message. Chaplain and author Alexander Ketterson wrote of his belief that the Canadian soldiers who had died in the war had not died in vain: "Gallant soldiers, what a glorious death; brave Crusaders, you have died in a noble cause!"[69] Ketterson included these words in his introduction to a collection of "uplifting" sayings selected by Canadian officers to express their feelings.

David Marshall includes a chapter about the war and the church in his 1992 book on the crises of faith in the Protestant churches in Canada.[70] He discusses a number of clergymen who went to the front to preach, some of whom made great efforts to adapt their services to respond to the despair of the men. One of the best-known Canadian chaplains of the war, Canon Scott, bent a few rules to be at the front with the men. When so many of the chaplains stayed well behind the lines, his presence alongside the men was respected, appreciated, and considered highly uncommon. A clear indication of the prevailing attitudes of the men toward most of the chaplains was that expressed by Noel Chavasse, double Victoria Cross recipient and son of the Bishop of Liverpool. He saw them as smug, unable to communicate with the men, and concerned only for their own safety. "As for parsons, they are no advertisement to the uplifting influence of the grace of God."[71]

In Scott's memoirs of the war, published in 1922, he mentioned the importance of one of his acts in his capacity as chaplain. "I used to distribute little bronze crucifixes as I went along … I told the men that if anyone asked them why they were at the war, that little cross with the patient figure of self-sacrifice upon it, would be the answer. The widow of an officer who was killed at Albert told me the cross which I gave her husband was taken from his dead body, and she now had it, and would wear it to her dying day. I was much surprised and touched to see the value which the men set upon these tokens of their faith."[72]

Although Scott may have had empathy for the soldiers, his job was to help maintain a fighting force at the front; to do this, he wielded the power of God and, sometimes, of women. In one of the cases where a man came to him asking to be sent behind the lines because of nerves, Scott relates how he told him that although he may have been a "weakling" in the past, with God's help he could become a hero and his mother and sisters would love him even more, "'For', I said, 'All women love a brave man.'"[73]

Other Canadian clergy persisted with a conventional evangelical Christian message of "repentance, sacrifice, and salvation."[74] More often this kind of message was reserved for those at home as opposed to the soldiers at the front, but not so for the evangelical-leaning Presbyterian minister, George Pidgeon, who was at the Front in 1918 with the YMCA. As David Marshall writes, "The idea that atonement – that through sacrifice comes life – permeated Pidgeon's message to the soldiers."[75] Pidgeon's religious interpretation of the war was in keeping with the general outlook of the YMCA, which in its newspaper, *Canadian Manhood*, supported the notion of sending soldiers to war "not as Canada's army but as representatives of Christ."[76]

Robert John Renison, a chaplain with the First Division and later Bishop of Moosonee and Metropolitan Ontario, felt that the war was "one of the shining moments of the great story of mankind" bringing out what was truly noble in people.[77] On the home front this militant idealism was encouraged and sustained by many of the nation's churches, "which like the churches of every belligerent nation mobilized all of their spiritual resources for battle."[78]

The messages of the nobility of Christian sacrifice in support of the war effort crossed over from pulpit to novel. For many writers, the war added another dimension to the Christian ethics embedded in their world view. Dagmar Novak, in her study of Canadian fiction and war, *Dubious Glory* (2000), argues it was for them "A holy war, a sacred cause, and a test of spiritual righteousness. Primed by the atrocity dispatches from London and Paris, they eagerly embrace the concept of 'Jesus in Khaki,' and represent the war as God's battle with the devil and involvement in it as a manifestation of faith, the supreme act of decision and sacrifice for Christ. Central in their treatment is the view that to die in the conflict is to die for Christ."[79]

A prime example of a religious depiction of the war came through the pen of Charles Gordon, who wrote extremely popular novels under the pen name of Ralph Connor. He had studied to be a missionary in Toronto and Edinburgh and worked as a Presbyterian minister in the west of Canada. He began to write fiction as a way to reach out to those who had little interest in formal religion. His novels were peopled by missionary heroes who stressed the "then popular themes of the nobility of sacrifice, moral regeneration and the influence of strong characters."[80]

Connor's first novel, *Black Rock* (1898), quickly sold through its initial print-run of 5,000 copies, a mark that still constitutes a best-seller in Canada. The book soon sold hundreds of thousands of copies when the American edition came out. Connor had a significant influence on his North American audience not only as a novelist but as a public speaker. Working for the Canadian government as a propagandist, he gave lecture tours in which, among other objectives, he tried to draw the Americans into the conflict.[81]

The close connection between Connor's fiction and his propaganda work is examined by Dagmar Novak, who notes that it was while he was involved in this work that Connor wrote two more popular novels,

The Major and *The Sky Pilot in No Man's Land*: "the ideas he developed [in those novels] were essentially the ones he was expressing from the public platform."[82] In *The Sky Pilot in No Man's Land* Connor explains that his heroes are of the "noble company of martyrs" since they are "uncommonly like God, for He did the same thing. He gave Himself to us."[83]

Novak argues that the Canadian novels of the war period fit easily into the romance tradition.[84] The defining characteristic of romance is, as Northrup Frye suggests, that it "avoids the ambiguities of ordinary life, where everything is a mixture of good and bad, and where it is difficult to take sides or believe that people are consistent patterns of virtue or vice. The popularity of romance, it is obvious, has much to do with its simplifying of moral facts."[85]

Romance authors were meeting the needs of Victorian readers who were looking to find moral law in action. Canadian novelists of the war and post-war era were loyal to this perspective and maintained that "romance was reality" long after their British and American contemporaries had moved on to an ironic understanding of the war.[86]

Novak found that "even the diaries, autobiographies, and letters of those who were involved in the fighting were replete with the sentimentality and propaganda characteristic of the novels" of the war.[87] Soon after the beginning of the war, on 8 September 1914, Lucy Maud Montgomery wrote in her diary, "Oh, we all come back to God in these times of soul-sifting – humbly, starkly, unconditionally. Perhaps this is why this awful war has come. The world was forgetting God. It had to be reminded of Him."[88] These sentiments were repeated through the voice of her heroine in *Rilla of Ingleside*, who states, "We all come back to God in these days of soul-sifting, ... There have been many days in the past when I didn't believe in God – not *as* God – only as the impersonal Great First Cause of the scientists. I believe in Him now – I *have* to – there's nothing else to fall back on but God."[89]

Montgomery saw the cause of the war as a failing relationship with God. Writing in *Everywoman's World* magazine in 1915 – the magazine with the widest circulation in Canada throughout the war[90] – she said she was not one of those who believed that "this war will put an end to war," for its cause was "moral degradation, low ideals, sordid devotion to money-getting ... Nothing short of so awful a calamity as a great war can awaken to remembrance a nation that has forgotten God and sold its birthright of aspiration for a mess of pottage."[91]

A marked increase in Sabbath observance during the war indicated that people were grasping at something to help them make sense of the slaughter. The culture of religion provided a ready philosophical framework for questions concerning ethical action. In *The Major*, Connor's narrator talks about people's renewed thoughts about the meaningfulness of churchgoing. "On the first Sunday of the war the churches of Winnipeg were full to the doors. Men, whose attendance was more or less desultory and to a certain extent dependent upon the weather, were conscious of an impulse to go to church. War had shaken the foundations of their world, and men were thinking their deepest thoughts and facing realities too often neglected or minimized."[92]

As to what people heard when they went to church, and how widely spread the message was, Connor carries on to say, "The newspaper press published full reports of many of the sermons preached. These sermons all struck the same note – repentance, sacrifice, service."[93] In *Sky Pilot in No Man's Land*, Connor specified what this sacrifice would look like in his description of the wounded: "At their country's bidding they had ascended that Holy Mount of Sacrifice, to offer upon the altar of the world's freedom their bodies as a living sacrifice unto God, holy and acceptable."[94] They came back shattered but "unconquered and eternally glorious."[95]

The call for repentance and sacrifice in Connor's novel mirrors that of George Pidgeon's sermons. Canada's sacrifice was made clear with the devastating casualty figures in the daily papers, and Christianity, as Montgomery made clear, could be relied on to answer the question of why there was a need to repent. This answer ran parallel to the political explanations for the war. Just as Christ had been sacrificed to save humanity from sin, so too were soldiers being sacrificed to save a world gone wrong. In his sermons to the Toronto Bloor Street Presbyterian congregation, George Pidgeon presented the death of a soldier and the consequent grief to his family as "comparable to the agony of Christ's crucifixion and the sorrow it brought to his mother," for both had a higher purpose.[96]

71

John Oxenham's poem, inscribed on a bronze plaque on the New-foundland memorial at Beaumont-Hamel, France, asks the visitor to tread softly on "this vast altar-pile" where the souls of men went up to heaven to gain immortality.[97] In *High Altars: The Battle-fields of France and Flanders As I Saw Them* (1918), Oxenham states, "We do not look upon this war as a punishment sent of God – except inas-much as all suffering is sin's own punishment. And punishment for all our falling away from the higher things we all undoubtedly deserved – and needed."[98] On the last page of the book is a poem called "Time's Altars." Oxenham places the sacrifices of the war on a time-line that begins in 1914 BC, when "Man sought redemption" through sacrifice. It carries on to AD 33 with the death of Christ, and then to the altars of World War I. Of the future he reasons, "if still the things of earth enthral us ... / Then, of a surety, shall still worse befall us."[99]

The idea that the war was God's justice paid out to those who had not led a truly Christian life was voiced by others in their effort to understand how such a horrible war could happen. Thus Montgomery wrote in her diary, "The world was forgetting God. It had to be reminded of Him."[100] Yet later she wrote that she was happy her son was not old enough to go to war. Embarrassed at her selfishness for being unwill-ing to make this sacrifice, she says, "Without shedding of blood there is no remission of sins. Without shedding of blood there is no *anything*! Everything, it seems to me, must be bought by sacrifice."[101]

In a war that produced poems like poppies, the most often quoted and most popular of all was "In Flanders Fields." First published on 8 December 1915 in *Punch Magazine*, these lines were translated into so many languages in McCrae's lifetime – he died of pneumonia 28 January 1918 – that he joked that only Chinese was left now.[102] The poem was used "for recruiting, raising money, attacking both pacifists and profiteers, and comforting the relatives of the dead."[103] It is sym-bolic for Canadians now of their participation in the war, and is quot-ed and sung every year on Remembrance Day. It was also used as propaganda in the election of 1917 to encourage continued participa-tion in the war. Much of the power of this poem comes in the poignant demand of the last verse:

Take up our quarrel with the foe;
To you from failing hands we throw
The torch; be yours to hold it high.
If ye break faith with us who die
We shall not sleep, though poppies grow
In Flanders fields

If the listener does not join the fight, then all those who have sacrificed themselves for the cause will have done so in vain. Because it was so effective in pulling the reader in to share the responsibility of the soldiers, it was used extensively in the United States when that country entered the war. It was often printed with a poetic reply, one of them by R.W. Lillard, who responded, "The torch ye threw to us we caught."[104]

The poem has been inscribed in words and images on the parliament buildings and Canadian monuments – a topic to be discussed in chapter 4. It is still used as a symbol of the war on the historic battlefields of the Western Front. The biggest, and arguably the best, museum of the war, housed in the reconstructed Cloth Hall of Ypres, is called "In Flanders Fields." The poem also gave the international emblem of the poppy to the war. The message of sacrifice and the need for future generations to remember has had great lasting power through this symbol.

"In Flanders Field," along with another poem by McCrae, "The Anxious Dead", which repeats the theme of the living having a sacred contract with the dead, was included in a 1919 volume, *The Great War in Verse and Prose*, published for use in Ontario schools. The collection gives a clear view of how Ontario schoolchildren were expected to interpret the war: with a strong sense of patriotism. In the introduction to the book, the minister of education, H.J. Cody, reiterated the notion of sacrifice and debt to the dead, saying, "Canada is dearer to us than ever, because it has been purchased anew at a great cost of precious blood ... A better Canada ... will come if there is kindled in the souls of our citizens the same bright flame of sacrifice and service which burned so brightly in the hearts of Canada's citizen-soldiers of the Great War."[105]

In the language of sacrifice, the soldiers were not trained to kill; rather, they were fighting for peace. As Jonathan Vance describes, the prevailing myth of the war in Canada was the belief that the conflict "had been thrust on peace loving people who were defending the weak."[106] As citizen-soldiers, or soldiers of peace, they were strongly supported by the propaganda of the time, which never lost sight of the fact that the Germans had invaded Belgium. After the war this interpretation of the soldier was further promoted with the view that veterans were men who "deplored war" but who, if needed, "would make any sacrifice to ensure a more lasting peace. The pacifist-soldier, then, was not a contradiction in terms."[107]

That it was not a contradiction was clearly understood by *Saturday Night* magazine's book-review editor, Tom Folis. In a review of Ralph Connor's *The Major*, Folis stated that the novel lacked a story compared with Connor's previous works, but "represent[ed] Canada's great response to the war."[108] Folis was impressed by the hero, the only son of a Quaker woman, who finally decided to go to war while still maintaining his pacifism. As will be seen in the next chapter, the theme of the "only son" is often repeated in war fiction, advertising, and propagandistic news stories. In Connor's novel the only son's decision to go to war meant that he was no longer a fool but rather, Folis maintained, "a fighting pacifist."

Soldiers are depicted as sharing with martyrs the characteristic of being lovers of peace. A remarkable thing about martyrs, in the traditional understanding of the term, is that they can have an immense impact on furthering a cause without physically hurting anyone. They do not seek their own or anyone else's death. It is through this peaceful means that they are able to strike a psychological blow at their enemy. All the might of the enemy is not enough to sway the belief of the martyr. For all their efforts the enemy gets only a dead body and a tarnished reputation. Canadian and other allied soldiers were presented by the propaganda system as defenders of the weak: of the women and children who were drowned when the Lusitania was sunk, of the executed Nurse Cavell, of the crucified Canadian, of the raped Belgian women and their bayonetted babies. By being characterized as defenders from the beginning of the war onward, the soldiers were able to appear as powerful as martyrs in their peace-loving ideals.

In summary, the Canadian public and soldiers were surrounded by the language of sacrifice issuing from the pulpit, newspapers, novels, poetry, and art. The martyrdom of Edith Cavell was widely reported and repeated in the Canadian press and resulted in the dedication of a mountain monument. The atrocity stories published in the Bryce Report and the tale of the crucified Canadian mirrored the tales of torture found in the traditional martyrologies and served the same purpose: to lift the public out of complacency and into battle. The very accessible images of cartoonist Louis Raemaekers gave a visual representation of these horror stories, thus adding to their impact. The atrocity stories were taken up by the chaplains serving overseas and added to their sermons to give the soldiers reason to carry on. Preachers, novelists, and poets at home assumed the right to give divine blessing to those fighting on their side. They provided a theological reason for the conflict – this is what happens when one turns away from God – and they gave clear direction to what act was necessary: sacrifice. These words and images simplified the issues, and presented them in terms that made it easier for their audiences to build conviction and to resist any desire to compromise.

The soldiers were not being attacked because they belonged to a particular religious faith. They were not offered the choice between death or conversion – an element often found in martyrologies, reinforcing a presentation of the act as being done in the name of a particular ideal or religious tradition. Even the curses they used, no longer focused on the power of the divine, were evidence of a disenchanted world. Instead of invoking the wrath of God on the enemy, they invoked the worst degradation they could think of to vent their feelings and describe their world. The predominant swear words were sexual rather than religious in character. As Brophy explains in his dictionary of World War I slang, "The obscenity satisfied, because the words blasphemed sex, even as war blasphemed life which is the child of sex."[109]

Any visions of glory and fighting for truth, justice and God that a young recruit might have entertained at the start of the war were soon wiped clean. The language of sacrifice, although it did permeate some of the writings of the soldiers, was for the most part imposed by those who were not doing the fighting. But, for all that, the hope that Christianity promised of death leading to a better life must have given a moment of comfort to many. Certainly, many mothers accepted the hope offered by this interpretation, whether through faith, compulsion, or the lack of ready alternatives.

Chapter 3

"You Are All I Have to Give":
War Mothers' Stories, Rewards, and the
Other Face of Loss

Maternal pride, military achievement, and a place in heaven were offered by the most famous of Canadian generals, Sir Arthur Currie, to the Canadian corps before the final German offensive in 1918. In his address to the troops he said, "To those who will fall I say 'you will not die, but step into immortality. Your mothers will not lament your fate, but will be proud to have borne such sons. Your names will be revered for ever and ever by your grateful country, and God will take you unto himself.'"[1]

Similarly, Mrs Mason, one of the characters in Nellie McClung's autobiographical novel *The Next of Kin: Those Who Wait and Wonder* (1917), described the conflict thus: "This is a holy war – holier than any of the crusades – for the crusader went out to restore the tomb of our Lord, and that is only a material thing; but our boys are going out to give back to the world our Lord's ideals, and I know they are more precious to Him than any tomb could be!"[2]

McClung begins her book by recounting conversations she had with women after giving a speech to the Red Cross Society. She presents herself as not the "author" but the "historian" of this book, commissioned by these women "to tell what we think and feel, to tell how it looks to us, who are the mothers of soldiers, and to whom even now the letter may be on its way with its curt inscription across the corner."[3] The inscription she speaks of is the words "Killed in Action," printed in red ink across the corner of an envelope addressed to a Canadian soldier fighting in France; these envelopes were returned to the sender, the dead soldier's mother, unopened.

The views of General Currie and of McClung's character, Mrs Mason, were echoed in many other public expressions of opinion. They open a window not only to the official justification of the sacrifices demanded by the war, but also to the extreme nature of the conflict and the role the mothers of soldiers had to play.

The mother-of-martyr role is, of course, contingent upon the story of the martyr. The previous chapter has shown that although the term "martyr" was rarely used by those outside the Church to describe the soldiers, their death was considered by many as a sacrifice for God and country. According to Jonathan Vance, "If Christ became the spiritual symbol of the ideals for which Canadian soldiers fought, an allegorical maternal figure became one of the most potent secular symbols."[4] The proximity of this maternal figure to the sacrificed son casts a spiritual glow on the mother as well.

The stories of the mothers during the war and of the mothers of martyrs from other times and places are alike not only in their ability to recruit followers to a cause, but also in the type of honour accorded to the protagonists. In more recent stories of mothers of martyrs from other parts of the world there is a record of honouring bereaved mothers not only with societal respect but also with material rewards. This was seen in Canada as well during and after World War I in various pension programs, in the devising and awarding of the Memorial Cross (or, as it is better known, the Silver Cross), and in suffrage for women. The fact that bereaved mothers of Canada and mothers of martyrs elsewhere both had public and private forms of recompense tied to their willingness to sacrifice their sons highlights similarities in the way that different societies, under extreme pressure, have used the special mother-son relationship to promote their own ends.

Early in the war, recruitment calls began to fail. The propaganda departments in Canada and Britain turned to women to help call up the men for service. The poster campaigns of these years bluntly used women in general to entice, shame, and cajole men to enlist. "Women of Britain say GO!" demands one of the best-known of these posters, showing an image of a woman standing by a window hugged by a girl and a small boy as they watch soldiers march off to war. A poster addressed "To the Women of Canada" lists four questions, the third of which was a toned-down reminder of the demand articulated in the British poster. After telling women of the atrocities in Belgium and the vulnerability of the home front, the poster asks, "Do you realize that the one word 'GO' from you may send another man to fight for our King and Country?" The final question relies on guilt and shame to encourage women to enlist their husbands and sons. "When the War is over and someone asks your husband or your son what he did in the Great War, is he to hang his head because you would not let him go?"[5]

Other posters directed their appeal to women identified by their specific relationship to the recruits. One, for example, called on mothers and sweethearts: "Do you expect other mothers' sons to defend you and your sons? Sweethearts: If you cannot persuade him to answer his country's call and protect you now, DISCHARGE HIM as unfit."[6] An early recruiting poster of the war,[7] originating in England and used in Canada, pictured a white-haired woman standing with a firm expression on her face. She is dressed in black and has her arm around a well-dressed young man. Once again the demand to "go" is presented as coming from a woman. The caption reads, "Go! It's your duty lad. Join to-day."[8] This elderly woman is not specifically labelled a mother but was likely understood as such, for mothers at this time were generally depicted as older women.

Another image of an older woman was used in the Canadian recruitment poster for the Irish Canadian Rangers Overseas Battalion, Montreal. Here the woman is depicted sitting in profile, wearing a black dress and lace cap. The demand "Fight for Her" accompanies the image.[9] The same picture was used as a British fundraiser with the caption "Old Age Must Come: so prepare for it in British War Savings

Certificates."[10] This woman is presented in a passive role, unlike the white-haired woman who urges her son to go.

A more militant image in both British and Canadian posters is of a woman in flowing robes with one bare shoulder and a veil on her head billowing behind her. She holds the scabbard of a sword, offering the hilt to the imagined recruit beyond the picture frame. Above her head are the words, "Take up the sword of justice."[11] Below her are ocean waters with dead or dying bodies floating in front of a sinking ship. Although this woman appears as an Athena figure urging men to battle, in some posters women referred to as mothers are dressed in the same type of clothing, thus amalgamating militancy and motherhood. In October 1917 *Everywoman's World* printed a message from the Food Controller, the Hon. W.J. Hanna, asking women to sign a Food Service Pledge to limit their use of certain foods so there would be enough for the soldiers. The right side of the page states, "Thou Shalt Not Want. The Undying Pledge of Canada's Mothers to Her Sons." This is balanced on the left with "They Shall Not Pass. The Immortal Cry of Canada at the Second Battle of Ypres." The mother in her Greek robe, sandals on her feet, and hat saying "Canada" on her head, protects her soldier sons behind her while staving off the figure of Famine, who wears a German helmet.[12] This image offers women a parallel role to men in the war. They too can fight and make sacrifices – in the kitchen.

Militancy also comes across in posters depicting Britain as a mother lion and the countries of the Commonwealth as her cubs. The lion and the unicorn are featured on the heraldic arms of Britain. During the Victorian era the more feminine symbol of Britain as Britannia was also used. The mother-lion portrayal conflates these images. Yet having a mother lion call to her cubs to defend her is a reversal of her stereotypical role; the lioness is usually the one who defends the cubs, and with a fierceness no male can match. Despite this role reversal the image came out in various posters with the hope of recruiting even Americans in the role of devoted offspring.

One version of the mother-lion image asks the question, "Are you answering the call?" The poster was used in the United States and advised those interested to apply at the "British-Canadian Recruiting

Mission" in Minneapolis, Minnesota.[13] A similar picture used on a British Recruitment poster calls to the men of the "overseas states" to enlist now.[14]

Another striking poster was used by the American Red Cross in a 1918 Christmas fund-raising drive. Entitled "The Greatest Mother in the World" and designed by Alonzo Earl Foringer,[15] it shows a woman sitting in front of a large red cross. She is dressed in the flowing white robes of a nurse, with the emblem of the Red Cross printed on the band of her white cap and on her scarf. The bare toes of one foot are shown at the bottom of the picture – reminiscent of a sandal-footed Athena – and the expression on her face is, like countless images of Mary, sad but understanding. An unmistakable *pietà* figure, she cradles in her arms a doll-sized wounded soldier wrapped with a blanket onto a stretcher. This image of a mother combines both ancient Greek and Christian iconography to persuade viewers to support the war effort. The Greek imagery alludes to the birthplace of Western civilization, the concept of democracy, and the notion of freedom associated with it, while the Christian imagery points to the ethical system by which the majority in Britain, Canada, and the United States professed to live.

Efforts at recruitment were made not only through visual means but also through popular music. In her study "The Music on the Home Front: Canadian Sheet Music of the First World War," Barbara Norman states that "recruitment was a dominant theme, reflecting the intense pressure exerted by government and society to enlist."[16] She also found in the songs a prevalent image of "the powerful role of the mother as recruiting agent."[17] Although some songs departed from this theme, a famous example being "I Didn't Raise My Boy to Be a Soldier,"[18] Norman writes that "even previously pacifist suffragette women rallied 'round the flag and pressed their sons into service."[19]

The onslaught of propaganda directed at women in Canada came when there was a steep decline in enlistment, particularly after huge casualty lists began to appear in the spring of 1915 after the First Battle of St Eloi and the Second Battle of Ypres. The military authorities required that women give written consent for their sons and husbands to enlist. Although many women had been supportive of the war

MOTHERS OF HEROES, MOTHERS OF MARTYRS

effort, it was known that others had been unwilling even from the beginning of the war to sign off their men. This problem for the recruitment officers was overcome when the demand for written consent was revoked in August 1915.

The regimental recruitment league for the 123rd (Royal Grenadiers) Battalion Canadian Expeditionary Force, was probably referring to this unwillingness when they mentioned "the selfish maternal appeal" that keeps a man at home. Their advertisement was addressed to "The Women of Canada," referring to them as "the mainspring of all masculine action." "Make your son, your husband, your lover, your brother, join now while he yet retains the remnants of honour."[20] Another example of the recognition of the power of the maternal figure to influence recruitment is found in an advertisement for the 118th Battalion published in the *Berlin News Record*[21] on 15 January 1916. It asked "Have You Mothered a Man?" and carried on to describe a real man as one who was wearing the King's Khaki somewhere in France and who is "upholding the most precious right that Britains are heir to, the right of freedom." Women are established as just as able as men to answer the call to arms. Here they do so by giving a man to the front. The words directed to mothers appeal to them "not to use their influence against the enlistment of sons who are able to take their places with the men who are fighting for Freedom and Liberty and for civilization." The men they encourage are fighting for "the sacredness of Home and Womanhood."

By this time, while some women were being accused of holding back their men, others were thought to be far too forceful in their efforts to encourage men to enlist. The White Feather Brigade was the most obvious example of excessive zeal. It began in England in August 1914 when Admiral Charles Penrose Fitzgerald asked thirty women to give white feathers to men not in uniform. The association of the white feather with cowardice derived from the 1902 novel *The Four Feathers* by A.E.W. Mason. If a game bird, bred for fighting, were to show a white feather on its tail, it not only indicated poor breeding but cowardice. In the story, a young man who is too scared to go into battle during the Boer War is sent three white feathers by his comrades; when his fiancée finds out, she leaves him.

Baroness Orczy, the British-Hungarian novelist, made a concerted effort to recruit men in Britain for the war and became closely associated with the White Feather Brigade. The practice spread throughout England and into Canada. Feathers were sometimes sent anonymously through the mail. In one case a "young gentleman" advertised in the *Berlin News Record* on 22 January 1916 for room and board. He received a letter in the mail with feathers in it and a note telling him that he could get free room and board if he wore a khaki uniform. He wrote a reply to the newspaper saying that he had been rejected because of his health but that his father and two remaining brothers (one had been killed) were in uniform.[21] One of the accounts included in Daphne Read's oral history of the Great War gives another version of the white feather story. George Wilkes, who was living in Toronto at the time, describes how the "ladies of Toronto" used a turkey feather duster filled with talcum powder to shower over anyone whom they thought was a slacker. He recounted how they mistakenly powdered a young man who had lost a leg in service when he was only 16 years old.[23]

Stories of young women pinning feathers on the wrong men quickly surfaced. There was one tale of a soldier who received a feather and the Victoria Cross on the same day.[24] Incidents such as this gave the campaign – already disliked by many – a bad name. After the war even more stories came to light and formed the basis for an angry backlash against the campaign and the women who had been involved in it. In reaction to this backlash Virginia Woolf wrote that the prominence of the white feather stories had more to do with male fear than with actual female activities.[25] Her views coincided with what Nicoletta Gullace refers to as the "Greenham Common" school of thought, which "tended to dismiss the white feather campaign as primarily misogynistic propaganda meant to discredit women and hide the more significant achievements of feminist pacifists."[26] Gullace believes this type of feminist perspective is the cause for so little scholarship on the white feather campaign specifically and, in general, on women's participation in recruitment campaigns that rested upon their ability to shame men into service. Gullace concludes that there were many episodes of men being pinned with a white feather up until 1916, when the

National Service Bill put conscription into effect, thus ending official recruiting appeals.

In the early recruiting posters I have described the state took on the guise of a woman. But this was a two-way street, for as women became involved in recruitment campaigns they "donned the aspect of the state as they used their own physical and rhetorical power in the service of the crown."[27] Gullace shows how the identification of woman and state in the service of militancy contradicted the traditional view of womanliness. Although Gullace is referring to the white feather movement, this was also true for mothers who encouraged their sons to be heroes. As a mother takes on a militant role she appears to step beyond her traditional place and to take on a potentially fearsome image. She may be seen as nurturing her community, in terms of seeing to its protection, and she safeguards her son's honour as well as her own, but in so doing she relinquishes her ability to protect the life of her son. Somehow the mother must live each day with this paradox, whether chosen or thrust upon her.

The question of honour is evident in many recruitment advertisements. An example previously noted in the poster addressed "To the Women of Canada" presented women as bringing shame to their husbands and sons if they did not let them go to war. An advertisement for the 123rd Battalion mentions temporal constraints on a man's honour, as if his quota of honour were slipping away as each day passed without him enlisting.[28] As well, a poster for the 118th Battalion attacks the mother's sense of honour, implying that if her son does not sign up she has raised a coward or a shirker.[29] Lady Sifton, the wife of Clifford Sifton, Minister of the Interior during the government of Sir Wilfred Laurier, spoke to an editor of *Everywoman's World* of the fear a mother has that she may have raised a coward. When sympathy was expressed to her regarding her great sacrifice of having four of her five sons in khaki, she replied, "It is very kind of you to express so much sympathy with me ... but I feel I should need it more if they had not shown a disposition to enlist in their country's cause."[30] Just as in the stories of mothers of martyrs of the past, honour rested on the relationship between mother and son; in this context, however, the relation of the mother's honour to her sexual purity was seldom openly discussed.[31]

—————

While the state and organizations such as the Red Cross and the Young Men's Christian Association (YMCA) made use of images of honourable women as recruitment officers and fund-raisers, and as some women "donned the aspect of the state" through their efforts in the White Feather Campaign, other women placed their honour at the "service of the crown" through pledges and proclamations. The most famous of these women, Baroness Orczy, founder of the Women's Service League, published an article in the *Daily Mail* that offered "To the Women of England, the Answer to 'What can I do?'" She asked women to pledge to "persuade every man [they] know to offer his service … and never be seen in public with any man who being in every way fit and free … has refused to respond to his country's call."[32]

The Baroness succeeded in enrolling 20,000 women to make this pledge and named them to the League's "Roll of Honour." Once again the question of honour came up – in this case with respect to defining what an honourable relationship was between the men in uniform and the women supporting them. Sisters and sweethearts shaming their men to war, and mothers offering their sons for sacrifice and speaking out proudly at their death, were an important part of this propaganda.

Much like the Women's Action League, the Mothers' Union produced a pamphlet entitled "To British Mothers: How They Can Help Enlistment." Women were asked, first, to pray, and after that to give their sons. There was a sense of urgency in the request, for "Not enough men are sent out and this largely because not enough mothers say to their sons, as one did lately, 'My boy, I don't want you to go, but if I were you I should go.'" The mothers were informed of how they should react if their sons come home from war or if they were killed. In case of the latter, the mother would have "a yet deeper cause for thankfulness that he is among the long roll of English heroes … [and] far better even than that – the welcome of the King of Kings will greet him – 'Well done, good and faithful servant, enter thou into the joy of the Lord.'"33

This sense of thankfulness appeared in an article written for the Canadian public at Christmastime, 1915. However, unlike the Mother's Union pamphlet, it was not written in the words of an outsider telling a bereaved mother what she should think and how she should feel. Rather, it was written with the power of the first person singular voice. Mrs E.A. Hughes published her story in the December 1915 issue of *Everywoman's World*,34 "I AM A PROUD MOTHER THIS CHRISTMAS And I Will Tell You the Reason Why."35 Her words reached into over 67,000 homes across the country, describing her reaction to the telegram she received from the British Government informing her that her son "Private Danny Hughes died in action yesterday." Initially she was in a state of shock at receiving the Christmastime telegram. But that "all passed and I was terribly, yet gladly sure that the messenger had not made a mistake ... I am a proud woman this day and, more, a proud mother. No other Christmas box would have been half so worth while." Because she cried at first she "could not see the triumph" that was hers. "I did not see the crown; the cross was omnipresent, Gethsemane was where I walked. But that has gone. I am a proud mother this Christmas. For I gave Canada and the Empire a Christmas present. I gave them my chiefest possession. I yielded what was more than aught else in the world to me. I sacrificed the life of my boy."

Although no reference to martyrdom is made, the association with Christ's death is explicit. Mrs Hughes was able to overcome the pain of sacrificing her son and feel the joy of the resurrection and the worth of the sacrifice. And, like other mothers of martyrs discussed in chapter 1, she takes full responsibility for the consequences of following her beliefs when she claims, "I sacrificed the life of my boy." Like the nurse in the Red Cross *pietà* poster, she has become "The Greatest Mother in the World." To tug further on her readers' heartstrings, Mrs Hughes tells us that Danny was all she had. "The rest, his Dad and a wee baby sister and a brother had all been taken."

This story is presented as autobiographical. The style, although highly melodramatic, would not have seemed so out of place alongside the propaganda surrounding the reader at the time. In the centre of the piece is a dramatic drawing, rather than a photograph. We see a woman, presumably Mrs Hughes, with her hands to her face leaning over a table while her son reaches toward her from behind. The caption under it says "'Oh, Mam,' he burst out again, 'I've got to go. I can't stay here, working and eating and sleeping and playing tennis and paddling and all, when the rest of the fellows are fighting, fighting for their mothers and fathers, fighting for England there, and all the vaster England in Australia and Africa and Canada.'" The melodrama in these lines makes them sound to a modern reader remarkably like an old Hollywood movie script.[36]

The enemy is never mentioned directly – at least in human form. What prompts this young man to enlist is a story told by a girl of her brother's death from "that damnable gas." The use of the "evil" gas, outlawed by international convention, was considered truly horrific in this time, as it is even now in an age knowledgeable of the atomic bomb. As in most martyrologies, the hero is forced to face death in the defence of his community and his values, and he knows he is on the side of ultimate justice.

Mrs Hughes tells us that Danny enlisted with the 15th Battalion, which was one of the first contingents to leave Valcartier, Quebec, in late 1914. They spent the winter training on Salisbury Plain and left for France in the spring of 1915. Now, unlike in 1915, it is easy to check the attestation papers of the Canadian Expeditionary Force as well as the Commonwealth War Graves Commission registry. No one with Danny's profile turns up in either archive. It is possible that Danny is a fictional character dressed with plausible details and designed to make an emotional impact on a receptive audience. The story highlights the bravery of a mother who, even if fictional, had her factual counterparts in mothers eager to dress their sons in khaki come what may.

Mrs Sarah Mead, the mother of William Benjamin Mead, was one of those mothers. She was a poor widow living in Campbellton, New Brunswick, during the war. Billie, her eldest child, was the income earner for his mother and sisters. In 1915, when he was only sixteen years old, his mother told him to enlist, saying, "I have nothing else to give to my country but you." Billie did not lie about his birthdate on his attestation papers, suggesting he may have had mixed feelings about signing up and perhaps hoped the officer in charge might see he was underage as well as undersized (he was 5′3″). From the moment of signing up Billie was designated as a bugle boy, a job he kept until the end of the war and his return to Canada on 6 June 1919. The words with which his mother sent him off to the enlistment office stayed with him. Years later, when he was ready to talk about the war, he shared this story with his daughter-in-law, Joan Meade, a professional story-teller from Fredericton, New Brunswick.[37]

Through the war *Everywoman's World*, the magazine in which Mrs Hughes' story was published, grew to be the most widely read period-ical in Canada. Audited circulation figures show an increase from over 67,000 copies in December 1914 to more than 125,000 copies in 1917 at its peak, far surpassing any other Canadian magazine. But, like the fame of novelist Ralph Connor, that of the magazine lives only with Canadian archivists and academics today.

A similar article was published in August 1916, less than a year after Mrs Hughes' letter, in the London *Morning Post*. Signed by "A Little Mother" and entitled "A Mother's Answer to 'A Common Sol-dier'"[38] it essentially provided a repeat of Mrs Hughes' sentiments but found a more lasting reputation. It was quoted in its entirety and commented on by Robert Graves after the war in his famous book, *Goodbye to All That* (1966). The existence of the Little Mother's let-ter provides further indication of how widespread was the expecta-tion and desire for maternal sacrifice in the Empire. Because of Graves' commentary on the letter we know more of the history of its reception at the time, as well as his later ironic attitudes toward the author's sentiments.

The editor of *The Morning Post* reprinted the letter in pamphlet form and sold 75,000 copies in less than a week.[39] Just as Mrs Hughes had only her Danny to give to the war effort, this "Little Mother" had only one child, a story element that serves both to increase the pain of loss and to raise comparisons in the reader's mind to Mary and the sacrifice of her only son. The Little Mother wished to speak out, for "we who mother the men" have the most important job in the world, of "uphold[ing] the honour and traditions not only of our

Empire but of the whole civilized world." She is clear about how mothers are to accomplish this task: "We women pass on the human ammunition of 'only son' to fill up the gaps, so that when the 'common soldier' looks back before going 'over the top' he may see the women of the British race at his heels, reliable, dependent, uncomplaining."[40]

Women are fulfilling their natural destiny in this role, the Little Mother claims, for they "are created for the purpose of giving life, and men to take it. Now we are giving it in a double sense."[41] All she asks for the mothers who have sacrificed their sons is that they be allowed a moment of quiet to share "the lonely anguish of a bereft heart" with the biblical mother of an only son, "Rachel the Silent." In the Genesis story, Rachel's love, Jacob, is first married off to her older sister Leah, by their father. Jacob has children with Leah but when he is finally allowed to marry Rachel it becomes apparent that she is barren. She agonizes over this, saying to Jacob, "Give me children, or I shall die!" (Gen. 30:1). Finally she gives birth to Joseph. Rachel, like other biblical women before her, waited so long for that which would give meaning to her life. By likening the mothers of soldiers to Rachel, the Little Mother tells the reader how dear their sons are to them. The story in the Hebrew Chronicles of a different Rachel, who as dicussed in chapter 1 sacrificed her four children, would also have evoked the image of the biblical mother.

Graves follows the Little Mother's letter with "Extracts and Press Criticisms." These quotations from newspapers and personal letters praise the sentiment of the letter and comment on its impact. One letter, describing the emotional reaction of "A Bereaved Mother," is reminiscent of the joy Mrs Hughes expressed in giving her son to her country. "I have lost my two dear boys, but since I was shown the 'Little Mother's beautiful letter a resignation too perfect to describe has calmed all my aching sorrow, and I would now gladly give my sons twice over."[42]

Robert Graves' commentary that prefaces the letter would lead one to think that these attitudes were well ingrained in the home-front population. From his post-war vantage point these emotions appeared as "war-madness" resulting from the desire for a "pseudo-military outlet." The outlet that people found was in stories. Graves describes these tales as speaking a "foreign language; and it was newspaper language." In other words, it was the language of propaganda. This is what his parents spoke, which he felt made it almost impossible to have a "serious conversation" with them. Graves' words are reminiscent of the backlash that arose in reaction to the White Feather Campaign. His anger with the Little Mother's letter was augmented years later by Jean Bethke Elshtain's book, *Women and War*, where she refers to the Little Mother's letter as the most "notorious" example of mothers being drafted into the propaganda service. Although Elshtain includes Graves in her comment, she seems to be even more incensed by the letter than he was. "Baldly proclaiming a sentiment carved on the mangled bodies of others, possibly her own son, 'A Little Mother' expresses bloodcurdling patriotism coated in vapid and lifeless pieties. Graves could not believe it; nor can we. But eager thousands did, including many mothers who saw themselves refracted through the Little Mother's 'longing for Spartan motherhood.'"[43]

It perhaps should not be surprising that the pendulum of social attitude swung from reverence of the Little Mother's bravery to disgust at her patriotism; from the ability of thousands to believe in the story, to subsequent incredulity. As in past times of social conflict and war, we can see once again how the political power of the mother was harnessed. One of the most vociferous American critics of the Iraq war is Cindy Sheehan, the mother of a dead soldier. To counter her protests, many other Gold Star mothers have spoken out in support of American participation in the war. We are again living at a time when many mothers are vocally supporting the choices that have led to their sons' deaths.

Beliefs stand behind the choices we make. The subject of belief was itself particularly interesting at a time when propaganda was ubiquitous and the Chief Censor asserted his control over the minutiae of the printed word. It was a well-worn joke in the trenches that you could believe anything except what you read. However, Jonathan Vance has convincingly shown in *Death So Noble* that those on the Canadian home front lived with the myth about the war of which his title speaks.

Like the eager thousands of British believers to whom Elshtain refers, the Canadian readers of Mrs Hughes' story were just as interested to accept it as truth. The public were willing to believe a story if its sentiments rang true, regardless of the factual details. Maybe this was the reaction Harold Lowrey was counting on in his February 1918 *Everywoman's World* story, "His Unknown Mother: The Story of a Victoria Cross." He declared that it was "one part fiction and three parts fact." Terrible Terry O'Malley, a giant devil of a man, is adopted at the train station just as he is leaving for the Front by a little old lady who had lost her only son at St Julien, the site of the first gas attacks. She is able to inspire terrible Terry to great Christian deeds, and he dies earning the Victoria Cross with just enough time before his last breath to say to his friend, "Jack, tell Mother I've kept faith, I'll wait for her in Hiven."[44] She is claimed by the whole of his battalion to be "the Empire's greatest and noblest Mother."[45] Having made the right choice to inspire her boys in battle, she is deemed to be unselfish in her mother-love.

Lowrey was not the first to claim the Canadian reader's attention with this story.[46] A year earlier, Nellie McClung's book *The Next of Kin* included a chapter called "War-Mother." Once again a tall, gruff soldier is adopted at a train station by a little old lady who had lost her sons – two this time – on the battlefield.[47] The main difference in this earlier version is that the mother seems to be in the habit of adopting soldiers and inspiring them to great acts of courage.

If Lowrey's story is a simple case of plagiarism it was not just the story that he copied, but also a willingness to fuse fact and fiction. In the foreword to McClung's autobiographical novel[48] the narrator says to a Red Cross meeting of women, "Remember that you women to-day made me promise to write down how this war is hitting us, and I merely promised to write what I heard and saw. I am not going to make up anything, so you are all under obligation to tell me all you can. I am not to be the author of this book, but only the historian."[49]

This blurring of fact and fiction in stories of mothers of the fallen echoes time-honoured questions that concerned the historians of ancient Greece. As seen in chapter 1, Aristotle's separation of history and tragedy was really an aberration. What audiences in classical times accepted as fact had to do not only with how a story was presented, but also with the terrible climate of tension and crisis of wartime, which clouds judgment. Similarly, readers in the time of the Great War felt an intense and overriding need for consolation in interpreting grievous losses. Fear, sorrow patriotism – all were magnified by the tensions of the day, lending credibility to stories that audiences might otherwise have dismissed.

This need for consolation at a time of great grief brought to the fore many references to the Spartan mother. When Elshtain refers to the Little Mother's longing for "Spartan motherhood" she assumes her readers are familiar with the story of the mother from Sparta who counselled her son to return to her from battle either with his shield or on it. Although the reference is Elshtain's and not the Little Mother's, this story surfaces many times in the literature of the war. It epitomizes the willingness and pride a mother can show in risking her son's life for his community and was used to illustrate both the height of patriotic fervour and, for those not supportive of the war effort, the depths to which propaganda could sink.

Although anti-war voices were a shunned minority they were present and indicated the intensity that infused public debate from many perspectives. One who spoke out against the war was Gertrude Richardson, an Englishwoman who moved to Swan River, Manitoba, in 1911. Richardson began her writing career in England by publishing anti-war articles in the *Times* about the Boer War. She continued in this vein in Canada, contributing to the socialist newspaper the *Canadian Forward*,[50] the voice of the Social Democratic Party. In an article entitled "Motherhood and War" she referred to a leaflet poem called "The Spartan Mother" that she had received from Fannie Buxley in California. "I know mothers who would send their sons to war. I read with a shudder the other day of one who said she 'would just push her son back into the trenches if he tries to escape.' God help the world if such an ideal of motherhood were to triumph."[51]

The Spartan mother would have displayed pride in a son's heroic death through her words and her demeanour.[52] This is alluded to in the Toronto *Globe's* 1916 article entitled "When bowed head is Proudly Held," which describes the National Council of Women's request to women who had lost men in the war not to wear black "but a band of royal purple on the arm to signify that the soldier they mourn died gloriously for his King and country."[53] It was thought that too much black might discourage enlistment.

A reference to the Spartan mother that glows with the fervour of propaganda is included in *Private Warwick: Musings of a Canuck in Khaki* (1915). The author, H.M. Wodson, admits his book is fiction but states in the preface that it was inspired by two young men and that he "believes there are many Private Warwicks bringing glory to Canada." The young private's girlfriend, Fanny, cries when he tells her he has enlisted in Winnipeg. But after the two of them attend a church service in which the parson "brightened up his sermon with the anecdote of the Spartan mother," Fanny is so moved that, as Private Warwick describes it, "she could almost see yours truly being carried into Westminster Abbey *upon* my shield."[54]

We are told in Wodson's preface about the other protagonist in the story, Private Warwick's mother. She is to "be found in ten thousand homes in Canada ... [she] who has given to the Empire that which she loves best." The book includes a number of letters from Mrs Warwick to her, once again, *only* son Richard while he is in training in England. In the first letter she reminds him of how he used to play with his grandfather's medals from the Crimean War. She has brought him up with stories of his grandfather's heroic fight and death for England, and so she feels it is in her son's "nature" to want to "wear the King's uniform."[55] However, she does not feel that his desire to go into service is entirely inherited. She sees herself as the one responsible for his lessons on the value of war, both in this world and as a "soldier for the King of Kings."

Mrs Warwick quotes a song her son used to sing as a little boy, which we must assume he learned from her: "I am a little soldier, / And only five years old; / I mean to fight for Jesus, / And wear a crown of gold."[56] To see him enlist is a reflection of her ability as a cultural teacher of morals and values. She thanks him "for giving [her] the *honour of being the mother of a young Canadian patriot.*"[57] Once again, we see the bond of honour joining the militant mother and her son.

Mrs Warwick leaves no doubt about her views on the righteousness of the cause for which her son is fighting. This strong faith is what allows her to overcome her "selfish" mother love.[58] "It is hard and I sometimes grow faint, but this is a just war, and the sword of God is in Great Britain's hand. The battle is for freedom, and God is the God of freedom. Of what worth are a mother's sacrifices in the rearing of her sons, if they do not make men noble and brave, and ready to make sacrifices for others? If my son should fall in battle, Christ's words will comfort me: 'Greater love hath no man than this, that a man lay down his life for his friends.'"[59]

Mrs Warwick may have been a fictional character, but there were real mothers who shared her views, including the compiler of the small volume *Mainly for Mother* (1919). This book consists of the collected letters of Armine Norris sent to his mother while he was serving overseas. This mother, like Mrs Warwick, was a soldier's daughter who passed on her belief that the right to fight for England "was a privilege to rejoice in."[60] There is something of the Spartan mother in Mrs Norris as well, for when she speaks of her mourning she says, "Let us remember to rejoice and be proud, for if the grief is ours the glory of great accomplishment is theirs."[61]

Hart Leech, who enlisted in 1914 in Winnipeg, made it clear to his mother just how he expected her to react if she received news of his death. In what he called his "post-mortem letter" of 13 September 1916, he said he would be "going over the parapet" the next day and knew he had little chance of surviving, so he wrote to his mother telling her to "cheer up, old dear, and don't let the newspapers use you as material for a Saturday magazine feature. You know the kind: where the 'sweet-faced, grey-haired, little mother, clutching the last letter from her boy to her breast, sobbed 'e was sich a fine lad,' as she furtively brushed the glistening tears from her eyes with a dish rag, etc. etc.'" Lieutenant Leech told his mother he was brave and good at his job; the implication was that she should be likewise.[62]

During the war Canadians were subjected to, and moved by, images of motherhood that joined ancient Spartan ideals with those of Victorian Christianity, but not all information directed at women asked them to support the war. Well into the beginning of the war, The National Committee of Patriotic Service, Council of Women, received what they referred to with some horror as "peace propaganda" that "call[ed] upon women all over the world to stop the war."[63] The Council's response, in March 1915, to this literature and its proposals of a peaceful solution to the war was that peace now would give victory to Germany. A few months later the Secretary of the National Committee of Patriotic Service, Mrs Plumptre, published her letter to the International Congress of Women at The Hague. She stated that the committee members, themselves leaders of nationally organized groups of women, were unable to accept an invitation to the congress because none of them believed the time for peace had come. The final paragraph of her letter joins the themes of ultimate values, democracy, and war: "We would ask you once more the old question, 'What shall a man or a nation give in exchange for his soul?' The soul of any nation is the value that it places upon the defense of the weak, the freedom of the many, and the keeping of its plighted word. It is to preserve our soul as an Empire that we are at war."[64]

Everywoman's World, consistently supportive of the war effort, ran its own election among readers on the issue of conscription and found that an overwhelming majority of woman were against it, although they were supportive of the war. The journal constructed the vote under the name of "The Women's Parliament of Canada." They printed an argument for each side and ballots that the readers were asked to fill out and send in. Counting on it to be a popular topic presented in a timely format that addressed women's suffrage, the publishers advertised this issue in the *Globe* in January and early February 1917. The published results showed a majority of 6:1 against conscription but unfortunately did not say how many ballots were returned. Those voting were from "every class and rank, and in every part of the country."[65] The article concluded that it was a truly representative vote.

Although this was a vote for all women, the section of the article that discusses "Who Voted" begins with poignant tales of mothers, such as "The mother who had given her only son, and she who had one son killed and three fighting." Those who spoke out against conscription did so for practical reasons, such as the need to have men on the farms,[66] and on the philosophical grounds of honour and freedom. One woman believed conscription would "disgrace the cause for which our sons have given all." Another insisted it would make "slaves of our young men." In a similar vein, another woman wrote that men would not consider their lives their own if conscription were the law. Others likened it to "Prussian Militarism."

Everywoman's World said they would carry the news of Canadian women's opposition to conscription to "seven hundred and fifty thousand readers and, with the aid of the newspapers, we shall reach every man and woman in Canada."[67] They also proposed to forward a resolution to the Prime Minister so that the government should know "the will of the wives, the mothers, and sweethearts of the man in khaki with regard to Conscription."

Behind the electoral scenes, Sir Robert Borden had been careful to ascertain how women would vote if given the opportunity. He did this by sending out a telegram to three representatives of large women's organizations. Mrs Torrington of the National Council of Women, Mrs L.A. Hamilton of the National Equal Franchise League and Win the War League, and Mrs Albert Gooderham, president of the Independent Order of the Daughters of the Empire, all received the telegram of 2 August 1917, which included the question, "Would the granting of the Federal franchise to women make conscription assured at the general election?"[68] In turn, women across the country were canvassed for their opinions, and the message was relayed back to Borden that the "granting of the franchise would imperil conscription."[69] Two alternatives to partial enfranchisement were suggested: the one eventually used was that the vote should be given to female relatives of enlisted men: the other was that it should be confined to those who already had it through provincial law, namely, in Manitoba, Alberta, and Saskatchewan.[70]

The government of Prime Minister Robert Borden passed the Wartime Elections Act on 20 September 1917 to extend the franchise[71] to the female relations of those who had served or were serving in the

Canadian or British military or naval forces. The Act increased the voter lists by approximately 500,000, but it also disenfranchised some women who already had the vote by virtue of provincial legislation.[72] The Act was designed solely to support the Union Government, a coalition of conservatives and some liberals and independents. Many of those who might have voted against it by reason of religious affiliation, ethnicity, or lack of family connection to the military lost the vote.

The government did its best through selective enfranchisement to ensure that the conscription legislation would pass, but pressure was also applied by the churches to both women and men to vote for the Unionists. The ministers in three out of four Protestant churches across the country spoke out in support of Borden's government on the Sunday before the election.[73] The outspoken leader of the Methodist church, Reverend Chown, presented a vote for the Unionists and their platform of conscription as a vote for true Christianity: "This is a redemptive war, and its success depends entirely upon the height of sacrifice to which our people can ascend. It is under this conviction that ministers of the gospel feel in duty bound to enter the political arena. We shall fail, and fail lamentably, as Christian people unless we catch the martyr spirit of true Christianity and do our sacrificial duty between now and the 17th of December." These words were published not only in the *Christian Guardian* on 12 December 1917, but across Canada as well.[74]

Those who had the vote and were inclined to cast it for the Liberals had to withstand a barrage of English-language media that blatantly supported the Unionists. Since many of the new voters were women, much of the media attention was paid to them, focusing on the themes of loyalty and, once again, honour. On 15 December 1917 the *Ottawa Evening Journal* ran a front-page banner reading; "If ye Break Faith with Us Who Die, We Shall Not Sleep Though Poppies Grow in Flander's Fields." Directly below was a photograph of Winnipeg war widows at a political meeting in support of the Union Government with the caption, "This reveals the keen interest of the woman voter."

A *Saturday Night* magazine editorial that clearly supported conscription emphasized the importance of men helping women to vote and not just "laugh[ing] at the ignorance of some women in the processes of voting." As for women, "Canada is asking the women-relatives of the soldiers to help maintain her honour before the eyes of the world."[75]

Many women did get the vote in the 1917 election, although of course the franchise went only to those who could reasonably be expected to vote for conscription. The government was essentially compensating them with a public voice for their support of the war effort and their willingness to, as Reverend Chown said, "catch the martyr spirit of true Christianity" and ascend to the "height of sacrifice."[76]

The vote was not the only compensation these women received. The Canadian Patriotic Fund was an organization set up by private citizens at the beginning of the war to help support soldiers' dependents.[77] Those who organized the Fund saw it as compensation for the bravery of the male members of the family, insisting "that an allowance from the CPF was not charity, but payment of the country's debt to its heroes overseas."[78] A pamphlet by member of parliament Herbert Brown Ames explaining the Fund stated that "The men may be the heroes, but the women are likely to be the martyrs of this War, and their sacrifice should be valued accordingly."[79] It may have been hoped that the female beneficiaries of the Fund would behave in a pure, noble, and martyr-like fashion, but to ensure this, their moral behaviour would have to be kept under scrutiny. If a woman's behaviour was found wanting – for example, if she had an affair while her husband was overseas – she risked having her payments reduced and her children taken from her and placed with a welfare society. One young man, Frank Bell, who boarded with a mother who was receiving twenty dollars a month from the Fund (and the same amount in separation pay from her husband) described how the payment was perceived: "This was a gift; it was charity, it wasn't from the government. This was administered by a group of rich men's wives, and if they found that a wife was running around, or that she was living beyond her means (they thought), or something, they would cut her off. One of the ways she could live beyond her means was to put in a telephone."[80]

Another expectation of the recipients' behaviour was that they would feel compelled by a sense of gratitude to act as recruiters. A pamphlet entitled "A Message to the Canadian Soldier's Wife" published by the Fund made this clear. "While your husbands are at the front helping to beat Germany, you also can bring up strong reinforcements by helping to get more men and more money."[81]

During the war, Parliament began discussing mothers' pensions. In November 1917, *Everywoman's World* published an editorial entitled "Canada Must Have Mothers' Pensions: As a Record of Service Rendered and a Safeguard for the Nation of Tomorrow."[82] The question was asked, "Canada's manhood is being sorely depleted on the battlefronts. What is being done at home to insure the filling of that void in national citizenship?" Although the article did not explicitly call upon the government to compensate mothers financially for the service they had rendered to the country by producing the soldiers who were being killed, it came close to it, just as it came close to saying that mothers needed to be supported so they could produce more citizens who might also turn into soldiers like their older brothers.[83]

At a time when national security was on everyone's mind, a "Safeguard for the Nation" must have been understood in a military sense. The editor pointed out that an essential aspect of the scheme was that the mother would receive the money herself "to conserve the home which is in danger because of the death of the breadwinner."[84] A parallel issue of the day was prohibition. Perhaps one reason the editor felt it was essential for the mother to handle the money was so it did not turn into an alcoholic libation for any older male relation. But there was a deeper issue involved here. If the money went directly to the mothers, it created a bond between them and the state, helping to ensure their mutual support. A state at war depends on young children being raised to believe that *"dulce et decorum est pro patria mori."*[85]

Although the federal government resisted the lobby for a national mothers' allowance program, provincial legislation was gradually adopted in Manitoba (1916), Saskatchewan (1917), Alberta (1919), British Columbia (1920), and Ontario (1920). Those who lobbied for the Ontario Mother's Allowance did so on the basis of a maternalistic ideology that "extolled the virtues of domesticity."[86] Just as moral guidance was involved in the distribution of the Canadian Patriotic Fund, the National Council of Women promoted a policy for the Ontario Mother's Allowance that would include investigations and moral regulation of the recipients. The moral authority previously exerted over the poor by private charities of the nineteenth century was now taken over by the government.

Mother's Allowances were also in part a way of compensating women who, after the war, were urged out of the workforce by the government to make room for returning veterans. An Ontario government pamphlet directed at women workers stated, "Who has the job you have before you took it? Was it a soldier? Then to him you owe the opportunity you had to gain a new experience, and some extra money. To his bravery and self sacrifice you owe the fact that you were able to work in peace and security. Now he has come back. He must have work to support himself and those dependent upon him. What is your duty? There is only one answer to that question. Of course you will go back to your home in order that the man may have a job."[87]

Thus the financial recompense that women in general and mothers specifically received in the form of funds such as the Mother's Allowance grew out of a need to support those who were bringing up the boys to fill the places of "Canada's manhood [which was] being sorely depleted on the battlefields."[88] Through these financial means and enfranchisement, women with a particular ideology and morality were being supported by the government and the well to do of Canadian society.

More than half a century later and half a world away, a similar form of compensation was given to Palestinian and Iranian mothers for the loss of their fighting children in times when their communities were involved in armed conflict or outright war. During the second Intifada we heard of Iraqi president Saddam Hussein's financial support of the families of the Palestinian martyrs, but the idea of this support had begun many years ago. In 1965 the Palestinian National Movement set up a committee of three headed by Intissar al-Wazir, also known as Umm Jihad, or "Mother of Jihad," a long-time political activist. The committee was set up in Amman, Jordan, to distribute allowances to the families of men killed in commando raids on Israel. This social-welfare program became known as the Families of the Martyrs Foundation. In a move that broke with Arab tradition and mirrored what had been called for in the Canadian experience of

World War I, the committee decided to give the money directly to the women. Umm Jihad realized that once the men of the household had been killed the family's connection to the revolution would be weakened. In a place where men were the primary wage earners, this was an astute move. By giving the money to the female head of the household, the committee helped secure the family's financial, social, and educational welfare and improved the status of women. Most importantly in Umm Jihad's mind, the program helped to maintain the spiritual connection of the families with the revolution.[89]

Another social-welfare program, the Palestine Martyrs Works Society, known by the acronym Samed, which has the literal meaning "steadfast," was developed for the vocational training of women. It was based on the same idea of empowering women. However, by its name it held the memory of those who died for the cause. Welfare programs designed to connect battlefield deaths with public financial support were also established by the Iranian government during the Iran–Iraq war. To help support the call for volunteers the government set up the Martyrs' Foundation (*Bonyad-e Shahidan*), which superseded the previous Foundation for the Oppressed (*Bonyad-e Mosta'zafin*).[90] Both drew their membership from the same pool of committed believers.[91] The support given by the foundation to the families of martyrs during the war was considerable. Journalist Anwar Nasir from the *Far Eastern Economic Review* stated, "Families of martyrs are virtually a privileged class."[92]

The families of the Canadian soldiers killed in World War I were by no means a privileged class. But there was a form of official recognition for which people began to lobby during the war: a recognition for the mothers who had lost their sons. The medal that was eventually designed to commemorate their loss was called the Memorial Cross when it was first struck on 1 December 1919 by an act of the Privy Council. The official recognition that the medal symbolized was an innovation at that time in the British Empire.[93] Officially, it was intended for both wives and mothers of men killed in action, but it has been mothers far more than wives who have captured the public's attention.[94] This has been true since the medal was struck – and was so even when it was still in the planning stage. The Canadian fiction author William Alexander Fraser (1859–1933) suggested to Prime Minister Robert Borden that a medal in the form of a silver cross be created to commemorate the sacrifice of bereaved mothers. An early reference to the medal was a small news piece entitled "Silver Crosses For Bereaved Mothers":

> The Canadian Mother who has given a life to the cause
> of right on the battle fields of France – a life more precious
> than her own – the life of her son, over whose grave she
> cannot place a cross, will wear a little silver cross over
> her heart that we may know she cherishes memory that
> is priceless, of one who faltered not at the call of his duty ...
> Canada will thus pay a simple tribute to a courageous
> motherhood that has laid its sacrifices on the altar of
> freedom, bearing its loss with splendid fortitude and
> unfailing courage.[95]

Not only does this short article tell us that it is the mother's loss that looms large and poignantly in the public mind, but we also learn that it was wrenching for the mothers not to have their sons' graves nearby. According to the policies of the Imperial War Graves Commission, details of which will be the subject matter of chapter 5, no soldiers' remains were to be repatriated to Canada. In the article calling for the commemorative medal to be struck, religion is not mentioned specifically, yet the symbolism is evident. The silver cross the bereaved mother wears over her heart is compared to the Christian symbol of the Cross over the grave. But thereafter in this brief text Christianity becomes indistinct and blends with a ritual of sacrifice that could belong to any number of traditions in which a mother offers her son's life in exchange for a value – in this case, freedom – upon which the life of her threatened community depends.

In September 1917, the Canadian poet and essayist Jean Blewett wrote in her editorial column in *Everywoman's World* of a "Mothers'

Recognition Committee." The group was centred in London, Ontario, and extended its membership all over the "Dominion." "The work of the Recognition Committee will be to see to it that the mothers who are giving their sons to fight and win, or fight and fall in this War receive tokens commemorating their sacrifice, and the heroism of their sons; tokens which stand for a public acknowledgment of the power their motherhood is in all that concerns the nation."[96] Once again, the power of motherhood is taken to extend over the whole community or nation. It is not only their power as mothers that the Recognition Committee is asking to be memorialized, but also the heroism of their sons. As the honour of the sons reflects on the mothers, so too the heroism of the sons gives the mothers a heroic quality.

In the same publication heroic mothers are mentioned by name in the article "They Know The Meaning of Sacrifice: Nine Canadian Mothers Who Have Sent Forty-Seven Sons to Fight."[97] The numbers in the title are meant to tell the real story: these women are giving all of what is most precious to them. A similar image was published after the war as a record of the sacrifice of another group of mothers. On Warriors' Day, 28 August 1920, a group of women travelled in an open car as part of a veterans' parade. A huge banner on the side of the car read, "These Four Mothers Gave To Their Country 28 Brave Sons."[98]

A less publicized story of maternal sacrifice was that of Mrs S.G. Ball of Vancouver. She came as a widow to Canada from Australia in 1910 with five sons and married a widower with eleven sons. In 1917 she petitioned the municipal authorities to extend the wooden laneway behind her house so that it would reach her door and make it easier for her to get around. Gradually details of her sad story emerged, and her case was taken up by a local alderman. She had been crippled by wounds received while nursing in the Boer War, and although her five sons and eleven step-sons had helped her in the past, they had all enlisted in the war and ten of the sixteen had already been killed.[99]

Among the many daunting stories of maternal loss, that of Mrs Charlotte Susan Wood of Winnipeg caused her to be chosen as the first Silver Cross mother. She was introduced in this role to King Edward VIII at the Vimy Ridge Pilgrimage in 1936. Two other mothers, Mrs T.H. Wardle and Mrs N. MacDonald, shook hands with the King, but

THEY KNOW
THE MEANING OF SACRIFICE

Nine Canadian Mothers Who Have Sent Forty-Seven Sons to Fight

Husband Greatest Recruiter

MRS. GORDON WRIGHT, London, Ont., President Dominion W.C.T.U., Vice-President London Red Cross, has sent three sons: Major Wright; Corporal Wright; Captain Wright, who is the youngest Divisional Quartermaster in the Service. Her husband, Chief Recruiting Officer, R.N.C.V.R., has secured more recruits than any man in Canada.

Seven Sons for King and Country

MRS. SCOBIE, Kars, Ont., has given seven sons: Private J. B. Scobie; Lieutenant R. M. Scobie; Corporal Sandy Scobie; Lieutenant A. A. Scobie; Private Russell Scobie; Sapper Sterling Scobie; and Dr. T. J. Scobie. One son remains at home as he is too young.

The Fighting Spirit Lives

MRS. LORNE McDOUGALL has four sons fighting for the Empire; Brigadier-General Alex. McDougall, Captain Kenneth McDougall; Captain Morris McDougall; and Lieutenant Archie McDougall. This young soldier was in the trenches for eleven consecutive months, but was wounded quite lately and invalided to the north of Scotland.

A Gifted Mother Sends Three Sons

MRS. ADAM INCH, President, The Woman's Institute, Mount Hamilton, Ont., has sent three sons to the Front. Mrs. Inch was greatly in demand as a platform speaker; but now work for the soldiers has crowded everything else out of her life.

Six Sons Answered the Call

MRS. BILLINGS, Hamilton, Ont., has six sons on Active Service; two in France; one in England; three in training. Mrs. Billings has one other son, a lad of thirteen, whose chief desire is that the War may be prolonged until he is of military age—he wants to strike a blow for the Empire.

Ten Men From One Family

THE Desormeau family is an example of Northern Ontario patriotism. Mr. Joseph Desormeau enlisted, but did not survive the sea voyage. Frank, Albert, James, and Joseph, Jr., have all been wounded. A brother and five sons are also in khaki.

No Need of Conscription Here

"I PRAY God to spare my boys to fight to the finish" said Mrs. Adolphe La France, a little French Canadian mother who has sent six sons: Private Joseph La France enlisted in 1914; Private Fred went a year later; Private Noe, and, in turn, the three younger brothers answered the call. Conscription makes no difference to this family.

Her All—Four Khaki-Clad Sons

LADY POPE, the charming wife of Sir Joseph Pope, K.C.M.G., Under-Secretary of State for External Affairs, is the proud mother of four khaki-clad sons: Major C. W. Pope, with the Royal Canadian Regiment; Lieutenant Maurice Pope, with the Canadian Engineers; Lieutenant Harold Pope, with the Canadian Army Service Corps; and Lieutenant Alfred Pope, with the Royal Canadian Regiment. Lady Pope's gift to the Empire represents her entire family.

Seven Sons Serve

MRS. LANGSFORD has given her husband, seven sons, and two sons-in-law. Her husband was invalided from the service and is now at a Military Hospital; one Son had has paid the supreme price; the others are scattered from France to Egypt, and figure in every kind of battalion from the Bantams to the Army Medical Corps.

From the August 1917 issue of *Everywoman's World.* "They Know the Meaning of Sacrifice: Nine Canadian Mothers Who Have Sent Forty-Seven Sons to Fight." Below the photographic portraits is a short biography detailing how many sons each mother had in uniform, how many had been invalided, and how many had been killed.

Mrs Wood was the one chosen to lay a wreath on England's tomb of the Unknown Warrior in Westminster Abby as part of the Vimy Pilgrimage ceremonies. She was the mother of twelve sons, eleven of whom fought in the war and five of whom were killed in action.

If circumstance has chosen one image to exemplify the Silver Cross mother, that image is a photograph of Mrs Wood, taken while she was on the pilgrimage. She is standing in a farmer's field facing her viewer while wearing her blue pilgrim's beret and all her sons' medals on her coat.[100] This is the photograph of Mrs Wood that hung in the old Canadian War Museum, and it is the most prominent one of her in the book *The Epic of Vimy* (1936). As testament to its lasting power, it is also the picture David Pierce Beatty chose for the cover of his book, *The Vimy Pilgrimage*.

Like many Canadians at that time, Mrs Wood was born in England. She was working as a laundress when she married the widower Frederick Louis Wood, who had six sons. Charlotte and Frederick then had one daughter and six sons together. In 1905 the couple emigrated to Canada with just four of the youngest boys. When war was declared, four of Charlotte's older stepsons, who were in England, immediately enlisted. The eldest boy, Richard, had already died in South Africa during the Boer War. By 1916, eleven sons had enlisted, the youngest two, Charles and Percy, being only 17 and 15 years old. Percy was killed at Vimy before he was 18 years old.

Mrs Wood's obituary, entitled "World War Mother Succumbs As Big Guns Roar Once More," states that her "family sacrifices during the Great War made her known throughout the British Empire." The obituary also mentions that she was "keenly interested in the welfare of returned men." She was active in a number of organizations, many related to the war, "honourary president of the ladies auxiliary, Imperial Veterans, BESL" – [the British Empire Service League, a precursor to the Royal Canadian Legion] – "mother of the Guards' association of Canada, and a life member of the Comrades of the World."[101]

As famous as Mrs Wood was after World War I, she is now almost completely forgotten in Canada. Fortunately, researcher Ceris Schrader recently spent years uncovering Mrs Wood's history after finding a photograph of her among her uncle's Canadian Expeditionary Force

Mrs Charlotte Susan Wood photographed during the Vimy Pilgrimage, 1936. (National Archives of Canada PA-148875.)

souvenirs. The photograph was inscribed only, "Lady Lost Five Sons." In a war where the remembrance and commemoration of names was so important, it is, as Schrader says, "a shame that someone could lose five sons in the service of their country and, just eighty years later, have almost no-one remember even her name."[102] In large part due to Schrader's advocacy, in June 2002 Mrs Wood's unmarked grave in Winnipeg was given a prominent marker explaining who she was: "Mother of the Guards and honoured by King and Country."

Of course there were and are many others who wore the Silver Cross. Following World War I, 58,500 Silver Crosses were awarded. During World War II, 32,500 were given out, and since Queen Elizabeth II ascended the throne, 500 have been awarded. The Cross has the cipher of the reigning monarch on the front and the name and service number of the son or husband on the other side. It hangs from a purple ribbon, has a crown at the top, maple leaves on the other three bars, and the whole rests within a wreath of laurel, which has long been used as a symbol of victory. In ancient Greece, warriors and athletes were crowned with laurel to signify their glory. Subsequently it entered into the world of martyrs in both Judaism and Christianity as a symbolic crown of piety.

Although Silver Cross mothers and wives have been laying wreaths on memorials across the country in memory of their sons and husbands since the end of World War I, it was not until the Second World War that Silver Cross mothers began to be presented in positions of honour.[103] The *Globe and Mail* from 12 November 1942, for example, mentions the position of prominence given to almost one hundred Silver Cross mothers at the Remembrance Day ceremonies in Toronto.[104] They sat just before the speaker's podium during the ceremony. It was at this time that the Royal Canadian Legion began choosing one Silver Cross recipient to represent all Silver Cross women from across the country in the laying of a wreath at the cenotaph in Ottawa.

Another example from recent times of the respect shown to Silver Cross mothers came in the form of a Nova Scotia parliamentary resolution calling for the congratulation of Mrs Margaret Langille for her participation in the 1996 Remembrance Day Ceremony as the Silver Cross mother: "Whereas Mrs. Langille has served her town, her province, her country and all mothers who lost their sons in battle proud as this year's Silver Cross Mother."[105] This form of official recognition of mothers of the fallen has also been given to Palestinian mothers of martyrs. They cut ribbons at opening ceremonies, sit beside dignitaries, and are thanked by leaders for their sacrifices.

After World War II the Silver Cross women of Canada founded their own association. Its name, the Remembrance Association, hearkened back to the official name of the Memorial Cross. The mandate of the association was "To forward the welfare of widows and mothers of former personnel of the Royal Canadian Navy, Royal Canadian Army, Royal Canadian Air Force and Fire Fighting Services who were killed in action or who died in consequence of service, and the welfare of such former personnel who are hospitalized or otherwise in need of assistance."[106]

Their charter was dated 29 October 1948. Different regions across the country set up their own chapters of the Remembrance Association, through which they raised money and planned local welfare programs. One member of the Ottawa chapter, Mrs Clara Twidale, gave a speech about the Silver Cross at the 26 June 1956 meeting. It seems that it was well received, as there are a number of copies kept in the chapter's scrapbook. Mrs Twidale placed the medal within a long history of rewards offered to those who have provided a service for their community. Beginning with a mention, by the first century CE historian Josephus, of a golden button used to commemorate military service, and carrying on through British history to the striking of the Victoria Cross, she ended with the Silver Cross of World War I. Twidale did not then go on to a discussion of bereavement – the deciding factor for the awarding of the Silver Cross – but discussed at length the war work women had done during the First World War.[107] Not only did she recognize that women had made "front page news" at the time for their work, but also that they had been involved in many tasks that they had never done before – from working the power machinery in plants, to driving ambulances and nursing in the actual war theatres.

It was only after a fairly lengthy list of women's wartime occupations that Mrs Twidale came to the subject of birth and bereavement.

She stated that God gave women a very important place in the universe – as is indicated by their bodies, which nurture and love all human beings before they are even born. She spoke of placing children "in God Almighty's care by our prayers throughout their formative years and when the need arose have we not returned them not without aching hearts, to God and Country?" Her words are reminiscent of Mrs Warwick's description of raising her son to know of God and connecting that teaching with military service.

By speaking at length about all the work and service Silver Cross women did in addition to losing their sons, it is as if Mrs Twidale was presenting a complete package for which they should be recognized. It may be that she saw the Silver Cross as a coming-of-age emblem for women. But she was speaking in 1956. It is notable that, although 26,000 more Silver Crosses were given to commemorate the dead of World War I than of World War II, it was not until after the latter war that the Association was formed with a mandate to develop social welfare programs for women who suffered directly from the war and in remembrance of the family members they had lost.

Perhaps the Association was not formed until then because women were strongly encouraged to return to their homes from the workplace after World War I and, as they were no longer gathering for wartime charity work, there were fewer opportunities for women to organize a Remembrance Association. The development of an association after World War II may, in part, have reflected a more utilitarian attitude toward commemoration: fewer monuments were erected, but more social programs were devised to commemorate the Second World War compared to the First. Twidale mentions "the institutions of learning and research whereby mankind may benefit by continued education and development" that were used to "perpetuate the memory of valorous deeds."[108]

The Association made a variety of efforts to promote their organization, the memory of their sacrifice, and their social programs. At a national meeting in 1949 they "resolved to bring pressure to bear on pensions for mothers."[109] At the same time, mention was made in the minutes of the Silver Cross Remembrance Association national meeting that some members would be discussing with government officials a plan to issue a stamp to commemorate Silver Cross mothers. The stamp was never made.

The American equivalent to the Silver Cross was the Gold Star, which was given to mothers and wives of servicemen who had died while serving in World War I. In the case of both medals, it was the mothers who held the primary position in the public mind. Gold Star mothers were represented by the Gold Star Association. Their appeal for funding for mothers emphasized the strength of the bond between mother and son. In her article for the American National Archives, Constance Potter goes so far as to say that in congressional debates "The bond between wife and husband seemed almost secondary. The bond between fathers and sons was barely considered – the association maintained that the maternal bond surpassed that of the paternal bond."[110]

The Gold Star Mothers Association was always ahead of its Canadian counterpart in organization and promotion. Gold Star recipients developed their association soon after World War I and, by the 1920s, had begun lobbying the government for a sponsored pilgrimage to Europe. In September 1948 the Gold Star mothers succeeded in having a stamp issued in their honour. In 1986 the Iranian government also made use of a stamp to publicly commemorate the women who supported the state in wartime. They issued a postage stamp in remembrance of "Woman's Day," celebrated on the anniversary of the birth of Fatima, the mother of the martyr Husayn. The stamp shows a woman holding a child with a headband marking him as a future martyr.[111]

The American Gold Star Mothers Association is still a thriving group that meets annually, promotes patriotism, and aids their membership. There has been some disagreement within the association as to whether non-American mothers and Gold Star Mothers for Peace are deserving of membership, but so far, since 1936, they have been celebrated by the nation each year on the last Sunday of September by presidential proclamation. The powerful American national identity is embedded in the symbol chosen to commemorate these mothers. They are the golden stars in a country that presents itself as a unity of stars.

In contrast, the main symbol of the Silver Cross medal points to a religion shared with others well beyond Canadian national borders.

The criteria for the awarding of the Silver Cross has been changed officially to include women who have been bereaved through peace-keeping missions. Chapter 5 will examine the notion of the Silver Cross mother of a peacekeeper and how it differs from the role of the original Silver Cross mother. From 1999 to 2001, the national representatives for the Silver Cross mothers were mothers of peacekeepers.[112]

Carol Isfeld, the national Silver Cross mother representative in 2000, has made the most of her profile. While her son Mark Isfeld was working on landmine clearance in Croatia, his mother sent him small scrap-wool dolls to give out to the children. He was, according to the Department of Veterans' Affairs, a mine-clearing expert who loved and was loved by children. Not only did Mark provide a role model for peacekeepers to uphold, but his actions reflected well on his mother. She, in turn, maintains his memory by still making the dolls to be given out by peacekeepers in Mark's name. Like the mothers and sons of World War I, this Silver Cross mother and her son were bound by honour and heroism. She has lived up to her role, proudly supporting the actions of her son and, consequently, those of the Canadian government.

Carol Isfeld has not had a Remembrance Association to help her. The local chapters of the Association across the country began closing as their members grew too old to participate in their programs. In 1974, the president of the National Association, Alta R. Wilkenson, wrote, "It will not be long now before our beloved Association will pass into history. Let us leave behind our records and 'footsteps on the sands of time.' We must never let the memories of this glorious time in the history of Canada be lost."[113] The National Association and the Ottawa Chapter deposited their scrapbooks, charters, and the minutes of the National Conventions in the Canadian War Museum Archives in the hope of preserving something of the honour and glory that they believed to be a part of their beloved soldiers and their Association.

It is difficult to imagine that any mother would not despair at the fate of her son dying on the battlefield, let alone merely "lament," as General Arthur Currie claimed they would when he spoke to the troops before the final battle of the war. But the mothers who supported the sacrifice of their sons in battle in World War I were portrayed in newspaper stories, fictional tales, and propaganda posters in Canada. Their images turn the stereotypes of the nature of mother-love on its head.

The bond between mother and son was laden with notions of honour. Recruitment advertisements promised honour to the men who enlisted and the mothers who supported them. Baroness Orczy formalized this production of honour with her Roll of Honour. The "Little Mother" tied honour and tradition together in the hands of mother and son to support the civilized world. Mrs Warwick was most blatant in claiming honour from her son's enlistment. The anti-conscription debates in *Everywoman's World* gave evidence that the honour of risking death in war was contingent upon the ability to freely choose that course of action. If these decisions are forced they lose power. This was so for the mother of the ancient sacrificial victim described in chapter 1 of whom Plutarch wrote. If she cried, the value of her child's sacrificial death was negated. Her offer must appear to come from her heart. Similar to those ancient mothers who were paid for their child to be sacrificed, the Canadian mothers of World War I soldiers could expect to receive some financial support, a public and political voice, and, if they were bereaved, a Memorial Cross.

Although the images used in recruitment posters, and the stories of Mrs Hughes, Mrs Warwick, or the "Little Mother," may now seem particular to their time, there is a sculptural depiction of a bereaved mother that still powerfully brings to the fore the values of the Silver Cross mothers. This "Spirit of Canada" stands at the front of the Canadian monument to the dead and the missing at Vimy Ridge – a subject for the next chapter.[114]

Chapter 4

Monuments and Memories
The Mother's Role in the Sad Work of Commemoration

A fter war comes the sad work of commemoration. Brave mourning for a child who has been sacrificed for a noble purpose such as "the war to end all wars" is a well-respected act with deep roots in many religious traditions. It is for this reason that the bereft mother is a poignant figure for a wide variety of people, whether she appears on the Vimy Ridge memorial or in the Memorial Chamber of the Peace Tower, or in each enactment of the Remembrance Day ritual.

In his writings on Jewish memory,[1] Yosef Hayim Yerushalmi comments on the importance of ritual in preserving the memory of an historical event. Historical details fade quickly, but the elements of a tale that have been woven into ritual and liturgy will last in the memory of a community. Remembrance Day and its evolution from Armistice Day provides an interesting backdrop to the story of the development of the role of the Silver Cross mother after the war. Applying Yerushalmi's ideas on ritual and the remembrance of history, it becomes clear that it is because the Silver Cross mother has a ceremonial part to play that her memory carries on. Long after Remembrance Association chapters across the country have closed down and their charitable works have ceased, individual Memorial Cross recipients will still be written about in papers across the country, interviewed on television, and honoured in provincial and federal parliaments. Their stories are important enough that the role of the Silver Cross mother has been adapted to modern times with the awarding of the medal to mothers of peacekeepers killed while on duty, and in this manner the bereaved mothers of the present are tied to those of the past. However, as more and more soldiers are being killed in Afghanistan, it may be some time before the medal is once again awarded to a mother of a peacekeeper.

———✦———

"On Armistice day, 1918, the world went mad for joy and business was suspended for a day; today, Armistice day, 1919, and the first anniversary of the cessation of hostilities, the world is too busy solving the problems of peace to take time for celebrations, and business will be suspended for two minutes."[2]

What we think of now as a moment of *silence* was originally an observation of a two-minute cessation of work. It was suggested by South African leader Sir Percy Fitzpatrick and subsequently made into a formal request by King George V to all parts of the British Empire. The request was read in the Canadian House of Commons on 6 November 1919:

> I believe that my people in every part of the Empire
> fervently wish to perpetuate the memory of that great
> deliverance and of those who laid down their lives to achieve
> it. To afford an opportunity for the universal expression of
> this feeling it is my desire and hope that at the hour when
> the armistice came into force, the eleventh hour of the
> eleventh day of the eleventh month, there may be for the
> brief space of two minutes a complete suspension of all our
> normal activities. During that time, except in the rare cases
> where this might be impractical, all work, all sound and all
> locomotion should cease, so that in perfect stillness the

thoughts of every one may be concentrated on reverent
remembrance of the glorious dead.[3]

The idea of a pause for commemoration was relatively new at the
time. It had been used to great effect in Cape Town during the four
years of the war, where all work stopped for three minutes at noon
every day so people could think of those who were fighting and those
who had died in the war.[4] After the war the quiet minutes were so well
respected in London that one observer was reminded "of the petrified
city of Pompeii."[5] Indeed, some even observed the day recklessly: one
airplane pilot flying from Manchester to London in 1922 turned off
his engines and the four passengers stood at attention while the plane
glided.[6] Canadians also respected the pause. The editorial in the *Winnipeg Tribune* commented that this form of commemoration fit the
mood of the times far more than the manner in which the first Armistice Day was celebrated. Peace was proving to be hard work for
many, and not only for the returning soldiers.

In 1921 Armistice Day was established rather prosaically as a legal
holiday under the Armistice Day Act. This legislation also stated that
Thanksgiving would be observed on the same day, the Monday of the
week during which November 11 occurred. The Liberal member of
parliament from South Renfrew had introduced the idea of a fixed holiday two years before, noting the support from business groups for
this idea.[7] The federal and provincial Commercial Travellers' Association of Canada, the Ontario Association Boards of Trade, and the
Retail Merchants Association of Canada all supported the proposal of
a fixed holiday Monday. It would be more convenient for employers
and, as Denise Thomson suggested in her comprehensive article on
"Commemoration of War in Canada," the holiday Monday would
"satisfy the powerful commercial travellers' lobby which wanted a
guaranteed long weekend in November."[8]

Thomson shows that even though there was a designated holiday
after 1921, because it did not necessarily fall on November 11, events
commemorating Armistice Day were divided between that date, the
holiday Monday, and the Sunday prior to the holiday. Legion members identified the problem and developed a resolution to submit to

Parliament requesting a change in date and name for the holiday. They stated that because the holiday was not on November 11, "the observance of this anniversary loses much of its significance and its sacred character is thereby much impaired."9 The importance of the holiday was emphasized through repetition of the word "sacred," for they hoped it would be a day "sacred to all ex-service men and women and which should be sacred to the people of Canada."10

A decade after the Act was passed it was amended so that Armistice Day would be celebrated on November 11 and would no longer be associated with Thanksgiving. This time, A.W. Neill, the independent member of parliament from British Columbia who introduced the bill, acted in response to increasing pressure from veterans, rather than business groups.11 The change of name from Armistice Day to Remembrance Day came at this time as well.

The new name suggested by the Legion emphasized the remembrance of the soldiers rather than "the Armistice, a political achievement in which rank-and-file soldiers were not directly involved."12 Through the years the veterans had worked diligently to keep Remembrance Day a living commemoration, but probably their most effective act was to pressure the government to have a holiday on November 11. In this way the day does not accommodate itself to anyone else's interests; in fact, it disturbs the regular pattern of life. If Remembrance Day had not been separated from Thanksgiving and, more importantly, if it had not been established as a statutory holiday on a designated day, it is likely it would not have survived as successfully as it has in Canada.

Another change that helped to bind people together in their act of commemoration and thus promote the lasting nature of Remembrance Day was technological. In 1931, the innovation of cross-Atlantic radio broadcasting allowed the Armistice Day Memorial Service in Albert Hall, London, to be broadcast across Canada via the Marconi Company and Canadian National Telegraphs. The *Globe*'s "radio editor" made it clear how exciting it was for North American audiences to be able to participate in the same celebrations as those attended so far away by their Majesties the King and Queen. What was of even greater significance than the proximity of royalty was the fact that this great technology of sound would, for a moment, be silent out of respect for something far greater: "Radio's thousands of monster broadcasting tubes will cease their white-hot oscillating, and radio's giant voice will fall silent in the loudspeakers all over Canada and the United States at the dramatic Eleventh Hour this morning. Radio, a child of Great Wartime, will thus for one moment pay tribute to the voices that were stilled in the Conflict which ended thirteen years ago."[13]

Unlike in Canada, in the 1950s remembrance celebrations in Britain were moved to the second Sunday in November, and because they were commemorated in churches they became more Christian and less national in character. Ronald Coppin noted that by the 1960s a decreasing number of people were observing Remembrance Sunday and that this seemed to be due to the fact that the day was no longer "an interruption of ordinary working life; instead it is an observance for the declining numbers who wish to make it."[14] In addition, the Peace movement of the 1960s would also have affected the number of people observing Remembrance Sunday.

The decline in Britain's observation of the day was also noted by Chadwick, who stated, "There is little doubt that by the law of history the commemoration of Remembrance Sunday will slowly die in emotion until the day is celebrated only in corners of the world."[15] His predictions have not yet come true in Britain – nor have they in Canada, and not merely because it is a "corner" of the world. One reason for this, as Yerushalmi has written in a Jewish context,[16] is the importance of ritual acts in keeping historic events in living memory. Although our national Remembrance Day services have changed through the years, we have developed rituals that are followed and expected. Yerushalmi argues that ritual and liturgy can be more important vehicles for memory than historiography. Remembrance Day observances in Canada seem to bear this out: even if the historical details of World War I are lost to many, the essential memory of this event still stands.

The Canadian national Remembrance Day ceremony is a religious service: television announcers do not speak at all from the time the Governor General arrives until the laying of the wreaths. Music is a large part of the ceremony and includes national, military, and religious songs. The core of the service consists of the playing of the Last Post – the end of the soldiers' day – followed by two minutes of silence. Then comes the bugler playing the Reveille – the soldiers' wake-up call. Two poems that have been a constant part of the program are "In Flanders Fields" and the middle verse of Lawrence Binyon's poem, "For the Fallen": "They shall grow not old, as we that are left grow old; / Age shall not weary them, nor the years condemn. / At the going down of the sun and in the morning / We will remember them." Seldom presented in its entirety, this poem, published in 1914, begins with a description of England as a proud mother mourning her dead children in much the same way as war-supportive Canadian mothers are presented in art and literature, "With proud thanksgiving, a mother for her children / England mourns for her dead across the sea."

The Remembrance Day ceremony continues with prayers and a benediction by military chaplains; finally, the wreaths are laid on the cenotaph. In recent years the wreath-laying has followed a standard order: first the governor general, followed by the Silver Cross mother, then the prime minister for the people of Canada, and representatives for the parliament of Canada, and for the veterans. Many dignitaries follow, but, significantly, the Silver Cross mother is second in status only to the royal representative in this event.

In the years after World War I, the bereaved who commemorated Remembrance Day were often pictured as women. In this way the poignancy of the women's stories of sacrifice during the war was maintained. Mrs Wood, the first Silver Cross mother, was remembered for her consistency in laying wreaths in memory of her five sons each "Decoration Day[17] and Armistice Day [which] meant to her far more than to almost anyone else in the dominion."[18] Although bereaved mothers are mentioned as attending ceremonies on November 11 during the interwar years, they were usually referred to as Silver Cross mothers only after World War II had begun and a new generation of women were joining the ranks of the bereaved. Even in Mrs Wood's October 1939 obituary in the *Winnipeg Free Press* there is no mention of the medal.

At the beginning of World War II the Legion became responsible for selecting the annual Silver Cross mother to represent all Silver Cross recipients in Canada in laying a wreath on the National War Memorial in Ottawa. The provincial branches of the Legion gather the names of the Silver Cross recipients each year, some of whom are chosen to lay wreaths in their communities. From this list the Legion chooses a national representative. In their decision they try to cover the different military services, all the provinces, and the different wars, although now the last consideration is moot, as certainly the Silver Cross mothers from World War I are all gone, if not all from World War II.

In the 1960s, the Canadian Broadcasting Corporation (CBC) began to televise the Remembrance Day ceremonies; in the 1990s, they began to include an interview with the Silver Cross mother as part of the television programming. This inclusion is probably in response to the increase in viewership since the fiftieth anniversary of the end of World War II in 1995 and the eightieth anniversary of the end of World War I in 1998. When a day of commemoration is significant enough to the public, other events of a similar nature will be added to the commemoration. The Remembrance Day programming of 2000 and 2001 included other religious remembrance services that took place during the year. In 2000 the CBC aired film from the previous May of the homecoming of the Unknown Soldier and, in 2001 they showed footage of the dedication of the National Military Cemetery at the Beechwood Cemetery, Ottawa. In 2004 the sixtieth anniversary of D-Day and the Battle of Normandy were remembered.

Yerushalmi refers to this act of joining together events for commemoration as "homologization."[19] In the context of Canadian history, this process has been called "annexation" by D.M.R. Bentley in his article, about Canadian memorials. He refers to the memory of General Brock and other, lesser, military heroes, who gained by having their names associated with his. At the time of the War of 1812, Brock was famous for his death in the defence of Canada. His name was so "prominen[t] in the history, mythology, and landscape of Ontario" that it inspired poets to connect the names of others with that of Brock in order to augment the status of those with no monument.[20]

Clearly, the fit between Thanksgiving and Remembrance Day was not close enough to maintain their connection. But this was not true for World War I and the subsequent wars. Although there are important differences between World War I, World War II, and the Korean War, they are similar enough that Remembrance Day serves them all. That being said, commemoration in the aftermath of World War I was characterized by dreams of peace, while World War II was memorialized in a more pragmatic fashion. Schools, for example, were supported in preference to building new monuments, and the dates of the subsequent wars were added to the existing monuments. The amalgamation of the wars in Remembrance Day serves the memory of the wars in different ways. The immense death toll of over 66,000 Canadians in World War I lends weight to the sacrifice experienced in subsequent wars, and the more recent wars serve to reinvigorate its memory. They have brought their bereaved into communion with those from the past. Celebrating the memory of World War II and the Korean War together with World War I also adds a sad irony to thoughts of the Great War, which was hailed as the "war to end all wars."

In memory of the "war to end all wars," the Peace Tower, known originally as the Peace and Victory Tower, was built in Ottawa after the destruction of the Parliament Buildings by fire in 1916. On 3 August 1927, the Prince of Wales unveiled the Altar of Sacrifice, a gift from the British Government. A reporter of the day, writing for the *Globe*, described whom he thought the gathered crowd was remembering: those who "set their course 'through dust of conflict and through battle flame' to build for Canada, as nothing else could build, her present-day status of full nationhood."[21] The belief that the war had won Canada her status as a nation on the world scene was clearly in place by this time. In the design of the Memorial Chamber that houses the Altar of Sacrifice, religious imagery as well as numerous references to motherhood express the sacrifices that the country had made. Originally, the names of those who died in World War I were meant to have been inscribed on the walls of the Chamber, but there was not enough room. At the suggestion of Colonel A. Fortescue Duguid, the Book of Remembrance was commissioned. His influence for this idea was Malachi 3:16–17 in the Hebrew Bible "A book of remembrance was written before him of those who revered the Lord and thought on his name. They shall be mine, says the Lord of hosts, my special possession on the act, and I will spare them." The Book was not finished until 1942. A Book of Remembrance was also written for World War II and, when finished, was placed in the Memorial Chamber on Remembrance Day 1957. These books are accorded the status of religious relics through the use of ritual. Each day at 11:00 a.m. the glass cases enclosing the books are opened by a guard in ceremonial dress; the pages are turned so that each page is exposed once in the course of a year. The guard bows to and salutes each book, beginning with the book from World War I that rests on the Altar of Sacrifice before proceeding counter-clockwise around the Chamber to the other books.

The Chamber was designed by the architect John Pearson. In a letter to the Prime Minister, W.L. Mackenzie King, dated 24 June 1927, Pearson described the symbolism of the three windows of the Chamber: the East Window, "The Call to Arms"; the West Window, "The Dawn of Peace"; and the South Window, the "Assembly of Remembrance." The South Window contains a number of Christian symbols and characters. The Archangel Michael appears, calling the nation to battle; St George and the Dragon show the priority of right over tyranny; a figure with hands outstretched in the form of the Crucifixion presents the suffering that both sides endured; and Joan of Arc carries with her the symbols of France and French-Canadians. But the character who receives the greatest attention from Pearson is that of an Athena representing Canada:

In the third light of the lower part of the window is an heroic figure, armoured and helmed, symbol of Canada proudly contemplative yet sorrowful, holding in her hand the victor's laurel wreath, she is standing above looking down to the centre of the Chamber upon the sculptured marble altar with the incised frieze of "MY MARKS AND SCARS I CARRY WITH ME, TO BE A WITNESS FOR ME THAT I HAVE FOUGHT HIS BATTLES WHO WILL NOW BE MY REWARDER ... SO HE PASSED OVER, AND ALL THE TRUMPETS SOUNDED FOR HIM ON THE OTHER SIDE." This altar bears the Book of Remembrance", containing the names of her valiant dead. Behind the figure of Canada stands another, symbolic of Canadian Motherhood, holding the shield of faith.[22]

The "symbol of Canada" is similar to Athena only in her apparel, not her mien, for instead of having the features of a strong, bold heroine, she is sad and thoughtful as she looks down on the names of all those who died for her. Nevertheless, it is this female figure who stands for Canada and her ability, through the sons she has sacrificed, to defend herself and her values. And if "sons" is meant metaphorically vis-à-vis the nation, it is meant literally to the faithful mothers who provided the background support for the war effort. For, as we have seen, during the war mothers were presented as faithful to the cause both at home and in the giving of their sons to fight.

Another image of a mother and child is carved into the sixth panel on the walls of the Chamber. It is the figure of the Virgin and Child of the Basilica at Albert, France. The statue of Mary high up on the church was famous during the war. After the Basilica had been shelled, she hung almost parallel to the ground. A story spread among the Allied soldiers that, if she fell, the war would end badly. The superstition became prominent for both Germans and Allies. In the statue's now golden form she still stands as a landmark visible from quite a distance over the French countryside.

A sculpted precursor to this Athena-like symbol of Canada was created by Frances Loring in 1917 in the form of a patriotic monument to stand in the grounds of the Canadian National Exhibition (CNE) in Toronto. This work, entitled *The Spirit of Canada*, showed a figure of Canada sending her sons to war with an Imperial lion and cubs standing at her side. The statue was constructed of plaster and straw and thus did not survive the years. A CNE Association report at the time, praised this work for "symbolizing splendidly the Spartan like Canadian woman with her whole-hearted spirit of service and sacrifice."[23] Boyanoski discusses another allegorical female monument created by Loring and her fellow sculptor, Margaret Scobie, in 1917. The figure, *Miss Canada*, which had been commissioned to celebrate the fiftieth anniversary of Canada, stood outside the Eaton's store in Toronto. The patriotism of the sculpture is evident in the *Globe*'s description of it as "standing in an attitude of triumph ... holding proudly up the ensign of Canada in her right hand while in the left, posed on the pedestal, is a shield of all the Canadian Provincial arms."[24] Many of the motifs of this sculpture were repeated in Pearson's figures of Canadian motherhood and the symbol of Canada in the south window of the Memorial Chamber of the Peace Tower.

In recent Remembrance Day telecasts the Silver Cross mother is shown in the Memorial Chamber of the Peace Tower looking at the Books of Remembrance. Her visit there joins or "annexes" her, in the sense used earlier, with the mothers of those whose names are in the Books of Remembrance. When entering and leaving the Memorial Chamber, the Silver Cross mother, like the rest of us, walks under a stone archway from which hangs an oversized representation of the Silver or Memorial Cross. The image of motherhood is repeated at the top of the arch with a bas-relief representation of a mother with two children. These figures, with an angel below them, are a work of Frances Loring entitled *Recording Angel and War Widow* (1928). The mother holds the infant in her arm, like the Madonna holding Jesus; her other arm encircles a young child standing beside her. The modern Silver Cross mother brings the sacrifice of the mothers of history and mythology into view once again, and they add the depth of history and tradition to hers.

———⊷◆⊶———

Pearson's "symbol of Canada" and "Canadian Motherhood" appear to be models for "The Spirit of Canada," or "Mother Canada" as she is also known, who stands at the front of the Vimy Ridge memorial in France. The design for the Vimy memorial by Walter Allward was selected as the winner in a national competition whose conditions were set out by the Canadian Battlefield Commission in a document dated 20 December 1920. The Commission wanted to erect eight memorial monuments on sites in France and Belgium significant both in their relation to battlefields and in their visibility.[25] They hoped that on those sites "the visitor would readily recognize the characteristic Canadian monuments among the many to be erected."[26]

In August 1921 Pearson publicized his plan to include a Memorial Chamber within the Peace Tower. It may be that Pearson, knowing of the battlefield memorial competition, felt the need to have a monument on Canadian soil to balance the one that would be built in France.[27] Although it is unlikely that he would have seen Allward's description of "The Spirit of Canada" submitted to the selection committee, it sounded remarkably similar to his own vision of the figure of Canada. Standing on the wall of the Vimy memorial was to be, in Allward's words, "an heroic figure of Canada brooding over the graves of her valiant dead,"[28] a concept very much like Pearson's "symbol of Canada proudly contemplative yet sorrowful ... looking down ... upon the sculptured marble altar." It seems clear that both designers were united in the image of Canada that they wanted to project.

Like Pearson's "symbol of Canada," the Allward figure looks down over a stone carved like a sarcophagus on top of which lies a helmet, maple leaves, and poppies. Just as Pearson's "symbol of Canada" looks on the names of those who died, "The Spirit of Canada" presides over the monument that carries the names of the 11,285 Canadians whose bodies were never found.

Although the monument presented a modern design at the time, traditional motifs are used in the figure of "The Spirit of Canada." A chiton slips down over her right shoulder, exposing most of one breast. Initially, this seems a strange attitude for a mother in mourning, but the drooping clothing is not meant to be erotic but rather to convey the attribute of strength. In her study of the female figure in monuments, Marina Warner states, "the allegorical female body either wears armor or proclaims its virtues by abandoning protective coverings."[29] Pearson's "symbol of Canada" wears the armour, while "The Spirit of Canada" shows her power through her disregard of her clothing. Another point Warner makes regarding the symbolism of the exposed breast in Greek literature also seems applicable here. The breast often indicated "the claim of a mother's love upon a hero, the bond that still joins the private and the public worlds."[30] The breast of the private world is the source of nourishment for the future hero.

Walter Allward, "The Spirit of Canada" (detail). Vimy Ridge
Memorial, Vimy, France. (Photograph by Alan Cumyn.)

This ability to nourish also appears in public depictions of the virtue, Charity, whose bared breast shows her ability to care for others. The presentation of noblewomen in the form of Charity was a particularly common phenomenon after the seventeenth century.

Beyond nourishment and support for the men who have died for her, "The Spirit of Canada" also bears the attributes of mourning. In ancient Mediterranean funeral rites (still maintained in some places and cultures today), mourning women tore at their clothes, bared their breasts, pulled their hair, and slapped their faces. Unlike these women, "The Spirit of Canada" is contemplative, but, like them, she stands in the traditional female role of chief mourner. In her quiet contemplation she reflects many depictions of Mary. The sacrificial element of her character is highlighted by the male figure standing between the pylons of the memorial just behind "The Spirit of Canada." This statue with outstretched arms reminiscent of the Crucifixion is called "Spirit of Sacrifice."[31] "The Spirit of Canada" wears a cowl over her head, reminiscent of a veil worn in mourning; it covers one side of her face, and we can see underneath it that she holds her hand to her chin in a pose reminiscent of Rodin's *The Thinker*. The actual model for "The Spirit of Canada" was Edna Moynihan. Allward interviewed her at length and then carefully measured her before offering her the job. She was told by Allward that he wanted to create "a mother figure with shoulders wide enough to carry the sorrows of dead sons."[32]

The statue of "The Spirit of Canada" was draped in the flag at the unveiling ceremonies of the Vimy Memorial. W.W. Murray, who compiled and edited the 1936 pilgrimage commemorative book, *The Epic of Vimy*, estimated that 100,000 people attended the ceremony, or, as one English newspaper more poignantly said, "There were as many people at the ceremony as there had been on the ridge on 9 April 1917, the day of the battle."[33] The *Winnipeg Free Press* was not so grand in its estimation of approximately 50,000 in attendance.[34] Many of the pilgrims were the bereaved, set apart from all the others by their blue berets. The ceremony on 26 July 1936 at the Vimy monument was the culminating event for those on the Vimy Pilgrimage. Over six thousand pilgrims sailed from Montreal on 16 and 17 July. They met with

Canadians living overseas and toured cities important to the war before returning home in August.[35]

This was not the first organized tour of the post-war era to take the name of "pilgrimage." The largest pilgrimage in this period was in 1919–20, when two million people over the space of a year made their way to the Cenotaph in London. In 1922, the King had made a pilgrimage to the Imperial War Graves in France and Belgium and to several British monuments, while 30,000 people travelled on a pilgrimage to Edith Cavell's grave in Norwich, England, in November 1923. The American Gold Star mothers went on pilgrimages at the expense of their government over a period of years. In 1930, for example, 3,653 mothers and widows travelled between May and September.[36] Kurt G. Piehler notes in his article on the Gold Star mothers that this extraordinary financial gesture of the American government should be recognized, but it should also be remembered that the pilgrimage was "impossible to resist politically." At the same time that the government spent vast amounts on the pilgrimage, it refused to fund maternity clinics.[37]

Although it may be true, as Lloyd says, that "propaganda writers used the language of pilgrimage to give greater meaning to the loss caused by the war," he also describes the development of an "anti-tourist" sentiment in the nineteenth century that would have promoted the distinction between regular tours and travel undertaken for a more distinguished reason.[38] The tension that quickly developed over the understanding of pilgrimages versus tours is evident in the question asked in the poem, "Trippers in Belgium," published in the London *Evening News*, 18 June 1919: "Yet is it well that high and sacred things, / The scenes of martyrdom, the hero's grave, / Should furnish forth a trippers' holiday?"[39] These doubts also coincided with the opening up of the Holy Land to tourists, a natural destination for a trip promoted as a "pilgrimage." Another factor that would have encouraged people to accept a tour as a pilgrimage and not merely another example of battlefield tourism was the language of sacrifice that surrounded the war. If the struggle had been a spiritual battle against evil and for goodness, truth, and justice, then certainly the battlefield could be considered a sacred site, the monument a shrine with its central icon of a mourning mother, the road there a *via dolorosa*, and the ones who travelled it the disciples of those who had been sacrificed. The present-day Parks Canada sign at the Vimy Ridge Canadian Memorial Park still projects the image of the site's sacredness by stating that, "The grounds of the Canadian Vimy Memorial Park have been hallowed by the sacrifice of those Canadians who died to preserve Freedom."

However, the Vimy Pilgrimage had more in common with traditional pilgrimages than merely being couched in the rhetoric of religion. It included many of the characteristics of pilgrimages outlined by Victor Turner in his article "Pilgrimages as Social Processes."[40] A pilgrim's journey is transitory in nature and is marked by voluntary participation. Unlike other religious behaviour, such as church attendance, travel on a pilgrimage is not a mandatory activity for Christians.[41] A pilgrim leaves home and ordinary life to travel into the unknown. Turner believes that the pilgrim enters into a *communitas*, a feeling of shared identity with fellow travellers who are distinct from his or her regular group of acquaintances. This step into a new world, Turner believes, "liberates the individual from the obligatory everyday constraints of status and role, [and] defines him as an integral human being with a capacity for free choice."[42] For Turner, the closeness and equality pilgrims find is, "in theological language, a forgiveness of sins, where differences are accepted or tolerated rather than aggravated into grounds of aggressive opposition."[43] Although subsequent scholars have been critical of Turner's theories, it is likely that the Vimy pilgrims and the organizers of the pilgrimage would have approved of these descriptions. Whatever the status of the pilgrim, they shared the experience of having lived through the war; for most, if not all, it was a time when strong bonds were formed by people living lives fully committed to one cause. The pilgrimage was an opportunity to experience again something of those bonds for a short, and much safer, time.

The differences among the pilgrims were, however, clearly marked by their clothing, which reflected their varied experiences of the war.

The bereaved, mainly women wearing their blue berets, experienced the war on the home front, relying on censored letters from the trenches and on what Robert Graves called "newspaper language" for their images of the battlefields on which they now walked. This view of the war would have bound them to the land and particularized its sacredness in ways that the veterans, marked on the pilgrimage by their khaki berets, would have found difficult to understand. For the veterans, the pilgrimage may have reflected something of the feeling of the closeness of the men during the war – a comradeship that those at home during the war would not have experienced.

Although beneath its voluntary nature lies a variety of motivations, a pilgrimage can be summed up as "essentially a form of penance."[44] Many who travelled to Vimy may well have felt that they owed the dead at least the respect of a visit. Some may have believed they owed their lives, whether factually or figuratively, to those who died.

In Lloyd's comparative study of pilgrimages and war commemorations in Britain, Australia, and Canada, he notes that the Australian and New Zealand Army Corps celebrations privileged the achievements of servicemen over all others in society both in the war effort and in the creation of a national identity.[45] Canada, like Britain, allowed bereaved women a more important part in pilgrimages. The attention paid to the grief of the bereaved in the commemoration of war served as a consolation to those who had lost family members but also helped direct the public's attention away from their dissatisfaction with postwar life. In Canada, this focus on the bereaved also helped to deflect attention from the divisions between English and French Canadians that had been so exacerbated during the war. Bodnar explains in *Remaking America: Public Memory, Commemoration, and Patriotism in the Twentieth Century* that commemoration in general "helps to avoid disorder and massive change and assuage fears by the continual tale of progressive and orderly transitions in the past."[46] This is not to say that officially organized pilgrimages are always designed as a top-down control measure by governments in a bid for power. The pilgrimage, the monument, the ritual, the poem, or the parade must resonate in the public mind to affect thoughts and shape memories.

There are many indications that the image of bereaved mothers res-
onated with the British public in their remembrance ceremonies. Bob
Bushaway, in his description of the King's pilgrimage of 1922, tells the
story of the mother of Sergeant Matthews, who wrote to the Queen
enclosing a bunch of forget-me-nots and asking that they be placed on
her sons' grave in Étaples Cemetery. As the Queen was unable to go,
the King brought the letter with him, found the grave, and put the
mother's flowers on it. Harry Gosling, British MP and a member of the
Imperial War Graves Commission, accompanied the King on this pilgrimage. Gosling described this scene in his memoirs, adding that after
the King placed the flowers "reverently" on the grave, "then, with that
touch of completeness that characterizes all he does, he turned to the
gardener and said: 'Now see that you keep them watered as long as
possible.'"[47] According to Bushaway, "This remarkable piece of theatre, whether consciously staged or a spontaneous act, was a micro-
cosm of the whole visit."[48]

Adrian Gregory, making a similar point, quoted a British newspaper account of the Armistice Day ceremony in 1927. The story included the words of a mother who had lost four sons in the war, spoken
as she stood by the cenotaph: "I could see the Queen's face quite clearly and it seemed to me to be pale with the sorrow which she was feeling for all the mothers whose sons never came back home ... I felt
proud of my sons and of their courage; I felt proud that I was their
mother."[49]

The poignancy of the bereaved-mother image has great lasting
power. In a *Maclean's* magazine article from 20 November 2000,
Maryanne Lewell, a Parks Canada student guide at Vimy Ridge, wrote
of her feelings about "Mother Canada" in the "Over to You" column
that *Maclean's* reserves for public opinion. Saying that even though
she knew little about Vimy when she went, when she first saw the statue of "'Mother Canada', staring at the tomb of her fallen sons below"
she "had to blink tears away." She lets the reader know further on in
the article that she was not alone in this reaction. "'Mother Canada'
makes visitors cry. In the guide package, we are told she faces east,
towards the dawn – which brings the hope of peace."[50]

The Canadian pilgrims at Vimy were certainly not all women, but the bereaved mothers did have an exalted place. Not only did the Silver Cross mother lay the commemorative wreath, but in several speeches at the unveiling politicians appealed to the magnitude of the pain of the bereaved mothers as the best reason for achieving peace. The acting prime minister of Canada, the Hon. Ernest Lapointe, expressed the hope that the power of the "cries of mothers, the revolt of conscience and the right of the weak" would abolish force as the arbitrator of nations. "Humanity suffered too much during the War, martyrised both in soul and spirit" and, for this reason, peace must be attained.[51] This statement was made at a time of growing nervousness that war might again be close at hand. It is because of this atmosphere that in the rules of conduct laid out for the pilgrims in their guide book they were advised to take "care that no word or act – individually or collectively – on the part of our parties shall show evidence of anything other than the best of feelings towards everyone in Europe, whether former enemies or allies."[52]

In London, the Vimy pilgrims had a full program organized for them that included a ceremony at the Cenotaph. The music, hymns, and two-minute silence were much like the Remembrance Day ceremonies performed today. The Bishop of London, Winnington-Ingram, pronounced the benediction, and wreaths were laid. Before the blessing the Bishop said that in 1915 he "had addressed 10,000 Canadians before the Second Battle of Ypres. 'Of 72 young officers I spoke to before that battle, 42 were killed,' he said, 'and of those 10,000, half were either killed or wounded.'"[53] After the ceremony the pilgrims went to the Tomb of the Unknown Warrior in Westminster Abbey. Mrs Wood, in the company of three other Silver Cross mothers "representing Mothers of Canada who lost sons in the War", along with an escort of fifty pilgrims, laid a wreath on the tomb.[54] The guidebook explains how these women were chosen. "Each Party Leader will name sixteen pilgrims, a number of whom will be ladies, to represent the Pilgrimage at the Tomb of the Unknown Warrior. This party will consist of those who lost near relatives in the War and will include the mother on the pilgrimage who lost the most sons."[55] The diary of one of the Vimy pilgrims, Florence Murdock, mentions Mrs Wood, who must have appeared as a figure of some importance to the pilgrims.

It was not until 2000 that Canada brought home her Unknown Soldier from World War I. The interment of the Unknown Soldier in front of the Cenotaph in Ottawa was a millennial project of the Legion and a celebration of their seventy-fifth anniversary. They chose to retrieve the remains of a soldier from Vimy Ridge. Not only does Vimy have Canada's memorial to those who have no grave but the battle fought there in April 1917 has taken on great symbolism through subsequent years as the crucible for the birth of Canada. In the ceremonial interment, soil from Vimy, along with soil from the ten provinces and three territories, was dropped on the coffin before it was lowered into the sarcophagus. Many of the rituals of Remembrance Day were followed in this ceremony. Buglers, pipers, and a fly-past in the "lost man" formation framed the central benediction and two minutes of silence. The official program states that after the covering of the sarcophagus there was a "Common Prayer for all Faiths." This appeal to those beyond the dominant religious culture represents an effort that began in the early days of the commemoration of the war.

Over nine million soldiers of all nations died on the battlefields of World War I, and so many bodies were not found or identified that all the major combatant nations erected tombs of unknown soldiers. Closely related in concept to these tombs were the cenotaphs – monuments to people buried elsewhere. Just as many of the stories in the previous chapter stipulated how mothers were to behave during the war, the same brave face was hoped for afterward. In a poem by the Canadian poet, A.M. Stephen, entitled "The Cenotaph," the mothers of British Columbia are advised on how they should behave in front of this monument. "O, young proud mother of the mountain-born, / Weep not for these! ... No funeral dirge or plaintive strain forlorn / Should sound the passing of their chivalry. / Joyous, they gave their radiant youth to be / A light transcendent o'er an age outworn."⁵⁶ As in the early stories of the mother of martyrs in all the traditions discussed, these mothers are meant to be proud of their sons' "joyous" sacrifice.

In writings about war monuments, the question of the motives of those who erected them is often raised: Do these structures attempt to shape the public memory of the war in support of the status quo? Eric Homberger reflects in his article "The Story of the Cenotaph" that the situation in London showed more blind luck on the part of the government than well-thought intent in their production of the popular symbol of the war. The concept of a cenotaph (the word derives from the Greek for "empty tomb") was chosen for a memorial by the British in preference to a catafalque, which was to be erected in Paris for the celebrations over the signing of the Peace Treaty. The Latin root of catafalque relates to a scaffold and refers to an ornamental structure used in funerals for the lying-in-state of a body. The British Foreign Secretary, Lord Curzon, thought that the idea of a catafalque "would be rather foreign to the spirit of our people, however much in harmony it might be with the Latin temperament."⁵⁷

A few weeks before the peace celebrations of 19 July 1919, the architect Sir Edwin Lutyens was asked to design a non-denominational temporary shrine, which he called a cenotaph. The monument was immediately so popular that the government decided to erect a permanent version. In the fall of 1919 the British government was so deeply concerned with unrest in industry and in the army that minimal and hasty attention was paid to creating a war symbol. Homberger argues that in the case of the cenotaph "it was the people not the government who made it such an unparalleled object of respect."⁵⁸

Robert Shipley comes to the same conclusion with regard to Canadian monuments. They were built, he argues, as a matter of community consensus (but with none of the bumbling good luck that the British had experienced). Shipley was speaking not only of the National War Memorial in Ottawa but of the many monuments across the country, a great number of which were funded by community collections. These, so to speak, "ground up" memorials came in many shapes and drew on symbolism from a variety of cultures and times. Some of the more interesting examples he gives are: memorial stones that look like northern European menhirs or standing stones, the more than 200 cairns across the country (one of the oldest types of place marker known to humans), and the small versions of Egyptian pyramids and obelisks. Shipley has catalogued approximately 1,200 monuments in Canada and has ordered them according to their shape: "Stelaë and cut-stone constructions – 32 percent; Statues – 27 percent; Cairns – 19 per cent; Crosses – 8 percent; Obelisks – 8 percent; and Architectural Monuments such as towers – 6 percent."[59] Many of the larger cities in Canada built monuments modelled after Lutyens' design in London. In fact the one in London, Ontario, is an exact, although smaller copy of the one in its name-sake city.

From Shipley's calculations we can see that the overt Christian symbolism on the war monuments is less common than other motifs. In many cases, however, the symbolism does coincide with a Christian cosmology. The similarity between Christ's empty tomb and the cenotaph is evident and carries with it the associated hope of resurrection.[60] However, the symbolism of the laurel, so often portrayed on war memorials, originally had a pre-Christian significance. This is true of the palm as well: a symbol of victory that took on the meaning of victory over death. Other images, although not specifically Christian, have been read as such. The most famous symbol of the war, the blood-red poppy, was the first to grow from overturned soil on the sites of battle and hence has taken on the idea of resurrection as well. The archway, like the one in the National War Memorial in Ottawa, was used by Romans to commemorate victories, indicating a passing from one state of being to another: from war to victory and, in Christianity, from life to Paradise.

Although in shape and design many of the monuments display non-Christian motifs, Shipley chooses to interpret both the structures and the Remembrance Day ritual, as many others with a Christian background would, as an image of Christ's sacrifice.

> Like Christ and the Christian martyrs our soldiers died
> violent deaths. The Remembrance Day ceremony, like the
> Eucharist, attempts to account satisfactorily for their

passing. At a critical point in the service the bugle sounds
"The Last Post." That is the traditional end to the soldier's
day. The Last Post symbolizes death and is followed by two
minutes of silence ... During the silence we reflect on the
dead and mourn their passing. Their suffering in war is
reminiscent of the martyrs' torment and of Christ's descent
into hell. At the end of the two minutes, "Reveille" is
sounded. That bugle call begins the day. What is symbolized
by Reveille is an awakening and in fact a resurrection. The
soldiers, by their sacrifice, are identified with a martyrdom
that wins them eternal life.[61]

Although it is easy to see how this view fits with the language of
sacrifice during the war as well, the fact remains that Canadian soldiers are not remembered as martyrs and the services by which we
commemorate them seem only distantly religious. There are two reasons for this. One was a question of orthodoxy. The equation of the
soldiers' death with that of Christ, in its ability to redeem the living,
is not acceptable in orthodox Christianity, although it may have been
acceptable to those like the chaplain Capt. T.A. Patterson, quoted at
the beginning of chapter 2. Patterson gave voice to a common belief
that the lowly soldiers had a far better understanding of true Christianity than those who were doing the preaching inside churches. It
would not have been considered true to Christian teachings to allow
that the soldiers were sanctified by their death – a notion implicit in
the common language of sacrifice in the newspapers, in the stories of
the mothers of heroes, and even in the words of some of the religious
leaders. Despite the fact that someone with the stature of the Bishop
of London, Winnington-Ingram, called the war dead "martyrs," the
title has faded with time, and there are few like Shipley who would
still refer to even the form of the soldiers' story as a martyrdom. But
the soldiers' deaths, especially on such a massive scale, needed to be
given a positive value. The bereaved needed to be consoled; since most
religions are looked to for aid in this area, the format and sentiment
of a religious tradition were borrowed for commemorative purposes,
but without the strict theology.[62]

A strict and specific theology would not have sufficed, for World War I was an international war. It brought together people from a variety of places and religious cultures. Even within Canada, although a majority involved were of some Protestant denomination, also active were Catholics, Jews, Native Canadians, and people from different parts of the British Empire, bringing with them their cultures and religions. To commemorate only one religious interpretation of that war would have been to misrepresent it and to understate its comprehensive destruction and consequent sorrow.

Chapter 5

Governance of the Gardens of the Dead
War Graves, the Ancient Greeks, and the Need
to Remember and to Forget

As time passes after a catastrophic event, people's thoughts turn toward commemoration of the period of agony. What should be remembered, and what forgotten? What shape will the selected memories take, what will they sound like, who will be chosen to give voice to them, where will that happen, and at what time? Chapter 4 discussed some of the ways in which the First World War was commemorated and how the image of the bereaved mother fit into those structures. This last chapter will consider one more way in which the war was remembered: through its cemeteries. Once again, I will examine how the mourning mother's role adapted to this form of commemoration.

The millions of men who died during World War I lie in cemeteries and fields all over the world. A large concentration of them are in northern France and Belgium, on what was the Western Front. This is where most of the Canadians who fought and died in that war are now buried. Some have a tombstone in a graveyard; others whose bodies were never found lie without a marker. A few months into the war it became evident to the British that a plan would have to be developed to cope with the dead. The need became so great so quickly that a committee was formed to bury the men and register their graves. This committee grew into the Imperial War Graves Commission (IWGC), which under its new name, the Commonwealth War Graves Commission, still controls the cemeteries where Commonwealth soldiers from both world wars are buried.

As we have seen, during the war the Silver Cross mother, as a symbol of the bereaved relative, was a powerful recruiter for what was presented as a just and noble cause. After the war she added sanctity and support to the image of a war fought for peace. This image was in part constructed through the work of the Commission, which created beautiful, orderly cemeteries of identical tombstones in long rows, mirroring the memory of soldiers in uniform marching with purpose.

Much of the carnage of the war was covered over, and great efforts were made to identify the remains of the men, bury them, and erect tombstones. The atrocity stories, so well promoted by the British propaganda during the war, were to be forgotten. An example of this, discussed in chapter 2, was the sculpture *Canada's Golgotha*. This work, based on the widely spread rumour of the crucified Canadian, was put in storage from 1919 until 1992 to avoid raising old bitterness.

Similarly, the IWGC was careful in the choice of wording used on all memorials, so as not to incite any desire for revenge. In this manner it reflected some of the ideal of an amnesty in the original sense of the term – neither as pardon nor as grace, but as an act of oblivion. The first amnesty occurred in Athens in 403 BCE. Nicole Loraux discusses the specific case of this amnesty in *Mothers in Mourning* and its requirement that citizens remember to forget the previous horrors, for the sake of social stability. For the same reason, the mourning of mothers in the Greek city-states was controlled in quality, quantity, and location.

When mourning is encouraged and clothed in vengeance, dangerous hatreds can be sustained for centuries, as in the case of Serbian remembrance of the Battle of Kosovo and of Mother Yugovich's bereavement. Not only did the memory of this battle figure in the origins of World War I, but on the 600th anniversary of the Battle of Kosovo in 1989, Slobidan Milosovic, in conjunction with the Serbian

Orthodox church, created a Mother Yugovich medal to be given to mothers producing many sons to fight for the Serbian cause.

The role of the bereaved mother exists within the balance of remembering and forgetting with which each nation with a history of war must grapple. The Silver Cross mother's role was that of chief mourner asking Canadians to remember that the war was fought for the ideal of peace.

Recently, Memorial Crosses have been awarded to mothers of peacekeepers: keepers of the terms of amnesty. The symbol of this cross thus connects the national ideals of past and present. The national emphasis placed on World War I as the birth of Canada on the international stage is paralleled by the vision of peacekeeping as a quintessentially Canadian intervention with a positive impact on the world. As the Silver Cross mother lays her wreath in Ottawa on the Cenotaph on Rememberance Day or on the Peacekeeping Monument on United Nations day, she balances both remembrance and forgetting.

The framing of the commemorative architecture and understanding of the war with elements of Greek culture is evident in John Hundevad's *Guide Book* to the Vimy Pilgrimage of 1936.[1] Hundevad ends his short descriptive section on "The Gardens of the Dead" – the cemeteries – with a quotation from Pericles' funeral oration in praise of the Athenian heroes after the first battle of the Peloponnesian War (431 BCE). The oration was first quoted in Thucydides' *Peloponnesian War* (2:34–46). Thucydides prefaces Pericles' words by explaining that this panegyric was part of the prescribed ritual that Athenians followed in the burying of their war-dead. Three days before the ceremony, the bones of the dead were taken from the tents where they had been laid out and were put in coffins to be carried to the outskirts of Athens, where they were to be buried in a public sepulchre. The procession was open to anyone interested in attending, but it was expected that the female relatives of the dead would be there to wail at the burial.

Two details of Thucydides' description of the ancient Greek ritual were folded into the commemoration of the dead during World War I. In both wars the issue was raised as to how to remember those whose bodies could not be recovered. The number of missing in World War I was so immense that they became a large part of the character of the war. Of the 1,104,890 dead soldiers who were commemorated by the Imperial War Graves Commission, 517,773 were designated as missing.[2] Many nations built monuments to the missing with the names of the men inscribed on the walls. Combatant nations built tombs of the unknown soldier, symbolically pointing to all the soldiers who were buried elsewhere. In chapter 4 the Greek heritage of the cenotaph – the empty tomb – was discussed as one way in which many communities in Canada and England commemorated their war dead buried far away. The way the Greeks dealt with their missing war dead after the first battle of the Peloponnesian war was to decorate an empty bier to signify all those whose bodies could not be found on the battlefield. The bier travelled with the dead to the burial ground.

Thucydides mentions an exception to the rule of the dead being buried near Athens: the heroes of Marathon, "who for their singular and extraordinary valor were interred on the spot where they fell." As a guiding principle the IWGC attempted to give this mark of distinction to each soldier who died in the First World War. Considering the shattered state in which many of the bodies were found, it was often a difficult or impossible principle to follow.

As well, the monuments to the missing were to be located on or near the battlefield where these soldiers died. Of the 11,285 names of the missing Canadians on the Vimy Memorial, for example, not all had died during the battle for the ridge, but that is where many lost their lives.

The excerpt from the funeral oration that Hundevad chose to include in his *Guide Book* is appropriate to the themes of remembrance and of honouring the missing that gave direction to the work of the War Graves Commission:

Each has gained a glorious grave – not that sepulchre of each wherein they lie, but the loving tomb of everlasting

remembrance wherein their glory is enshrined, remembrance
that will live on the lips, that will blossom in the deeds of their
countrymen the world over. For the whole earth is the sepulchre
of heroes; monuments may rise and tablets be set up to them
in their own land, but on far-off shores there is an abiding
memorial that no pen or chisel has traced; it is graven, not on
stone or brass, but on the living heart of humanity.[3]

This section follows Pericles' description of why Athens was worth
fighting for. He asserted Athens' leadership among states in its democratic favouring of the many over the few, in its openness to the world,
and in its cultivation of knowledge. Knowing that the cause was a good
one, he argued, would help the bereaved to cope with their loss. In
speaking first to the parents of the soldiers, he pointedly offered them
comfort, not condolences. The comfort came from the pride they must
feel at their sons' noble death. He insisted that those who are young
enough should have more children, not only to help them forget their
loss[4] but, more importantly, because in making public policy, no one is
more fair than the man who brings with his decisions the interests and
apprehensions of a father. Thucydides, in his prefatory remarks, does
not mention the mothers who, of course, were not citizens in this
democracy. The only reference he makes to the female relatives of the
dead concerned the expectation that they would be there to wail.

Where the women were allowed to wail, and for how long, was
governed by the state. Loraux's reading of Thucydides' description of
the funeral ceremony suggests he does not include women in the procession to the burial site because women, and particularly mothers,
must be dealt with firmly so that they do not have an adverse effect on
public support for the war and hence in the safety of the city. Loraux
has compiled a summary of laws limiting women's mourning in Sparta,
Athens, and Rome. As one might expect from the stories of the Spartan mother, Sparta allowed the shortest period for women's mourning: twelve days. Athens and Argos allowed one month. In Rome, the
period lasted for nine or ten months, unless the city was dealing with
exceptional circumstances such as a great defeat, in which case mourning was curtailed to thirty days.[5]

Loraux agrees with a common interpretation of funerary laws as "antiaristocratic measures aimed at curbing luxury and expenses" and argues that they had the most effect on women, who were the most prominent mourners."[6] Because these laws served to control the public expenditures of the nobility, they worked toward evening out the financial disparity among the people. In this way funerary laws were linked with the democratization of the state, providing for an equality of expression among citizens – that is, men. Loraux finds proof for this interpretation in those democratic regimes of ancient Greece where "women [were] even farther removed from the political sphere … than under other constitutions."[7]

Taking this argument one step further, Loraux emphasizes that the main concern in the limiting of mourning, which essentially means the limiting of the role of women, is to ensure the stability of the city. If a mourning mother turns her passion into anger against the state, she may become volatile and dangerous.

Loraux begins her discussion on the power of the bereaved mothers of ancient Athens with a reference to Shakespeare's *Richard III*: the "scene of mothers" in which three queens lament the death of their sons. One of the queens states that her sorrow is "general," meaning that a mother's sorrow "contains all mourning within itself."[8] This is a powerful emotion that can turn into a desire for revenge. Queen Margaret takes her own hatred and turns it into a vengeful lesson (4.4.118–23):

> Forbear to sleep the night, and fast the day;
> Compare dead happiness with living woe;
> Think that thy babes were fairer than they were,
> And he that slew them fouler than he is:
> Bettering thy loss makes the bad-causer worse:
> Revolving this will teach thee how to curse.

In general, monuments are constructed in peacetime, when it is no longer state policy to "nurse" the desire for revenge. One does not often see war memorials commemorating a hatred leading to a curse. An exception is in Péronne, France. A memorial inscribed "À Nos

War memorial in Péronne, Picardie, France. Inscribed "À Nos Morts," the statue is called *Picardie Maudissant La Guerre*. (Photograph by Alan Cumyn.)

Morts" depicts a woman in peasant clothes on her knees beside a dead soldier.[9] The woman looks grimly forward, holding out one arm in front of her, a clenched fist facing upward. She curses those who brought war and death. These could be seen as both the leaders and the enemy. At no time is it profitable for the state to allow the power of bereaved mothers turn against it, whether in wartime, discouraging others from sending their sons to battle, or in peacetime, condemning decisions the state has made.

During a war, mourning must serve to improve the state's ability to fight, calling on the honour and courage of men to defend their home. Afterward, it must not endanger the peace by either inciting revenge against the enemy or by prompting a backlash against the decisions of the leaders and their right to lead.

Loraux examines the power of mourning during the Amnesty of 403 BCE. This amnesty was devised after the rule of the Thirty Tyrants, when civil war had ripped Athens apart. Originally the decree of amnesty, which forbade the recollection of misfortunes, was upheld by oath only. Each year senators and dicasts took the oath against re-membrance. Women, not being citizens, would not have been expect-ed to take any oaths to forget, yet, according to Loraux, they were commonly known as the "keepers of memory."[10] But if memory turns to anger, as it does in the cursing mothers, it can be a danger to the state: "anger as mourning makes the ills it cultivates 'grow' assiduous-ly, and it is a bond that tightens itself until it resists all untying."[11] Thus the keepers of memory and, specifically, the mourning mothers must have their emotions controlled for the sake of the community.

Adrian Gregory, in his book on the development of Armistice Day, perceives a similar circumscription of mourning behaviour during World War I. He comments that "the requirements of national morale pre-vented extravagant mourning in wartime."[12] Public mourning behav-iour as exhibited by the proud mother of the sacrificed represents not just a repression of mourning but a change of parameters to accom-modate the needs of the bereaved, both the individuals and the state, so that they participate in the creation of a story that makes sense of the loss and finds something positive in it.

An example of the containment of mourning is found in the work-ings of the IWGC. And, just as Loraux unites the control of women's mourning with the growth of democratization, so too, we can see that the strict control asserted by the IWGC is associated with their efforts to assert a sense of equality among all who were sacrificed in the war. The IWGC was faced with an immense physical task and needed to reach beyond their immediate cultural experience to create the principles that would govern their work. As will be seen in the next section, elements of ancient Greek thought run parallel to the scheme they developed.

The Imperial War Graves Commission had its origins in the Joint War Committee of the British Red Cross Society and the Order of St John of Jerusalem. The committee began its work in September 1914 by sending out a mobile unit to the battlefield to search for missing soldiers. For the next year, until the work was taken over by the army, the committee was supplied by the Red Cross with the means to mark and register British graves.[13] By 1916, Dominion representatives had been appointed to share in the decisions concerning the graves, and in 1917 a charter constituting the IWGC was adopted. The guiding principles set out in 1918 were described by Fabian Ware, vice-chairman of the Commission: "(1) the memorials should be permanent, (2) the headstones should be uniform, and (3) there should be no distinction made on account of military or civil rank."[14]

The historian Edmund Blunden emphasized the efforts of the Commission to remember the names of fallen soldiers.[15] The only precedent for this act came during the American Civil War, when a general of the Union army ordered that each battlefield have a spot for burial and that the soldiers be buried as soon as possible in graves marked with their names. "By 1866 there were forty-one such cemeteries containing over 100,000 Union soldiers."[16]

The naming of the dead served not only to recognize the efforts of each man but also to democratize one of the most hierarchical institutions in the world – the military. In the past, only military leaders had been remembered. In the commemoration of World War I each soldier's life was to be seen as equal, whether he had been a general or a private.[17] Longworth argues in his history of the Commission that the principle of equality developed under Ware's leadership reflected the servicemen's experience of comradeship in the field.[18]

This feeling was certainly present in many situations – even among the men peacefully crossing enemy lines, as was evidenced in the famous Christmas truce of 1914 when the soldiers played and sang together and shared their supplies. But the divide between officers, mainly from upper-class families, and their men was often deeply resented by the men, and so the equality of all soldiers in death may reflect a vision more than a reality. Still, it was an extraordinary vision for the time. In setting aside military hierarchy, the IWGC was also choosing to set aside the class structure embedded within the military.

Early on in the war the Commission recognized that dealing with the dead was only part of their responsibility. The concerns of the bereaved relatives also had to be met. Thus, they appointed members who would keep in touch with the relatives, who were, as Ware describes them, "the natural guardians of the graves."[19] The "natural" rights of the relatives to have some control in the burial of their dead sons was also understood by the horticulturalists who developed a policy of planting the graves with flowers and grasses, originally from Red Cross funds, and saw themselves as acting "*in loco parentis.*"[20]

Although mourning and burial practices were seen as a family matter, the development of policy for the IWGC was not. There were no women included among the names of the commissioners from all the Dominions in Ware's history of the Commission's first twenty years. Women's organizations had pressured the Commission to have a female representative, but to no avail. Longworth reasoned that in the early days of the IWGC members were Victorian "gentlemen" whose values were insulted by the women's suffrage movement and who were blind to the work women had done during the war. Although one of the original members of the Commission, Harry Gosling, a Labour member of parliament, had brought up the issue of female representation at a Commission meeting, "others hinted at female inefficiency and the matter went no further."[21] In the end, Gosling felt confident that "the Commission is as representative of every different political view and social class as it is possible for any body to be."[22] This belief would have easily enabled him, and the others on the Commission who likely shared his view, to dismiss the "thought that bereaved mothers and wives had a right to formulate policy."[23]

The family did have the right to have an inscription of their choice added to the bottom of the tombstone. The inscription had to be quite short to fit into the small space and the Commission had the final say on whether it was acceptable. The general rule for the words on the tombs was that "nothing was allowed to be said in any inscription which would tend to perpetuate international ill-will."[24] Although most of the German dead who are buried in Belgium or France lie in German cemeteries, some German soldiers are buried alongside the Commonwealth dead. Friends and families from all over the world, including Germany, would be visiting these cemeteries, so the Commission did not want words of revenge or great emotion.

The IWGC's control over the actions and words of the bereaved extended beyond their prohibition of extravagant inscriptions on the tombstones to a prohibition against building personal monuments near the graves that may have marked class and financial differences. The guiding principles of permanency also meant that no bodies would be repatriated but would stay on or near the spot where the men died. Although the IWGC committed considerable energy and finances to the burial and registration of the dead soldiers, it would have been far more demanding to repatriate the bodies and, considering the conditions of battle, it was often difficult to identify remains. The American government offered the families of dead soldiers the choice of whether or not to repatriate their bodies. About seventy per cent chose to repatriate, although the difficulties in accomplishing this were indicated by the resignation of the head of the American war graves service, who "could not guarantee that the right bodies would go to the right relatives."[25]

The decision not to repatriate any remains of Comonwealth soldiers was made during the war, yet some did try to circumvent the rule. The remains of the grandson of the British prime minister, W.E. Gladstone, for example, were sent home after pressure was exerted on the IWGC. Ware did not want to see a situation develop where those with the finances could remove the bodies of their sons and those without could not. To ensure that this would not happen again he succeeded, by giving reasons of hygiene, in having a ruling put in place against exhumations. Where the local people in France were able, they were encouraged to care for the soldiers' graves. Ware hoped that their interest would have an effect on the relatives after the war so they would be less likely to want to move the remains of their sons. For the most part, families were content to leave their sons buried in the graveyards, but there were a few stories of Canadian parents digging up the remains of their boys after the war and attempting, unsuccessfully, to bring them home.[26] Many were unhappy not to have their sons brought home, but for the purposes of the IWGC keeping the soldiers from all over the Commonwealth together in immense graveyards served to magnify and unify the effect of the sacrifice – a message that the Commission was intent on communicating.

The Commission is as firm in its resolve today as it was during and just after World War I to leave the graves undisturbed.[27] Poignantly, Ware explained that soldiers had been promised that if they brought back their dead comrades, at some risk to themselves, to designated cemetery sites, their friends would stay there permanently. Even now, the French government has had difficulty promoting its plan to put in a new airport near Paris, possibly necessitating the relocation of 1,250 Commonwealth graves. This plan has been taken very seriously by the Commission.[28]

The policy of not moving bodies once they were buried was acceptable to Muslims who disapproved of exhumation. But the Commission had more difficulty in coming to a happy compromise regarding the distinctive grave markings wanted by both Muslims and Hindus. Baker and Lutyens were to design mosque and temple memorials, but this idea was abandoned when further requests were made by Sikhs and Gurkhas to have their own commemorative monuments; such commitments became more than the Commission was willing or able to take on.

One area, however, where the Commission succeeded in bringing together the emblems of all the countries of the Empire was in a memorial plaque. It was, according to Ware, "the only sculptural memorial to express the union of the partner nations of the Commonwealth."[29] Ware's description of "partner" nations indicates a hope of equality among the countries of the Commonwealth that few of those countries would have seen either before or after the war. Yet the symbol of unity was so important that the plaques were known as the Commission's "coping stone." These plaques, erected throughout France as well as in Westminster Abbey, stated, "To the Glory of God And to the Memory of One Million Dead Of the British Empire Who Fell In the Great War 1914–1918 And of Whom the Greater Part Rest In France."

⸺⸻⸺

The words that have come to be associated with the commemoration of the war dead were for the most part composed or selected by the

British author Rudyard Kipling. The message of equality among soldiers and among armies made up of men from a wide variety of cultures is apparent in both the words chosen to frame the memory of the war and their visual presentation. Hundevad, for example, stated in his *Guide Book* to the Vimy pilgrimage, "By their very uniformity they speak in one voice of one death, one sacrifice, for a cause that was common to all."[30]

Most of the tombstones of the Commonwealth cemeteries were carved from Portland stone with a slightly rounded top to help preserve them against the elements. All the stones are on a cycle such that they receive upkeep every twelve years. Originally, the graves were marked with wooden crosses, as in John MacCrae's line, "between the crosses row on row," but stone was necessary to replace them as the names disappeared from the quickly rotting wood. During the transition these crosses were piled up beside the cemeteries and were often taken away as souvenirs by pilgrims. Some of these relics can be found in churches in Canada, such as St Paul's Anglican Church in Toronto, as well as in museums such as the Canadian War Museum.

The shape of the tombstones was significant to the philosophy of the IWGC and the message it was trying to convey. One might have expected them to retain the original symbolism of the Cross, as did the French in their graveyards. Some say that the idea of the crosses was rejected because it left too little room for inscriptions.[31] Although this may be true, it is likely that the uniformity of the shape for all Commonwealth soldiers was more important to the IWGC. By choosing a non-denominational shape, the Commission was able to promote the idea of uniformity while at the same time inscribing each stone with the religious symbol of the soldier. The Commission asked the families what religious insignia they wanted on the tombstones. The "default" religion was Christianity: if the family could not be contacted, a cross was cut into the stone. Most of the stones display Latin crosses; some have nothing at all; on others, the Star of David, or symbols from Buddhist, Hindu, Sikh, Islamic, Baha'i and Zoroastrian traditions are carved. There was also room for the insignia of a soldier's regiment or the symbol of his country, his name, date of birth, and date of death.[32] The decision to have the regimental insignia put on the stone allowed the IWGC to maintain uniformity while declaring the individuality of each soldier, a balancing act that was new at the time in the commemoration of dead soldiers.

Each missing man was remembered through the inscription of his name on the memorial to those without a grave, but some of these soldiers were also remembered in another way. Over 150,000 war graves contain unidentified dead, whose tombstones record what personal information was available, such as nationality and date of death; all of these stones also bear the words composed by Kipling, "Unknown Soldier" or "A Soldier of the Great War" followed by "Known Unto God."

Kipling also chose "Their Name Liveth For Evermore" to be written on the Stone of Remembrance. This quotation from the Hymn in Honour of our Ancestors in Ecclesiasticus (44:2–13) deliberately omitted the preceding phrase, "Their bodies buried in peace," which might have offended Hindus, whose funerary observance requires cremation. The Stone of Remembrance and the Cross of Sacrifice are two standard memorials that vary only according to the size of the cemetery. The former was designed by Lutyens, who had in his mind "a great fair stone of fine proportions, twelve feet in length, lying raised upon three steps and bearing in indelible lettering some fine thought or words of sacred dedication."[33] When Ware wrote his history in 1937, 560 Stones of Remembrance had been set up. They are placed either in cemeteries containing 400 or more war dead, or close to memorials to the missing.[34] Most of these stones, which look very much like altars, were cut from the same Portland stone as the tombstones. Having no reference to any particular faith, they serve as an emblem of sacrifice for all.

Although efforts were made by the IWGC to be at best inclusive of other faiths and cultures and at least inoffensive, the predominately Christian influence is seen in the other memorial that stands in Commonwealth cemeteries, the Cross of Sacrifice designed by Reginald Blomfield. By 1937, close to a thousand Crosses of Sacrifice had been erected.[35]

The words that are probably the best-known symbols of the war, "Lest We Forget," have taken on a life beyond World War I but were actually part of a poem written before that conflict. In 1897, Kipling wrote his "Recessional" for the Queen's Golden Jubilee. The first four verses end with the line, "Lest we forget, lest we forget!" Although composed at the height of the British Empire, this was a cautionary tale warning its readers that the Empire's strength could melt away in a moment and that faith should be placed in God and his "ancient sacrifice" rather than in the iron of the Empire.

> Far-call'd our navies melt away –
> On dune and headland sinks the fire –
> Lo, all our pomp of yesterday
> Is one with Nineveh and Tyre!
> Judge of the Nations, spare us yet,
> Lest we forget, lest we forget.[36]

The context of a Christian world view has faded, and the words "Lest We Forget" are now used throughout the documentation of commemoration. Yet embedded in the warning to remember is the demand to forget. The stories of atrocities that were once so important during the war must now be consigned to oblivion lest the flame of an old fight be relit. On the other hand, it is important to remember the number of dead, to honour their names, and to beware human weakness and the possibility of falling into war again.

The work of the IWGC was designed to promote a message of unity among equals in the sacrifice of men. In their efforts to convey this message, the IWGC appropriated the voice of the bereaved. Nevertheless, the voices of mothers were heard in other places, just as had occurred in ancient Greece. Despite the control on women's mourning in ancient Greece, stories of anguish were told during times of war. Loraux argues that what was repressed in the public and political realm was expressed in the theatre. Moses Hadas comments in his introduction to Aristophanes' plays that in Athens "the amazing thing is that plays attacking the war policy when the state was at war could be given under state auspices."[37] An example of this was Aristophanes' *Lysistrata*. Its comic treatment of the deeply serious topic of war speaks to perennial issues surrounding the experience of war. The play was presented just after the disaster of 413 BCE, when Athens failed in its efforts to take over Sicily. The solution it offers to end the war is a sex strike by the women. The women argue it is time they were heard despite their lack of citizenship for, as they say in the voice of the Chorus, "It should not prejudice my voice that I'm not born a man, / If I say something advantageous to the present situation. / For I'm taxed too, and as a toll provide men for the nation."[38]

Canada, given its censorship laws during World War I, was not so free to present criticism of the war effort, but the political right of mothers to be heard was argued nonetheless. In an *Everywoman's World* article of April 1915, twelve well-known Canadian women were asked what "they hope[d] to see as the outcome of the war." This article was billed as the first national expression of opinion by Canadian women, and it was thought that the wide selection of contributors would represent women in Canada, the United States, and all over the world. L.M. Montgomery, a frequent contributor to *Everywoman's World*, wrote, "I do hope that [the war] will in some measure open the eyes of humanity to the truth that the women who bear and train the nation's sons should have some voice in the political issues that may send those sons to die on battlefields."[39] Montgomery thus states more directly the view of the women of *Lysistrata*.

Nellie McClung tied women's role, or lack of it, in the democratic state to the state's inability to find peace. She gives particular importance to the mother's voice. "Man's pride in masculine statecraft has received a jolt, and they are not so sure of things as they were four months ago! There can be no true democracy where one-half of the race is ignored, and this war, if it has any significance at all, is a war against autocracy. The mother's point of view will be represented in the days to come – the good days to which our longing eyes are turning in hope and faith."[40]

Flora MacDonald Denison, Honourary President of the Canadian Suffrage Association, also hoped that a stronger democracy would evolve out of the war. This would come when the "female constructive mind" and her "maternal instinct" were given equal political and economic rights. Most of the women did see a greater political role for women, both as an outcome of the war and as a means to improve the world and its possibilities for peace. The democratic ideal that the IWGC wanted to display in its commemoration of the war was, like that of ancient Athens, the promotion of equality among men. Canadian women at this time were arguing for an equal voice for men and women in the governance of the state.

———⟶●⟵———

Many of the women published in *Everywoman's World* wrote in grandly idealistic terms of hopes of a new internationalism through which nations would join forces and prejudices would dissolve. Emily Murphy, known by her pen name Janey Canuck, pinned these same ideals on particular solutions, such as the arbitration of international issues by the Hague Court, the establishment of an international police force, disarmament, and equal status for women. But before these tactics could be contemplated she hoped to see an "amnestia."

> When in the year 400 BC, at a time of great bitterness of
> feeling, Thrasybulus, one of the chief men of Athens, came
> to the head of affairs, he exerted his influence to secure the
> passage of a law they called *amnestia*, from a Greek word
> signifying no recollection. The law provided that all former
> quarrels and offences be forgotten, and that the people
> take a pledge to live peaceably towards each other as if the
> offences had never taken place. Yes! Let this be the way of
> it – that John, Jean, Johann, and Jack sponge off their
> memories all red-written records.[41]

It was in this spirit that the IWGC tried to do their work. The Commission was trying to live up to a phrase coined in 1914 by H.G. Wells describing the war as "The War that will end War." Initially this was meant to refer to the end of Prussian militarism, but it came to mean the war that would bring peace forever.[42] This phrase, although it mutated slightly into "the war to end all wars," stuck throughout the war and in the interwar period as a hopeful description of a redeeming purpose of massive destruction.

We know that World War I famously failed in this task, as have subsequent wars, yet Remembrance Day focuses on peace, a theme that Jonathan Vance identifies as emerging during the interwar years. Part of this emphasis arose from a suggestion by the National Council of Women and the Canadian Legion in 1938 to "observe Remembrance Day as a day of thanksgiving for peace."[43] This suggestion was taken up by Prime Minister Mackenzie King, with the resulting addition to Canada's mythology of the First World War of the soldier viewed as "the guardian, even the servant, of peace."[44]

The peace terms at the end of World War II came closer to the ideals of the original amnesty, making political room for a functioning United Nations and for the development of an international peace and police force. The Canadian Secretary of State for External Affairs, Lester B. Pearson, announced the idea of this force to the United Nations General Assembly in November 1956. A man of his times, Pearson went beyond the belief that war would eventually bring peace. "The best defense of peace is not power, but the removal of the causes of war, and international agreements which will put peace on a stronger foundation than the terror of destruction."[45] He made this statement on 11 December 1957 in his Nobel Peace Prize lecture in Oslo, Norway. Pearson received the Peace Prize in view of his years of work for peace, but this is not how it is remembered in Canada. According to Pearson's editor, S. Pierson, he is remembered for having received the prize for the development of peacekeeping forces. Because of this, peacekeepers have become "Canadian" – at least as far as Canadians are concerned![46]

In September 1988, the Peacekeepers of the United Nations themselves received a Nobel Peace Prize. Building on the heightened profile of the peacekeepers, and ensuring that Canada would be clearly associated with them in the minds of Canadians, the suggestion arose to erect a monument to Canadian peacekeepers. The "Canadian Monument to Honour Peacekeepers, Past, Present and into the Future" was unveiled in 1992. It is the only monument of its kind in the world.

Peacekeepers are still promoted by government agencies as having a special connection with Canada. The Canadian soldiers who fell in World War I were presented as having fought for peace; their death was taken as payment for Canada achieving the status of nationhood in the eyes of the world. Peacekeepers are now presented by government as carrying an image of Canada onto the world scene. The Canadian Department of Foreign Affairs makes explicit what they see as the connection between Canada's international reputation and its history of peacekeeping: "Peacekeeping is an important aspect of Canada's national heritage and a reflection of our fundamental beliefs ... Canada builds on our established peacekeeping tradition to make strong and imaginative contributions to international peace and security ... Peacekeeping is also a significant component of Canada's foreign policy and our contribution to the multilateral security system."[47]

The Silver Cross mother provides a connection between these two positive notions Canadians have of themselves as actors on the international stage. In both cases her image acts, if not as an agent for recruitment, as during World War I, then at least as a reinforcement of the values upheld by the state, as in the case of the peacekeepers. And that image commands respect, now as in the past. If a Silver Cross mother of a peacekeeper can support the sacrifice of her son or daughter, then how can anyone question the government that attempts to foster the peace in whose name her child died?

The Silver Cross mother who lays a wreath on the War Memorial reminds us of all Silver Cross mothers. Cloaked in the ideals of peace, she asks us to remember Canada's involvement in wars and missions as honourable and necessary. Like the mothers of ancient Greece whose mourning was controlled, the Silver Cross mother seems to remind us selectively of our past. For the sake of peace, attained through amnesty, her image, quietly supportive of the state, encourages us to forget the side of war that incites revenge. The atrocity stories of the Bryce Report are now remembered only by military historians, just as Mount Cavell is significant only in its scenic beauty.

During World War I the stories in Canada of proud, bereaved mothers were inextricably tied to an understanding of a war steeped in notions of Christian sacrifice and divine purpose. Surrounded with this world view, some of the 58,500 women who were awarded the Memorial Cross of World War I presented their loss as a gain on the side of truth and divine justice. One can cite Mrs Hughes, whose story was presented in chapter 3. Some, such as those who responded to the letter of the "Little Mother," went so far as to say that if they had had more sons to give, they would have. But many women gave to the war effort in other ways. These activities reflected on all women collectively. It was on the basis of what they gave as proud mothers of sacrificed sons and as hard-working women in hospitals and munitions factories and on farms that women felt they had the right to ask for political equality. Unlike the demanding voice of women in the Greek chorus, they did this outside of the theatrical realm. Unlike mothers of martyrs, enough women in Canada looked to the balance of justice and tied their sacrifices to demands. As even the fairly conservative L.M. Montgomery stated, women "should have some voice in the political issues that may send [their] sons to die on battlefields."[48] Women did achieve some acceptance in the public and political sphere of the country. The federal vote was granted to women in 1917 – as long as they were related to men in the forces. The vote was initially therefore tied more to blood than to action. Thus it was easier at the end of the war for the veterans to demand that women return to the home and relinquish their jobs.

This has been a common and much commented-upon scenario for women involved in revolutions and wars around the world. One of the most straightforward and unabashed responses on behalf of male fighters toward female revolutionaries was made at the end of the Algerian struggle for independence from France (1954–62). The imprisoned female resistance fighter, Djamila Boupacha, who had been raped and tortured by the French for her role in the war, asked the revolutionary leader Mohammad Khider about the future of women after the revolution. "'And how about us women? Our status must change now that —' Khider interrupted the young woman, 'Women after independence? Why, you will return to your couscous, of course.'"[49]

The Silver Cross mothers were encouraged to return home with the medal they received in recognition of their loss. It would seem a paltry payment, but it comes with its own story of consolation. In its shape it is tied to the concept of sacrifice at the heart of the Christian faith. In this connection death becomes worth something, a means to a better world both for the living as well as for the sons who will go to heaven as their reward. Pericles said in his funeral oration that he intended his words to give not consolation but rather comfort to bereaved parents. Their comfort was to rest on pride – a pride in what their sons had died for. Although Pericles does not consider his words "consolation," he, like the authors of Islamic, Jewish, and Christian consolation literature,[50] recognized the need for practical aids to help parents overcome their intense pain over the loss of a child and counselled calm acceptance without excessive emotion.

This is, in essence, the position of the Silver Cross mother. She is not an hysterical, wailing, hair-rending presence, but is stoical in her grief, a pillar of dignity, honouring her dead child and sanctifying the struggle by ensuring that we remember – but not too much.

Conclusion
Mothers and Memories

War and religion have been constant companions for millennia. They support each other, providing proof of the other's validity and poignant stories to ensure their place in memory. One aspect of the relationship can be seen through the stories that have arisen from different cultures, faiths, and times of the mothers of sacrificed heroes. Mothers said to have supported their children's martyrdom include the joyful mother of the Maccabees, the mothers of sorrow, Mary and Fatima, the poet al-Khansa, and the grandmother Mata Gujari. Whether with joy or sorrow, these mothers are portrayed as accepting the necessity of the sacrifice of their children.

Ancient tales of child sacrifice have been retold and reinvented according to the needs and the culture of specific times and situations. The historical theorists of ancient times recognized the motivational potential of these stories. Martyrologists from different religious traditions have made this appeal in similar ways. All the old mothers-of-martyrs stories rely on the assumption of an intense bond between mother and child – a bond that the mother, when put to the test, is willing to sever for the sake of her faith and her community. This sacrifice is taken as proof of the ultimate truth of the cause for which it is made.

Similar stories, now mainly forgotten, were reproduced in English culture in Canada during World War I in public art, newspapers, magazines, and sermons steeped in the language of sacrifice. These stories and their high diction were given high credence during the war, but were rejected afterward as propagandistic – as the "foul language of glory," in Bertrand Russell's phrase. Soldiers were described sometimes specifically as Christ, or more generally as martyrs. From today's standpoint, the atrocity stories of the Bryce Report are comparable to the tortures found in martyrologies, in that both were designed to reveal the evil nature of the enemy. The tales of the martyrdom of Edith Cavell and the rumours of the crucified Canadian had an impact on recruitment and morale. Both were martyrs in the popular imagination, and the causes for which they suffered, as in earlier martyrologies, reached to the ultimate of truth, justice, civilization, and God. And although soldiers were trained, more or less, to kill, they were depicted as peace-loving defenders of truth, much like the ancient martyrs.

The stories of Canadian mothers from the war were grounded in a particularly patriotic social context reflected in images of mothers and women supporting the war effort that appeared on posters, in advertisements, and in initiatives such as the White Feather Campaign. This context made the letter from "A Little Mother" and Mrs Hughes' happy Christmas telegram, as well as repeated references to the Spartan mother, appear less "over the top" and more believable. The recruitment activities of women who participated in the White Feather Campaign were comparable to those of the mothers of martyrs and heroes. Theirs were not the voices of the pacifist women reviled in their day but recovered and saluted in the post-war era. For women who presented views supportive of the war – however deep their beliefs were – there were forms of compensation similar to what Palestinian and Iranian women have received in more recent times, ranging from financial support and formal respect in the shape of the Silver Cross to political enfranchisement.

After the war, mothers of soldiers continued to have a role in commemoration. Once again they were depicted in works of art, such as the Vimy Memorial and the Peace Tower's Memorial Chamber, as sad but proudly supportive of the state's choice to participate in the war. The role of bereaved mothers was highlighted in another dramatic fashion in 1936 on the Vimy Pilgrimage, when Silver Cross mother Mrs Wood was chosen to lay the wreath in Westminster Abby and was introduced to the King.

During World War II the image of the heroic Silver Cross mother was once again called up to support the value of sacrifice. Since 1939, the Canadian Legion has chosen one Silver Cross mother to lay a wreath on the War Memorial in Ottawa on behalf of all the war-bereaved mothers of Canada. This ritual is televised, and in recent years the Silver Cross mother has been highlighted in an interview prior to the Remembrance Day ceremonies, in part taking place in the Memorial Chamber amidst the Books of Remembrance. The Silver Cross mothers and their association with peacekeepers represent to Canadians a positive image of their country's actions on the international stage. Through the rituals of Remembrance Day they remind us of the sacrifice of mothers from previous wars, but particularly World War I, which now represents in popular Canadian history a significant rite of passage for the nation and Canada's entrance onto the international stage.

After the war, the huge task of burying the dead was taken on by the Imperial War Graves Commission (IWGC). In devising their principles, the Commission decided not to include women, those who are traditionally considered responsible for mourning. Thus the men of the IWGC effectively took control of the mourning process. In many ways they were following the precedent established by the ancient Greeks for burying war heroes. As Nicole Loraux argues, the voices of the mourning women in Athens and other city-states were also controlled for fear of the emotions they would raise. The IWGC made a great and creative effort to commemorate the one million dead in a manner that reflected what they saw as the international nature of the war, the solidarity of the British Imperial Empire, and the unity of purpose with which the war was fought.

The image of the Silver Cross mother and that of "The Spirit of Canada" on Vimy Ridge balance our needs and desires to remember and to forget. The reason most often given for the need to remember the sacrifice they signify is that remembrance will help us to cherish what we have and not go lightly into war. In addition, by remembering those fallen soldiers and their mourning mothers, we give their death and pain a purpose and a place in history.

As one would expect from a more militaristic culture, the remembrance of war-bereaved mothers has been taken a step further in the United States. Since 1936, on the last Sunday of September, Gold Star Mother's Day, the President is required to issue a proclamation to the people that they display their flags and hold meetings in their homes, public places, or places of worship so that they might express their respect for the Gold Star mothers.

When the need for a strong sense of patriotism and support for the military was required in the lead-up to the Gulf War in 1990, George Bush Sr. reminded the American public of the sacrifice of the Civil War mother, Mrs Bixby, in his Gold Star Mother's Day proclamation. Eight years later the Steven Speilberg movie *Saving Private Ryan*, in which American soldiers are ordered to find and bring home the last remaining son of a mother who has lost three others, provided another prominent reference to Mrs Bixby. Her loss is remembered because of the letter of respect she received from Abraham Lincoln on 21 November 1864 during the American Civil War, a letter that reflects the sentiments of pride and honour found in Pericles' funeral oration of 403 BCE. Lincoln addressed Mrs Bixby:

> Dear Madam: I have been shown in the files of the War
> Department a statement of the Adjutant-General of
> Massachusetts that you are the mother of five sons who have
> died gloriously on the field of battle. I feel how weak and
> fruitless must be any words of mine which should attempt to
> beguile you from the grief of a loss so overwhelming. But I
> cannot refrain from tendering to you the consolation that may
> be found in the thanks of the Republic they died to save. I
> pray that our Heavenly Father may assuage the anguish of your
> bereavement, and leave you only the cherished memory of the
> loved and lost, and the solemn pride that must be yours to

have laid so costly a sacrifice upon the altar of freedom.
Yours very sincerely and respectfully, Abraham Lincoln.[1]

A number of historians now believe that Lincoln did not write the
letter, that Mrs Bixby's five sons did not all die, and that she did not
sympathize with Lincoln. But the letter and purported story behind it
live on, untouched by this professional skepticism.

In the context of the Middle Eastern conflict, Palestinian mothers
of martyrs are also having a place in history asserted for them, particularly by radical leaders, in an increasingly dramatized and unforget-
table manner. In June 2002 a low-budget video caught the attention
of the world press. The story-line was reminiscent of the film *Some
Mother's Son*, discussed in the introduction, but in this case the actors,
Naima al-Abed and her son, Mahmoud, played themselves. Naima,
like the Irish mother who chose to maintain her unconscious son's
hunger strike until his death, also chose to support her son's death in
upholding a cause. In this video, designed and distributed by Hamas,
Naima al-Abed makes clear her belief in the close and winning relationship between martyrdom and the land. She says to her son, "I am
not losing you, because you are going to paradise ... Our sons whom
we love are no more dear to us than our land. Their blood will redeem
it."[2] Through the influence of video and newsprint, the story of Naima
and her desire for redemption has been recorded and, her supporters
hope, will live on in the minds of others long enough to inspire them
to follow in her and her son's steps.

The fear in remembering is that the memory will constantly rekin-
dle the desire for revenge. The atrocities of war must be forgotten,
because peace cannot be built on the memory of hatred. What helped
us to forget the atrocities that took us to war in World War I was the
post-war knowledge that many of them, said to have been committed
by the enemy, never occurred. With this knowledge came a realization
that the atrocity was the war itself and how it was conducted. Mrs
Wood, the most notable Silver Cross mother of the war, voiced the
agony of this understanding. Upon meeting King Edward VIII while
on the Vimy pilgrimage in 1936 she said, "Oh! Sir, I have just been
looking at the trenches and I just can't figure out why our boys had to

go through that."[3] It is likely that George Bernard Shaw would have added Mrs Wood's name to those of Edith Cavell and Joan of Arc on his list of arch-heretics, had she made this statement during the war. But the King responded with a gracious although, as it turned out, empty hope. "Please God, Mrs Wood, it shall never happen again." These words are now carved into the new headstone marking Mrs Wood's grave.

Charlotte Wood died a month after the beginning of World War II. Until 2003, this first Silver Cross mother was buried in an unmarked grave in Lot 113, Section 52, Brookside Cemetery, Winnipeg. Despite the new gravestone that has been erected for this once famously bereaved mother, she remains all but forgotten in this country of relative peace.

Will the stories of her sacrifice be resurrected and polished up in some future time of national crisis? The scenario is not implausible. Societies under attack band together and use whatever weapons are available, be they the latest military hardware or, at last resort, suicide bombers. Certainly propaganda and national mythmaking are crucial parts of the mix. Yet in an era when Irish blood is still brought to a boil over the outcome of the Battle of the Boyne, and bombs still rock the streets of old Jerusalem in a conflict centuries old, it is hard not to take some strange comfort in the peaceful obscurity of a figure like Mrs Wood. If history is a struggle between remembering and forgetting, then what is remembered is a battleground in itself, and forgetting is sometimes the sanest relief.

NOTES

ABBREVIATIONS
AO   Archives of Ontario
CWM   Canadian War Museum
DND   Department of National Defence
NAC   National Archives of Canada
Biblical quotations follow the New Revised Standard Version.

INTRODUCTION
1 Vance, *Death So Noble*, 147.
2 Klausner, "Martyrdom," 237.
3 Newman, "We'd Rather be Clark Kent," 87.
4 Ibid.
5 Gray, "No Idol Industry Here," 83.
6 Young, "'We Throw the Torch,'" 21.
7 Canada, Privy Council Office, PC 1976-2724, 2.
8 Thurer, *Myths of Motherhood*, 6.
9 Ibid.
10 The "Spirit of Canada" and "Canada mourning" are expressions used
   to describe this sculpture in Hundevad's *Guide Book of the Pilgrimage
   to Vimy*. "Mother Canada" is a colloquial term found in present-day
   media. "The Spirit of Canada" was also the title of a sculpture done in
   1917 by Frances Loring; it stood on the grounds of the Canadian
   National Exhibition, Toronto, but deteriorated over time.

CHAPTER ONE

1 Boyarin, *Dying for God*, 94.

2 In Frend's words, "martyrdom in Judaism remained something of a *Hamlet* without the Prince. However much the Jew might regard the Law as 'pre-existent,' and 'the breath of the power of God,' his sufferings on its behalf were in hope and anticipation only. The Law remained God-created and majestic, but impersonal, and for deep-thinking minds an 'occasion for sin' rather than a means of salvation." *Martyrdom and Persecution*, 67.

3 Bowersock argues that 2 Maccabees does not include the documentation of legal hearings, which are a necessary element in making "narratives of resistance to authority and heroic self-sacrifice" into martyrologies. *Martyrdom and Rome*, 27.

4 Boyarin, *Dying for God*, 96.

5 I use the male pronoun to refer to God because that is how the divine was described in all of the stories included in this book. If any of the gods had generally been understood to have been female or sexless it is likely that the stories of mothers of martyrs, which themselves developed in strongly patriarchal societies, would be very different.

6 Jowett and O'Donnell, *Propaganda and Persuasion*, 218.

7 Rubio and Waterston, *Selected Journals of L.M. Montgomery*, 102.

8 Salisbury, *Perpetua's Passion*, 51.

9 Plutarch, *Plutarch's Moralia*, trans. De Lacy and Einarson 2:493.

10 Robin Darling Young's article "'The 'Woman with the Soul of Abraham': Traditions about the Mother of the Maccabean Martyrs" discusses the philosophical and metaphysical attitudes toward women at the time 2 Maccabees was written. She states, "an ancient philosophical commonplace claimed the feminine element in the human constitution to be weaker and more subject to the emotions than the manly, reasonable element" (72, n.5).

11 Goldstein, *II Maccabees*, 21.

12 Doran, *Temple Propaganda*, 84.

13 Ibid., 86.

14 The Maccabean mother is described as joyful in: Pesiq. R. 43, b. Git. 57b and Midr. Lam 1:16. All of these sources refer to Ps 113:9. I have confined my comments to the chronicle written between 1140 and 1146 and most commonly ascribed to Solomon bar Simson (although scholars suspect that the work had more than one author). My quotations from this chronicle are from Eidelberg's translation. It is the longest of the three Hebrew chronicles of the First Crusade.

15 Eidelberg, trans, *The Jews and the Crusaders*, 35.
16 Ibid., 36.
17 Ibid.
18 A story strikingly similar to Rachel's surfaced recently, although with a change of place and culture. The Canadian doctor, James Orbinski of the international aid organization, Médecins Sans Frontières, described his experiences in Rwanda, where parents came to him either begging for or offering to pay to have their children killed before they were captured and put to death by the enemy (CBC *Ideas* "Taking a Stand: The Ethics of Intervention" part 3, 30 May 2001). Orbinski told this first-hand and very emotional story in the context of a speech calling for people "to speak out against the moral hollowness of political inaction."
19 Although the books were brought to Palestine by the Christians from Egypt, William Rueben Farmer points out in *Maccabees, Zealots, and Josephus* that we have no way of knowing whether this literature circulated in Palestine during the first century CE prior to its importation. However, even without the written documents of either 1 or 2 Maccabees, the history of the Hasmoneans probably survived in oral form. As well as the oral tradition there may have been other written texts, now lost, presenting different versions of this story.
20 Winslow, "The Maccabean Martyrs," 23:78-9.
21 Origen, *Prayer and Exhortation*, trans. John J. O'Meara, 126.
22 This sorrow can be seen in lamentations of the Sumerian goddess, Innana, and her Babylonian counterpart, Ishtar, as they weep for their lost son/spouse. See Briffault, *Mothers*, (93) for lamentations and Warner, *Alone of All Her Sex* (207) for similarities with Mary.
23 Musurillo, *Acts of the Christian Martyrs*, 77.
24 Ibid.
25 Salisbury, *Perpetua's Passion*, 91.
26 Cunneen, *In Search of Mary*, 188. Warner makes the point in *Alone of All Her Sex* (209) that although the *pietà* did not enter Christian imagery until the Middle Ages, one of the original visual influences was the figure of Isis holding her dead son Osiris from the Egyptian cult that lasted into the Christian period.
27 Newman, *From Virile Woman*, 83.
28 Ibid., 80.
29 Warner, *Alone of All Her Sex*, 210.
30 Tydeman, "Introduction to Medieval English Theatre," 20.
31 Ibid., 211.

167

32 Ibid.

33 Tydeman, "Introduction to Medieval English Theatre," 6.

34 Witt, *Contrary Marys*, 2.

35 Tydeman, "Introduction to Medieval English Theatre," 18.

36 Ibid. The battles being waged over the souls of the British audience took a twist in 1534 when Henry VIII established himself as head of the church, but this did not mean an end to the religious content of the plays. The efforts designed to support Henry's takeover made good use of the stage. The propagandists of this time recognized that in a largely illiterate population, especially in rural Catholic regions, drama conveyed ideological messages in an entertaining and accessible manner. The Passion plays did carry on, being performed into the 1600s, but gradually the scripts were revised to conform to Protestant orthodoxy.

37 Ibid., 27.

38 In the N-Town cycle, notable for its emphasis on Mary, the angel Gabriel spends some time urging her to accept the Incarnation. All souls living and dead wait in anticipation for her response for their salvation weighs in the balance.

39 Witt, *Contrary Marys*, 164.

40 Bevington, *Medieval Drama*, 156–60.

41 Ibid., 580. Examples of these laments can be found in the Passion play from Benediktbeuern, which has an extended section on Mary at the foot of the Cross, where she wishes "Let my little one live for my sake. And let me die, his mother, / Mary, most pitiable woman. / What use are life and body to me?" (Bevington, *Medieval Drama*, 220). Mary's lament is also like that of mothers in "The Slaughter of the Innocents" from Fleury. This play describes Christ's flight into Egypt and the killing of all the suckling children by Herod's order, an atrocity parallel to that of Pharaoh. In this story the bereaved mother is advised to understand that her grief rests on her joy. In another parallel of history the main mother of the play (cf. Matt. 2:18) is called Rachel, and like the Rachel of Genesis, she now suffers from childlessness. She is comforted and asked to restrain her tears, for "although you grieve, rejoice that you weep. / For, truly, your sons live blessed above the stars" (Bevington, ibid., 70).

42 Witt, *Contrary Marys*, 165.

43 Ibid., 134.

44 Ibid., 132.

45 Cunneen, *In Search of Mary*, 266.

46 Fussell, "Fate of Chivalry," 238.

47 Ibid., 222.

48 Ibid., 241.

49 Ayoub, *Redemptive Suffering in Islam*, 71.

50 Ibid., 71.

51 Vaglieri, "Fatima," 3:847.

52 Pelly, *Miracle Play of Hasan and Husain*," 113.

53 Vaglieri, "Fatima," 3:845.

54 Ibid., 3:847.

55 Ayoub, *Redemptive Suffering in Islam*, 144.

56 Friedl, "Ideal Womanhood," 150.

57 Ibid., 149.

58 The mourning ceremonies, songs, and poetry commemorating the death of Fatima's son Husayn are thought to reflect ancient Babylonian ideas concerning the cult of Tammuz and the Persian legend of the death of Siyavush. Siyavush, a young prince, escaped his father's anger by going to Turan, where he ended up being murdered. This pre-Islamic story has survived through the writings of Islamic historians who, although they stripped much of the religious content from the tale, do mention some details that allude to the sanctity of this hero, who became the centre of a cult that included annual sacrifices at his grave amidst much weeping and, some sources say, face cutting. See Yarshater, "Ta'ziyeh and Pre-Islamic Mourning Rites," 90–1. Briffault (*Mothers*) suggests the possibility that the term *ta'ziya*, the name of the ritual commemorating the death of Husayn, and which means mourning and lamentation, is "a corrupt reminiscence" of "ta'uz" or "Tammuz."

59 Pelly, *Miracle Play of Hasan and Husain*, iii.

60 Pelly follows in what Chelkowski refers to as "the tradition of scholar-diplomats." There were a number of other foreign observers who had previously written about the Iranian Muharram celebrations. Through their works one can see that the celebrations developed from "a mourning ritual into full-scale theatre" (Chelkowski, "Ta'ziyeh," 1979:259). A major aspect of this development was the addition of the spoken element to the drama augmenting what had previously been a silent staging of tableaus.

61 I have used this, the more common spelling of Husayn's name in recent times, but left Pelly's spelling of Husain as it was published in 1879.

62 Pelly, *Miracle Play of Hasan and Husain*, v.

63 Like Jesus' anointing before his death, this act serves to purify the sacrifice (the martyr, in this case) so as to make it acceptable to God. This,

along with fasting, was also a custom of warriors on the battlefield when they expected to die.

64 Pelly, Miracle Play of Hasan and Husain, xiv.

65 Ayoub, Redemptive Suffering in Islam, 117.

66 Chelkowski, "Ta'ziyeh," 2. It is likely that the annual Muharram mourning ceremonies developed with some ease because of the long Persian tradition commemorating dead heroes. The pre-Islamic legendary hero Siyavush was venerated with sacrificial offerings and weeping at his grave with special singers.

67 Baktash, "Ta'ziyeh and its Philosophy," 96.

68 Ibid.

69 Ibid.

70 Pelly, *Miracle Play of Hasan and Husain*, 130.

71 Ibid., 131.

72 Chelkowski, "Ta'ziyeh," 8.

73 Ayoub, *Redemptive Suffering in Islam*, 42.

74 Sa'id Ibn al-Nili, in Ayoub, *Redemptive Suffering*, 179.

75 This statement was originally printed in *Enqelaley Eslami*, 24 May 1981 and was here quoted by Afshar ("Khomeini's Teachings," 61).

76 Afshar, "Khomeini's Teachings," 62.

77 Shariati was very popular in Iran, especially with younger people. When the ban on his writings was lifted in 1978, his works were so sought after that stalls selling his writings emerged on street corners throughout Iran.

78 Ibrahim, "Burning Cause."

79 Omid, *Islam and the Post-Revolutionary State*, 122.

80 Agence France Presse, "Tehran's vast monument."

81 The details from the tribal traditions that state that al-Khansa led a deputation to meet with Mohammad and that she was present at the battle of al-Qadisiyya are, Gabrieli states in his *Encyclopaedia of Islam* article about the poetess, "very suspect to western critics" (1027). Nevertheless, they have some currency, for because of them she was called forth as a model of behaviour in the Palestinian resistance to the British Mandate, as well as being written about by the commentator on that period, Mogamman. These stories are repeated in the work of the modern author Elizabeth Warnock Fernea and are available on the Internet. They also have been remembered in the work of the modern Palestinian poetess Fadwa Tuqan.

82 Mogannam, *Arab Woman*, 22.

83 Fernea and Bezirgan, *Middle Eastern Muslim Women*, 4.

84 See, for example, www.witness-pioneer.org/vil/Articles/compan
ion/18_umar_bin_al_khattab.htm (accessed 30 April 2006).

85 DeYoung, "Love, Death," 51.

86 Ibid.

87 Rowley, "Soldiers in a Holy War." Stories of replacement children go
back to the Hebrew Bible: see Genesis 4:25 and Samuel 12:24.

88 Eickelman, *Middle East*, 184.

89 Rowley, "Soldiers in a Holy War."

90 Tertullian, *Apology*, 50.

91 Singh, *Illustrated Martyrdom Tradition*, n.p.

92 *Supreme Sacrifice of Young Souls*, an illustrated English- language
comic-book style publication describes Mata Gujari's behaviour toward
her grandsons during this interval. She encourages her grandsons to be
true to their traditions. In this behaviour she is portrayed in a manner
strikingly similar to that of the Maccabean mother in 2 Maccabees and
Pesiq. R. 43. Another interesting point of comparison between the two
stories is the trickery shown on the part of the ruler. In both cases the
scene is the court of the rulers. For the young Sikh boys the test was in
how to enter the court through the small opening down at the bottom
of the great gates without bowing down and appearing as though they
were submitting to Nawab Wazir Khan. But, being presented as intelli-
gent as well as brave, they put their feet in first and avoided bowing. In
the Midr. Lam 1:16 version of the Maccabean story, the King calls the
youngest of the boys to him and suggests that he could just throw his
ring down on the ground and the boy could pick it up. This would
look as if he were bowing to the king, but he would know that he was
just picking up the ring. As one would expect, the boy does not accept
this offer.

93 Fenech, *Martyrdom in the Sikh Tradition*, 3.

94 Singh, *Anecdotes from Sikh History*, 15.

95 Strikingly similar images of the fate of babies appear in World War I
atrocity stories to be discussed later, the only difference being that they
were impaled on bayonets instead of swords.

96 Giani Gian Singh (1880), cited in Fenech, "The Mother as Heroic
Icon."

97 Doran, "Martyr," 192.

98 Singh, *Anecdotes from Sikh History*, 17.

99 Ibid., 7.

100 Mahmood, *Fighting for Faith*, 105.

101 Ibid., 106.

102 Fenech, *Martyrdom in the Sikh Tradition*, 46.

103 Juergensmeyer, *Terror in the Mind of God*, 94.

104 Although Briffault sees mothers as being very powerful in the creation of society, the intellectual abilities of women are, he says, "deficient in the qualities that mark the masculine intellect ... The critical, analytical, and detached creative powers of the intellect are less developed in women than in men" (*Mothers*, 507). He assumes the reason for this "arises in all probability from the subordination and sacrifice to maternal functions which limits the physical growth of the mammalian femal." (ibid). In these thoughts he appears to be to be a man of his era, although the changing attitudes of the time are reflected in his response to the women's suffrage movement: to achieve independence from subordination, he states, women must defend their own interests and men must unlearn much of their "patriarchal theory."

105 Ibid., 509.

CHAPTER TWO

1 Although Winnington-Ingram was the Bishop of London, England, he had strong connections to Canada, where he was well received. Before the war he had taken two trips to Canada combining official church business and visits with relatives. He describes his travels through Nova Scotia, New Brunswick, Quebec, and Ontario in his autobiography, which was published in Toronto as well as in London. Large crowds came out to hear him speak in both urban and rural locations. In the years leading up to the war the British Archbishops' Western Canada Fund sent hundreds of English clergy to Canada; Winnington-Ingram was said to have considered volunteering himself.

2 Patterson, "An Ex-Chaplain," 3.

3 Lasswell, *Propaganda Technique*, 197.

4 Ryder, *Edith Cavell*, 231.

5 Ibid., 226.

6 Ibid.

7 Lasswell, *Propaganda Technique*, 198.

8 Horne and Kramer provide an explanation for the "outpouring of British emotion" for Cavell, stating that "apart from the fact that as a nurse she embodied wartime female selflessness ... her tale particularized the surrogate relationship of British opinion with the invasion of Belgium by providing a direct victim" (*German Atrocities*, 311).

9 Ryder, *Edith Cavell*, 251.

10 The enlistment figures from Colonel Nicholson's *Official History of the Canadian Army in the First World War*, including officers and other ranks are as follows. For 1915: October, 12,837; November, 17,993; December, 23,683. For 1916: January, 29,187; February, 27,662; March, 34,892 (*Offical History*, 546).

11 Quoted in Ryder, *Edith Cavell*, 188.

12 Ibid., 228.

13 Ibid., 214.

14 Shaw, *Seven Plays*, 773.

15 The plaque below the relief says "Edith Cavell and the Canadian Nurses who gave their lives for humanity in the Great War: 'In the midst of darkness they saw light.' Lest We Forget." It was erected by Societá Italo Canadese, 11 November 1922.

16 Chown, "Pacifism at Chautauqua," 13.

17 Buitenhuis, *The Great War of Words*, 27.

18 Tuchman, *Guns of August*, 314.

19 See Tuchman, 319-22.

20 Horne and Kramer, *German Atrocities*, 76.

21 Lasswell, *Propaganda Technique*, 88.

22 Ibid., 81.

23 Peel, *How We Lived*, 43.

24 Ibid., 44.

25 Lasswell, *Propaganda Technique*, 190.

26 Godwin, *Why Stay We Here*, 189.

27 Bryce, *Report*, 51.

28 See Knightley, "The Disinformation Campaign."

29 Connor, *The Major*, 366.

30 Bloch, *Historian's Craft*, 107.

31 Ibid., 108.

32 Brophy and Partridge, *Songs and Slang*, 135.

33 Remarque, *All Quiet*, 15.

34 Bloch, *The Historian's Craft*, 110.

35 "Canadian Crucified by the Germans?," 4.

36 Tippett, *Art in the Service of War*, 82.

37 Chambers, in Feldman, *Canada's Golgotha*, 6.

38 Coppard, *With a Machine Gun*, 76.

39 Chesterton, in Raemaekers, *Raemaekers' Cartoons*, 32.

40 In Tippett, *Art at the Service of War*, 23.

41 Ibid., 81.

42 The statue was exhibited at the Canadian War Museum from 30 March to 8 October 1992 in the show "Peace is the Dream" and then from 20 December 1992 to 28 September 1995 in the show "Conservation Is?". It was in the minister's office of the Department of National Defense from 20 June 1996 to 2 July 1997 and was shown as a part of Canadian Museum of Civilization's show "Under the Sign of the Cross" from 5 November 1999 to 18 March 2001.

43 Sinclair, in Feldman, *Canada's Golgotha*, 9.

44 Ponsonby, *Falsehood in War-Time*, 92.

45 NAC RG 24, vol. 1749, "Canadian War Records Office Official Report," 31 Aug. 1919: app. I, "Canadian War Memorials Report of Executive Committee," 1.

46 Morton, *Silent Battle*, 4.

47 Feldman, *Canada's Golgotha*, 18.

48 In McMartin, "Kin of Crucified Soldier," B4.

49 Feldman, *Canada's Golgotha*, 22.

50 *Sacrifice* now hangs in Regeneration Hall of the new Canadian War Museum, opposite Allward's maquette of "Hope" from the Vimy Memorial and a slender window facing the Peace Tower on Parliament Hill.

51 Konody, *Art and War*, plate I.

52 There were well-known Canadian cartoonists of the time, for example Arthur Racey and Ben Batsford, publishing with the *Montreal Star* and *Winnipeg Free Press* respectively, who tackled the subject of war. Their comments were filtered through the lens of politics in Canada and were not related to Christian ideals of sacrifice. Racey, for example, condemned Canadian politicians for quibbling at home "while our boys are fighting for liberty and the flag at the front." Batsford produced a pre-election cartoon with the caption "Make every ballot a bullet for Bill" under an image of a fleeing Kaiser Wilhelm (Desbarats and Mosher, *Hecklers*, 74).

53 *Raemaekers Cartoons*, 1915.

54 *Raemaekers' Cartoons with Accompanying Notes*, 1971.

55 *Raemaekers' Cartoons with Accompanying Notes* includes commentary by well-known authors of the time facing each cartoon. A book similar in style was published by Raemaekers in the United States, entitled *America in the War* (1918). Once again, each cartoon was faced with a page of commentary by American writers.

56 Horne and Kramer, *German Atrocities*, 297.

57 Craig, *But This is Our War*, 33.

58 Raemaekers, *Raemaekers Cartoons*, 39. This is a small, comic-book style publication of only forty pages.

59 Raemaekers, *Raemaekers' Cartoons with Accompanying Notes*, 251.

60 Ibid., 24.

61 Raemaekers, *Raemaekers Cartoons*, 11.

62 Ibid., 29.

63 Punch, *Mr. Punch's History of the Great War*, 7.

64 "The Very Stones Cry Out" is a reference to Luke 19:40.

65 Vaughan, in *Raemaekers' Cartoons with Accompanying Notes*, 20.

66 Winnington-Ingram, "A Word of Cheer," 353.

67 He also mentions Poland, Serbia, and Armenia.

68 MacDonald, "The Cause of God," 6.

69 Ketterson, *On Active Service*, ix.

70 See Marshall, *Secularizing the Faith*, 156–181.

71 Clayton, *Chavasse — Double VC*, 182.

72 Scott, *The Great War As I Saw It*, 105.

73 Ibid., 151.

74 Marshall, *Secularizing the Faith*, 171.

75 Ibid.

76 In Hopkins, *Canadian Annual Review*, 254.

77 Renison, *Canada at War*, 361.

78 Bliss, "The Methodist Church," 39.

79 Novak, *Dubious Glory*, 22.

80 Wilson, *Charles William Gordon*, 28.

81 See Gordon, *Postscript to Adventure*, 286, 294–302.

82 Novak, *Dubious Glory*, 11.

83 Connor, *Sky Pilot*, 256.

84 See Novak, *Dubious Glory*, 7-51.

85 Frye, *Secular Scripture*, 50.

86 Novak, *Dubious Glory*, 51.

87 Ibid., 36.

88 Rubio and Waterston, *Selected Journals of L.M. Montgomery*, 154.

89 Montgomery, *Rilla of Ingleside*, 125.

90 This monthly magazine was published in Toronto from 1909 to 1921 and is described by John Craig as "the most popular and outspoken magazine of women's opinion in the era" (*Years of Agony*, 89). By 1915 it was available by subscription in the United States, England and "foreign countries." It billed itself as the magazine for "the Canadian Woman who thinks and feels," and by 1917 it claimed a circulation of 130,000 (although audited figures allow for 125,000), surpassing the

combined circulation of all other major Canadian magazines at the time.

91 Murphy et al., "What Twelve Canadian Women Hope," 7.

92 Connor, *The Major,* 333.

93 Ibid., 335.

94 Connor, *Sky Pilot in No Man's Land,* 174.

95 Ibid.

96 Marshall, *Secularizing the Faith,* 163.

97 At the time of the war Newfoundland was Britain's oldest colony and had raised its own army. During the Battle of the Somme on 1 July 1916 at Beaumont Hamel, Newfoundland's total casualties were 733 out of 801 troops (Gwyn, *Tapestry,* 1992:304). The poem on the plaque does not have a title but in *High Altars* Oxenham calls it "Vimy Ridge"(1918:31).

98 Oxenham, *High Altars,* 76.

99 Ibid., 78.

100 Rubio and Waterston, *Selected Journals of L.M. Montgomery,* 154.

101 Ibid., 160.

102 Prescott, *In Flanders Fields,* 107.

103 Ibid., 106.

104 Ibid.

105 Wetherell, *The Great War In Verse,* xiv.

106 Vance, *Death So Noble,* 136.

107 Ibid., 33.

108 Folis, "The Major: Book Review," 7.

109 Brophy and Partridge, *Songs and Slang,* 18.

CHAPTER THREE

1 Quoted in Freeman and Nielsen, *Far From Home,* 175.

2 McClung, *Next of Kin,* 148.

3 Ibid., 14.

4 Vance, *Death So Noble,* 150.

5 AO C 233-2-0-4-199.

6 Rickards and Moody, *First World War,* 19.

7 A 1914 photograph published in Barker and Jackson shows this poster prominently draped over a recruiting table in front of Trafalgar Square, London (*London,* 356).

8 CWM 56-04-11-083.

9 CWM 56-05-11-091.

10 CWM 56-04-11-072.

11 CWM 56-04-11-087.

12 Hanna, "They Shall Not Pass," 27.

13 CWM AN 19820554-006.

14 CWM 56-04-11-044.

15 Gilbert, *Soldier's Heart*, 213.

16 Norman, "Music on the Home Front."

17 Ibid.

18 This song was written in opposition to the establishment of the cadet corps in New York schools.

19 Norman, "Music on the Home Front."

20 NAC, RG 24, v. 4301, file 2D. 34-1-59.

21 The name of the Ontario town "Berlin" was a casualty of the war. On 1 September 1916 it was changed to Kitchener.

22 Wilson, *Ontario and the First World War*, xci.

23 Read, *Great War*, 104.

24 MacDonagh, *In London During the Great War*, 79–80; Gullace, "White Feathers," 179.

25 Gullace, "White Feathers," 180.

26 Ibid. Gullace cites Claire M. Tylee as an example. Tylee's article "'Maleness Run Riot'– the Great War and Women's Resistance to Militarism," implics that all women were against the war but were powerless to prevent it.

27 Gullace, "White Feathers," 186.

28 NAC, RG 24, v. 4301, file 2D. 34-1-59.

29 *Berlin News Record*, 15 January 1916, 8.

30 Sifton, "About People You Know," 17.

31 A woman's sexual purity was an issue for wives of soldiers with regard to their eligibility for financial support from the Canadian Patriotic Fund. This fund was set up in 1914 based on similar funds collected in Canada during the Crimean and Boer Wars. If a woman had an affair while her husband was away, she risked having her children taken from her and/or her financial support being reduced. The belief in the necessity of the moral regulation of female dependants during the war carried over into the governing structure of the Mother's Allowance programs after the war.

32 Orczy, "To the Women of England," 1914.

33 Rickards and Moody, *First World War*, 20.

34 Hughes, "I am a Proud Mother," 11.

35 Mary Macleod Moore also wrote of the pride felt by Canadians in the women's pages of the Christmas 1915 issue of *Saturday Night*. It was a

"heartbreaking" time "because from end to end of that vast country, pulsing with high patriotic feeling and glorious by self-sacrifice, there are men and women mourning for sons, lovers, husbands, brothers" but for Canada this moment is also "proudest because the whole country, including the bereaved, exults in the fact that young Canada counted life itself but a small thing when the trumpet's call was heard" ("What this Christmas Means").

36 Not surprisingly, American movies made during and about World War I had as their most prominent female role that of the mother. Isenberg writes of this role, "If at times she grieved over her lost soldier boy, her role also was interlaced with the idealization of motherhood as a biological sanctification of the national spirit." He argues that their role in the war effort was to bear sons to send off to fight. The depiction of their fertility as sacred was, he believed, more of a European concept than a reflection of American values (*War on Film*, 191).

37 Interview with Joan and Robert Meade, 9 November 2003, Ottawa, Ont.

38 The *Morning Post* had a long history in London, beginning in 1772. Its chief competitor for the upper-middle class market was the *Times*. Although remembered as a conservative newspaper, it supported such institutions as income tax and national education. In general it reflected both British society and its taste in literature. Rudyard Kipling, famous during the Great War, was one of its well-known contributors (see Hindle 1937:1–6). One of the editors of the *Morning Post* was Fabian Ware, who went on to head the Imperial War Graves Commission.

39 Graves, *Goodbye to All That*, 202.

40 In Graves, ibid., 203.

41 In Graves, ibid., 204.

42 In Graves, ibid., 205.

43 Elshtain, *Women and War*, 193.

44 Lowrey, "His Unknown Mother," 28.

45 Ibid., 6.

46 A popular institution that developed most fully in France, was that of the *marraines* (godmother or adoptive mother). It began early in the war when women began knitting socks and sending letters with their parcels to the men. Some realized that there were men with no family and offered to act as mothers for those without. The institution took on an erotic tone for a time but then was taken over by old women and little children writing to the soldiers.

47 In a war fought in the trenches it was not an asset to be tall. The mention of the height of the soldier in both stories would not have been an indication of a happy ending.

48 The perception of a blending of history and fiction in this book is apparent in Hopkins and Castell's *Canadian Annual Review of Public Affairs*, which lists the book under "Canadian Books on the World-War" (a category that included many books by military officers) and under "Fiction and Novels." In a contemporaneous review, *Saturday Night* editor Tom Folis took the opportunity to blast Nellie McClung for her suffragist ideas, thus reacting to the book more as an extended essay than as fiction.

49 McClung, *Next of Kin*, 17.

50 This avowedly anti-conscription and anti-war newspaper did have a difficult time with the censors. Richardson tells us that Mr I. Bainbridge, the editor, was imprisoned on the charge of circulating literature with intent to prevent recruiting and circulating seditious libel. (Richardson, 24 February 1918, 6.)

51 Richardson, "Motherhood and War," 5.

52 The ancient Greek states had designated time limits governing the behaviour of mourners, most of whom were women. As one might infer from the story of the Spartan mother, Sparta allowed the shortest time: 12 days (Loraux, *Mothers in Mourning*, 31 n8, 32).

53 "When bowed head," 10.

54 Wodson, *Private Warwick*, 15. Another "light-hearted" reference to a female character shaming a man into enlisting is included early in Private Warwick's musings as he describes meeting a man in khaki walking down the street with his wife and children. Private Warwick overhears the wife saying to her husband that just because some men were not signing up to save the Empire did not mean that married men had any excuse. Warwick remarks that if a manhole had been in front of him it would have been appropriate to drop into it. "It takes a woman to stick the bayonet into your vitals, and to give the steel an artistic twist. *Women of that type breed fighting men*" (ibid, 9).

55 Wodson, *Private Warwick*, 20.

56 Ibid., 95.

57 Ibid., 23.

58 The selfishness of mother-love is the topic of the editorial from *Everywoman's World*. "Though it have selfishness at its base, mother-love is the sweetest, strongest, passion in the world" ("Mother-love," 3). As in

the recruitment leagues' literature, the power of the maternal bond is viewed with ambivalence. Although a sweet love, it must adapt to the needs of the time and release young men to go to war.

59 Wodson, *Private Warwick*, 45.

60 Norris, *Mainly for Mother*, 9.

61 Ibid., 8.

62 Unfortunately Mrs Leech did not receive her son's letter until 1928: after his death it had been placed inside his captain's valise without the captain's knowledge. It was not until Captain King was cleaning out the valise that he found the letter and sent it to the Leech family with a letter of explanation. Both letters were published in the Manitoba Free Press. http://web.mala.bc.ca/davies/letters.images/H.Leech/letter.Nov3 .1928.htm (accessed 17 March 2005).

63 "National Committee," *Saturday Night* 27 March 1915, 23.

64 Plumptre, "Canadian Women and the 'Peace Congress,'" in *Saturday Night* 27 March 1915, 21.

65 "Women's Parliament of Canada [Conscription]," 19.

66 To overcome this common objection, the Union Government, beginning in November 1917, promised that farmers, farmers' sons and farm workers would be exempt from conscription. They took out full-page advertisements in newspapers to inform the public of this, but on 20 April 1918 the government rescinded the exemption in response to the final German offensive.

67 These claims seem optimistic, considering that the subscription rate by 1917 was only 125,000. However, in 1915 the magazine claimed to have 500,000 "readers" (as opposed to "subscribers"), and so it may be that the 750,000 figure includes subscriptions, newsstand sales, and the hope that other members of the household and neighbours would be reading that issue in particular.

68 In Geller, "The Wartimes Election Act," 101.

69 Ibid., 102.

70 The idea of a partial franchise had been raised in 1916 by Nellie McClung, who suggested to Borden that the vote be given to women born in Britain and Canada (Geller, "Wartime Elections Act," 101).

71 The Military Voters Act was adopted at the same time. Both Acts required closure of debate in order to pass. The Military Voters Act gave the vote to nurses serving in the war and stated that military voters could assign their vote to any riding they had lived in or have the party for which they voted choose in which riding to place the vote. What made this freedom to choose a riding most important was the

fact that, included in the Act, was the provision that the overseas votes were to be counted 31 days after the election. At that time, when the votes had been counted in Canada, the government redistributed the military votes (90 percent for Borden) in such a manner as to win fourteen more seats (Canada. Office of the Chief Electoral Officer of Canada, *History of the Vote*, 58–68).

72 The Act also excluded conscientious objectors from voting as well as many who had become British Subjects after 31 March 1902 or who had been born in what by then had become enemy territory (ibid., 59).

73 Ibid., 60.

74 Hopkins and Castell, *Canadian Annual Review, 1917*, 629.

75 "If Union Government is Beaten," 2.

76 Hopkins and Castell, *Canadian Annual Review, 1917*, 629.

77 Parents were entitled to a pension on the death of their son if there were no other eligible dependants; even after the war the CPF continued to support the parents (McCallum, "Assistance to Veterans," 165).

78 Ibid., 160.

79 Ames, *Our National Benefaction*, 14. The Fund organizers made it clear that if a man did not fight he must pay. To clarify this point Ames drew a comparison with the American Civil War, stating that at that time it was customary for men to buy other men to take their places on the fighting line. "I know a man who bought two other men to go the front for him and paid each man $500.00 for the purpose" (Canada, House of Commons, *Debates* 24 February 1915:402).

80 Read, *Great War*, 189.

81 Canadian Patriotic Fund, *A Message*, 7.

82 Dr Helen MacMurchy (1862–1953), a great social activist in the area of public health care, particularly for mothers and children, connected the battlefield with the importance of child care when she stated, "We are only now discovering that Empires and States are built up of babies. Cities are dependent for their continuance on babies. Armies are recruited only if and when we have cared for our babies" (in Arnup, "Educating Mothers," 191).

83 A call for financial support for war-bereaved mothers in another form came from Rev. George Williams. He demanded that "every mother who lost her son is entitled to as least as much as the best of us has who stayed at home" ("Victory Loans," 1). This not-so-subtle tactic was intended to shame people into investing in Victory Loans.

84 The idea of public support for mothers did not arise in a vacuum. Pensions were an important issue at this time. In 1918, Stephen Leacock

wrote an editorial in *Everywoman's World* on the need for soldier's pensions. His argument for the support of a variety of social pensions rested to a large extent on the change in the relationship between the government and the people in light of conscription. If the government could compel men to sacrifice themselves for the country, then the people had the right to compel the government to support those men. "The old creed of every man for himself has broken down. In place of it has come a new doctrine of social solidarity in which the welfare of each is the common cause of all" ("What of Soldiers' Pensions?", 3).

85 "It is sweet and proper to die for one's country" (Horace). This phrase was used in an ironic sense as a title in a poem by one of the best-known British war poets, Wilfred Owen, but many took this sentiment seriously during the war.

86 Little, *No Car, No Radio*, 26.

87 AO, RG 7-12-0-11, file: Employment, General, 1918–1919, 'To Women Workers.'

88 "Canada Must Have Mothers' Pensions," 3.

89 See Kawar, *Daughters of Palestine*, 41–3.

90 The prototype for this foundation was the Palestinian Families of the Martyrs Foundation.

91 Chubin and Tripp, *Iran and Iraq at War*, 133.

92 Nasir, "Khomeini Faces Crunch," 37.

93 Jocelyn, *Awards of Honour*, 243.

94 This is still true today, as is clear from an article printed in a local newspaper in Okotoks, Alberta, the *Western Wheel*, about a Silver Cross representative who was chosen to lay the wreath at the Remembrance Day ceremonies in her town. In introducing her and explaining why it was a wife rather than a mother who was chosen, the reporter, Gillian Beckett, said, "Traditionally the role of Silver Cross Mother has been reserved for a mother whose son(s) had served in the two world wars." She reasons that because the mothers are dying off, "to carry the legacy of an honoured tradition, the role has been extended to the wives of such soldiers." It is easy to see how this understanding of the role came to be. Beckett is merely giving voice to a message which has been prominent since before the medal was even struck – a mother's loss was considered the most heartbreaking and thus the one to call in the most respect ("Resident Named Last Silver Cross").

95 "Silver Crosses For Bereaved Mothers," 3.

96 Blewett, "Mothers' Recognition Committee," 53.

97 "They Know," 5.
98 Pringle and Booth, NAC PA-60562.
99 "Of Sixteen Sons," 12 December 1917.
100 NAC PA-148875
101 "World War Mother," 2.
102 Schrader, "Lady Lost Five Sons."
103 There are newspaper references before 1942 that mention mourning women at Armistice Day celebrations but do not refer to the Silver Cross. The *Toronto Daily Star* mentions hundreds of Toronto mothers "giving vent in common to pent up grieving for war stricken sons" ("Mother Bears her Burden," 1927).
104 "Busy Tempo," 4. Jonathan Vance mentions an earlier example of the priority shown to bereaved mothers at the unveiling of the Yarmouth Town and County War Memorial, Thursday, 11 November 1926. These women were given special consideration in the seating arrangements for the ceremony (*Death So Noble*, 149).
105 Nova Scotia, Legislature. *Official Report.*
106 CWM 19800700-005 58C 1 31.3
107 A thorough discussion of the work in which women were involved during the war was included in the women's section of *Saturday Night*'s Dominion Day issue of 1916. It was so full that the magazine published a special issue the following week, on July 8, devoted solely to the work of Canadian nurses ("Dominion Day").
108 CWM 19790335-001 58E 6.
109 CWM 1947–77. 19810790 58E 3.
110 Potter, "World War One Gold Star Mothers," 4.
111 See Eickelman, *Middle East*, 197.
112 From 2002 to 2005 the national representatives of Silver Cross mothers were mothers of the four soldiers killed by "friendly fire" in Afghanistan in 2002.
113 CWM 19790335 001 58E 6. Ottawa Chapter Scrapbook.
114 In contrast to the image of contemplative mourning portrayed in Allward's "The Spirit of Canada" is a memorial in the German cemetery of Vladslo, just a few kilometers from Vimy. *The Mourning Parents* (1932) by Käthe Kollwitz presents a father clutching his arms around himself while the mother bows her head and grasps her cloak tightly with her right hand. It rests in the graveyard where Kollwitz's son Peter was buried after he was killed in the first year of the war. Kollwitz draws out the weight of agony in her image of bereavement rather than pride in sacrifice.

CHAPTER FOUR

1 Yerushalmi, *Zakor Jewish History*.
2 "One Year of Peace," 1.
3 Canada. House of Commons, *Debates*, 6 November 1919: 1835.
4 Owen Chadwick cites this example and two early twentieth-century American examples of the commemorative pause ("Armistice Day," 323).
5 Chadwick, ibid., 325.
6 Homberger, "Story of the Cenotaph," 1430.
7 Canada. House of Commons, *Debates*, 23 May 1921, 3773-4.
8 Thomson, "Commemoration of War," 9.
9 "General Resolutions: Remembrance Day," 25.
10 Ibid.
11 Canada. House of Commons, *Debates*, 18 March, 1931.
12 Thomson, "National Sorrow," 11.
13 "Radio: A Department, " 13.
14 Coppin, "Remembrance Sunday," 527.
15 Chadwick, "Armistice Day," 328.
16 Yerushalmi, *Zakor Jewish History*, 51.
17 Decoration Day was a precursor to Remembrance Day celebrated in parts of Canada. The day began to be celebrated in the United States when, after the Civil War, the relatives of the dead would decorate the graves with flowers.
18 "Mrs. Wood is Dead," 2.
19 Yerushalmi, *Zakor Jewish History*, 49.
20 Bentley, "Monumentalités," 6.
21 Oliver, "Shrine is Dedicated," 1, 3.
22 Pearson, Office of the Parliamentary Curator, file 124928.
23 *Report and Financial Statement for 1917,* as quoted in Boyanoski, *Loring and Wyle*, 19.
24 20 June 1917, as quoted in Boyanoski, *Loring and Wyle*, 21.
25 Sixty-one years after the unveiling, an Interpretive Centre was opened at the Vimy Memorial. The Veterans' Affairs Web site states that the goal of the display is to "wrap the visitor in the atmosphere of Vimy in 1917, drawing on ones' emotions and senses to enhance ones' understanding of the facts" ("Interpretive Centre," 2000). The importance of the interplay between reason and emotion framing the presentation of this memorial is taken into consideration, even down to the level of the placement of the trees in the "theatre" of this historic battlefield. The Commemorative Integrity Statement written by Parks Canada for

Veteran's Affairs acknowledges that the Vimy Memorial Park has been developed in such a way that it "enables dramatic vistas of the monument to approaching visitors, creating a sense of drama and contributing to the spirit of the place" (Desloges, *Conservation and Preservation*, 4.0–11).

26 Walter Allward Artist File, Canadian War Museum Archives.

27 See Hucker, "Lest We Forget," 92.

28 Canadian War Museum Archives, Walter Allward Artist File, vol. 2. Much of this file in the archives is now full of newspaper clippings of reviews of Jane Urquhart's novel *The Stone Carvers* (2001). This fictional account of World War I, its aftermath, and the building of the Vimy Memorial has renewed interest in that period of Canadian history as well as in the monument. Not only are ritual and liturgy important for the memory of historical events, but the drama of fiction and art allows history to appeal to a wider audience, thus keeping it in the public memory.

29 Warner, *Monuments and Maidens*, 277.

30 Ibid., 282.

31 To one side of the crucifixion-style figure stands another man who, by holding his torch high with what looks to be all his strength, reminds the viewer of the lines, "To you from failing hands we throw / The torch; be yours to hold it high" from John McCrae's poem "In Flanders Fields."

32 Drusilla Mason told Paul Chapman the story of how her mother, Edna Moynihan, got the job with Allward (Chapman, *Spirit of Canada*, np).

33 Murray, *Epic of Vimy*, 65.

34 Coo, "Vimy Ceremony," 4.

35 *Epic of Vimy* (1936), published by the *Legionary*, the official national magazine of the Canadian Legion of the British Empire Service League, included information concerning many of the small details of the journey, such as the numbers for the provincial quotas, the names of the pilgrims and their province (or state if they were living in the United States); the cost – $160, which represented a 20% reduction off a third-class fare; a list of pilgrimage equipment, including the blue beret for bereaved relatives; and the khaki beret for ex-sevicemen and women and directions on exactly how to wear them. The cost of the trip was further offset for some of the pilgrims in the form of paid leave. The pilgrims were given reminders concerning their behaviour, urging them to show "typical Canadian cheerfulness." This was thought to be particularly important because of the "shadow of bewildering crises"

hanging over the world at that time (Hundevad, *Guide Book*, 18).

36 Potter, "World War One Gold Star Mothers," 5.

37 Piehler, "The War Dead," 177.

38 Lloyd, *Battlefield Tourism*, 19–25.

39 In Lloyd, ibid., 39.

40 Turner's model of pilgrimages has had a strong influence on subsequent scholars, yet critiques have arisen concerning some of the interpretive concepts Turner used, particularly that of communitas, "the direct, immediate, and total confrontation of human identities." Turner suggests that pilgrims tend to relate to each other with this kind of immediacy through the suppression of their differences (*Ritual Process*, 183). M.J. Sallnow takes the concept of communitas to be actually detrimental to understanding pilgrimages because it tends to "inhibit an appreciation of the contradictions" he finds there ("Communitas Reconsidered," 183). Mary O'Connor, on the other hand, found that although pilgrimages do reinforce some differences, pilgrims are united by a belief in the sacredness of the place they have gone to visit ("Pilgrimage to Magdalena," 375).

41 A point that Mary O'Connor makes in her study of the Mexican pilgrimage to Magdalena is that the rituals involved in it were not related to Church teaching but, rather, fall under the category of folk Catholicism ("Pilgrimage to Magdalena," 371). The Vimy pilgrimage was certainly not a form of folk religion, but the rituals were presided over by both Protestant and Roman Catholics as well as by secular representatives, thus allowing the pilgrimage to expand in meaning beyond the confines of one particular church's interpretation of the event.

42 Turner, "Pilgrimages as Social Processes," 207.

43 Ibid., 208.

44 Sallnow, "Communitas Reconsidered," 188.

45 A pilgrimage of bereaved mothers was organized in Australia with high hopes that it "should be possible to achieve the peace of the world by a union of mothers." But with only four mothers going to the battlefield, that hope did not live long (Lloyd, *Battlefield Tourism*, 196).

46 Bodnar, *Remaking America*, 246.

47 Gosling, *Up and Down Stream*, 223.

48 Bushaway, *Name Upon Name*, 152.

49 *Daily Mail* 12 November 1927, 12, as quoted by Gregory, *Silence of Memory*, 39.

50 Lewell, "My Turn," 9.

51 Lapointe, in Murray, *Epic of Vimy*, 94.

52 Hundevad, *Guide Book*, 9.
53 Murray, *Epic of Vimy*, 126.
54 Ibid.
55 Hundevad, *Guide Book*, 24.
56 Stephen, *Land of Singing Waters*, 124.
57 In Homberger, "The Story of the Cenotaph," 1430.
58 Ibid., 1429.
59 Shipley, *To Mark Our Place*, 191.
60 Both Shipley and Bushaway mention this.
61 Shipley, *To Mark Our Place*, 142.
62 Lloyd mentions that, in England, the development of this secular religious mix in the commemoration did not happen without a struggle. Despite barriers of theological interpretation, the Church of England made an effort to have greater control over the memory of the war by having the Unknown Warrior buried in Westminster Abbey. This was an attempt to create a rival shrine to the cenotaph (*Battlefield Tourism*, 87).

CHAPTER FIVE

1 Hundevad, *Guide Book*, 44.
2 Ware, *Immortal Heritage*, 26.
3 Thucydides, in Hundevad, *Guide Book*, 44.
4 See note 38. The concept of replacement children has a long and wide history as a means of consolation. ·
5 See Loraux, *Mothers in Mourning*, 31–2.
6 Ibid., 19.
7 Ibid., 20.
8 Ibid., 3.
9 Picardie is the region of France in which Péronne lies, in the centre of what was the Western Front.
10 Loraux, *Mothers in Mourning*, 16.
11 Ibid., 98.
12 Gregory, *Silence of Memory*, 21.
13 Ware, *Immortal Heritage*, 23.
14 Ibid., 30.
15 Blunden wrote the introductions to two books on the Commission, the first by Ware in 1937 and the second by Longworth in 1967. In both cases he stressed the novelty of the Commission's work.
16 In Longworth, *Unending Vigil*, xx.
17 Another institution that served the men as equals was Talbot House in Poperinge, Belgium. The house was bought by Neville Talbot in

remembrance of his brother, Gilbert, who had been killed in the war. It was set up as a safe haven for any soldier and is still running as a hostel and museum. Veterans of World War I were travelling there to visit as recently as the last ten years. With help, even those over 100 years old were able to make it up the tiny staircase to the third-floor chapel.

18 Longworth, *Unending Vigil*, 13.
19 Ware, *Immortal Heritage*, 61.
20 Longworth, *Unending Vigil*, 15.
21 Ibid., 29.
22 Gosling, *Up and Down Stream*, 223.
23 Longworth, *Unending Vigil*, 29.
24 Ware, *Immortal Heritage*, 38.
25 Vance, *Death So Noble*, 61.
26 Ibid., 62-3.
27 There were times when soldiers' bodies were exhumed to be placed in a graveyard if their bodies had initially been buried in places where the graves could not be maintained. But, if the graves were near a designated cemetery, they would be left. Many of the cemeteries have a majority of the graves in one spot in rows and a number of single graves in dispersed locations, indicating that the latter stayed where they were initially buried.
28 Campbell, "Graves," 1-2.
29 Ware, *Immortal Heritage*, 36.
30 Hundevad, *Guide Book*, 37.
31 Laqueur, *Memory and Naming*, 161.
32 The Registry of Names provided one other area for the families to present more information about their dead relatives. In each cemetery these books are kept in a small box in the graveyard wall or in a small monument and contain the names of the men buried there together with biographical information submitted by the families.
33 In Ware, *Immortal Heritage*, 54. Lutyens carries on to give details on the measurements of the surfaces and planes of his design, describing how the vertical lines converge at a point $1,801'\ 8''$ above the centre of the spheres. Longworth states that this design was based on a study of the Parthenon (*Unending Vigil*, 36).
34 Gibson and Ward, *Courage Remembered*, 230.
35 The crosses come in four sizes, depending on the size of the cemetery. The smallest are usually on sites where there are forty or more graves (ibid., 219).
36 Kipling, "Recessional 1897," 327.

37 Hadas, *Complete Plays of Aristophanes*, 8.

38 Aristophanes, *Lysistrata*, trans. Lindsay. A voice of one "taxed" in this manner was heard many centuries later when she spoke out after the American Civil War. Julia Ward Howe, author of the "Battle Hymn of the Republic," was also the originator of the celebration of Mother's Day, which in 1872 was called Mother's Peace Day. Although her first claim to fame was her effort to encourage the soldiers during the war, she later questioned the value of war and the role of war mothers. "Why do not the mothers of mankind interfere in these matters, to prevent the waste of that human life of which they alone bear and know the cost?"(Howe, *Reminiscences*, 328). Her efforts to join motherhood with a movement to support peaceful resolutions of conflict were subdued by the common belief that women did not have a place in the political realm (Illick, "Mother's Day 2000"). The version of Mother's Day that we now celebrate in Canada had its origins in Mothers' Work Days in the early twentieth century. The American Anna Jarvis proposed that mothers be involved in a day of community service to help improve their world (Illick, ibid.).

39 Murphy et al., "What Twelve Canadian Women Hope," 7.

40 Ibid., 33.

41 Ibid., 6.

42 Gregory, *Silence of Memory*, 122.

43 Vance, *Death So Noble*, 218.

44 Ibid.

45 In Pearson, *Four Faces of Peace*, 13.

46 The historian and former head of the Canadian War Museum, Jack Granatstein, sees this "ownership" taking place as early as 1960, when troops were sent to the Congo (Granatstein and Lavender, *Shadows of War*, 188).

47 "Canada and Peace Support Operations."

48 Murphy et al., "What Twelve Canadian Women Hope," 7.

49 Quoted in Minai, *Women in Islam*, 76.

50 The history of consolation writings goes back to ancient times in the Mediterranean world. The Roman and Greek writers Seneca, Lucretius, and Plutarch patterned their consolation writings after Crantor, but the tradition extended to Homeric times and through the tragedies and public funeral ceremonies of Athens (De Lacy and Einarson, *Plutarch's Moralia*, 7:577). The call for patience when facing death is found in the Muslim literary genre of comfort stories designed for consolation, dating back to the Middle Ages. Within this group of

writings existed a subgenre of comforting tales dealing specifically with bereaved parents (Gil'adi, "'The Child was small,'" 367). The Islamic comfort books were so popular that they "entered Jewish literature via Judeo-Arabic, either in the form of themes and genres or – by way of translation – whole works" (Brinner, Introduction, xvii). A number of medieval Christian writers referred to the death of a child as a divine mercy. In doing so they rebuked parents for excessive weeping, but at the same time consoled them with the assurance of a life in Paradise for their child. In *Childhood in the Middle Ages* (151–2), Shulamith Shahar mentions Jean Gerson, Humbert de Romans, John Wyclif, and Thomas Cantimpratanus as examples of those who condemned bereaved parents for their show of grief, as it indicated a rebellion against God's will.

CONCLUSION

1 Lincoln, "Lincoln's Letter to Mrs. Bixby."
2 Her words were quoted in an article by Alan Philps written for the *Daily Telegraph* and reprinted in the *Ottawa Citizen* 17 June 2002:5.
3 Halton, "His Majesty Voices Hope," 1.

BIBLIOGRAPHY

ARCHIVAL MATERIAL
Archives of Ontario
"To Women Workers." RG 7-12-0-11. In file: Employment, General,
   1918–1919
"To the Women of Canada." C 233-2-0-4-199

Canadian War Museum Archives
"Canada on Vimy Ridge" [booklet]. Reprinted from *The Canada Year
   Book*, Ottawa: J.O. Patenaude, 1936
Recruiting posters: 56-04-11-083; 56-04-11-087; 65-04-11-091; 56-05-11-
   072; 56-04-11-044; AN 19820554-006
Remembrance Association Silver Cross Women of Canada. Minutes of
   National Conventions 1947-77: 19810790 58E 3; 19800700-005 58C
   130.3; 19800700-005 58C I 31.3
Ottawa Chapter Scrapbook 1954-78: 19790335-001 58E 6
Walter Allward Artist File

National Archives of Canada
PA-148875 [photograph] Mrs Charlotte Susan Wood

University of Ottawa Archives
The Memorial Chamber in the Peace Tower, House of Parliament Archives [pamphlet]. 01-CRC-1931-76

BOOKS AND PERIODICAL ARTICLES

[118th Battalion Poster]. *Berlin News Record,* 15 January 1916, 8.

Abbott, John S.C. *Mother At Home; or The Principles of Maternal Duty.* New York: American Tract Society, 1833.

Afshar, Haleh. "Khomeini's Teachings and Their Implications for Women." *Feminist Review* 12 (1982) 1: 59–73.

Agence France Presse. *Iranian.* 15 December 1997. "Tehran's vast monument to a deadly conflict." 15 December 1997. www.iranian.com/News/Dec97/bzahra (accessed 02/05/06).

"Al-Khansa." Witness-Pioneer Virtual Islamic Organization. www.witness pioneer.org/vil/Articles/companion/18_umar_bin_al_khattab.htm (accessed: 30/04/2006).

Ames, Herbert Brown. *Our National Benefaction: A Review of the Canadian Patriotic Fund.* Ottawa: n.p., 1915.

Arnup, Katherine. "Educating Mothers: Government Advice for Women in the Inter-War Years." In *Delivering Motherhood: Maternal Ideologies and Practices in the 19th and 20th Centuries,* edited by Katherine Arnup, Andree Levesque and Ruth Roach Pierson, 190-211. London: Routledge, 1990.

Ayoub, Mahmoud. *Redemptive Suffering in Islam.* The Hague: Mouton Publishers, 1978.

Bajwa, Sandeep. "Mata Gujari ji, Biography." Sikh History Online, 2004. www.sikh-history.com/sikhhist/martyrs/matagujari.html (accessed 02/05/06).

Baktash, Mayel. "Ta'ziyeh and its Philosophy." In *Ta'ziyeh: Ritual and Drama in Iran,* edited by Peter Chelkowski, 95–120. New York: New York University Press, 1979.

Barker, Felix, and Peter Jackson. *London: 2000 years of a city and its people.* London: Papermac, 1974.

Beatty, David Pierce. *The Vimy Pilgrimage July 1936: From the diary of Florence Murdock Amherst, Nova Scotia.* Amherst: Acadian Printing, 1987.

Beckett, Gillian. "Resident Named Last Silver Cross Mother of Millennium." *Western Wheel* (Okotoks, Alberta), 10 November 1999.

Behrman, Cynthia F. Introduction to *Raemaekers' Cartoons with Accompanying Notes by Well-Known English Writers,* 5–12. New York: Garland Publishing, 1971.

Bentley, D.M.R. "Monumentalités." *Canadian Poetry* (1993): 32: 1-16.

Bevington, David, ed. *Medieval Drama*. Boston: Houghton Mifflin, 1975.

Binyon, Lawrence. "For the Fallen" *Times* (London), 21 September 1914. www.spartacus.schoolnet.co.uk/FWWbinyon.htm (accessed 25/09/02).

Blewett, Jean. "Mothers' Recognition Committee." *Everywoman's World*, September 1917, 53.

Bliss, J.M. " The Methodist Church and World War One." In *Conscription 1917*, edited by Carl Berger, 39–59. Toronto: University of Toronto Press, 1969.

Bloch, Marc. *The Historian's Craft*. Peter Putnam trans. Manchester: Manchester University Press, 1954.

Bodnar, John. *Remaking America: Public Memory, Commemoration, and Patriotism in the Twentieth Century*. Princeton: Princeton University Press, 1992.

"Books of Remembrance." Government of Canada, Veterans Affairs. www.vac-acc.gc.ca/remembers/sub.cfm?source=collections/books/history#fwwbook (accessed 02/05/06).

Bowersock, Glen. *Martyrdom and Rome*. Cambridge: Cambridge University Press, 1995.

Boyanoski, Christine. *Loring and Wyle: Sculptors' Legacy*. Toronto: Art Gallery of Ontario, 1987.

Boyarin, Daniel. *Dying for God: Martyrdom and the Making of Christianity and Judiasm*. Stanford, California: Stanford University Press, 1999.

Brandon, Laura. "History as Monument: The Sculptures on the Vimy Memorial." Ottawa: Canadian War Museum. *Dispatches*, issue 11. January 2000. www.warmuseum.ca/cwm/disp/diso11_e.html (accessed 09/05/00).

– *"Resurrection: images of belief in Canada's War Memorials."* Unpublished paper, 1998.

Briffault, Robert. *The Mothers: A Study of the Origins of Sentiments and Institutions*, vol. 3. 1927. Reprint, London: George Allen and Unwin, 1969.

Brinner, William M. Introduction to *An Elegant Composition Concerning Relief After Adversity*, by Nissim ben Jacob Ibn Shahin. New Haven: Yale University Press, 1977.

Brockett, L.P. *The Camp, the Battlefield and the Hospital*. Philadelphia: National Publishing Co., 1866.

– *Women's Work in the Civil War: A Record of the Heroism, Patriotism and Patience of Women in the Civil War*. Philadelphia: Zeigler, McCurdy & Co., 1867.

Brophy, John, and Eric Partridge. *Songs and Slang of the British Soldier: 1914–1918.* London: Eric Partridge Scholartis Press, 1930.

Bryce, Viscount James. *Report of the Committee on Alleged German Outrages.* Ottawa: Government Printing Bureau, 1916.

Buitenhuis, Peter. *The Great War of Words: British, American, and Canadian Propaganda and Fiction, 1914–1933.* Vancouver: University of British Columbia Press, 1987.

Bushaway, Bob. "Name Upon Name: The Great War and Remembrance." In *Myths of England,* edited by Roy Porter. Cambridge: Polity Press, 1992.

"Busy Tempo of Toronto Slows as Citizens Pay Tribute to War Dead on Remembrance Day." *Globe and Mail* (Toronto), 12 November 1942, 4.

Campbell, Jennifer. "Graves: Commission to Fight Airport Plan." *Ottawa Citizen,* 8 March 2002, A1–2.

Canada. House of Commons. *Debates,* April–June 1869, vol. 2; 24 February 1915, 402; 23 May 1921, 3773–4; 6 November 1919, 1835; 18 March 1931.

"Canada Must Have Mothers' Pensions: As a Record of Service Rendered and a Safeguard for the Nation of Tomorrow." *Everywoman's World,* November 1917, 3.

Canada. Office of the Chief Electoral Officer of Canada. *A History of the Vote in Canada.* Ottawa: Minister of Public Works and Government Services Canada, 1997.

Canada. Parks Canada. *Canadian National Vimy Memorial Conservation and Presentation Plan.* Ottawa: Parks Canada, 1997.

Canada. Privy Council Office. *Order Respecting the Award of the Memorial Cross to Mothers and Widows of Sailors and Soldiers – World War One.* PC 1976-2724, 2.

"Canada and Peace Support Operations." Government of Canada, Department of Foreign Affairs International Trade. Updated 2003/02/06. www.dfait-maeci.gc.ca/peacekeeping/menu-en.asp (accessed 02/05/06).

"Canadian Crucified by the Germans?" [editorial] *Globe* (Toronto), May 1915, 13.

Canadian Patriotic Fund. *A Message to the Canadian Soldier's Wife* [pamphlet]. Ottawa: Canadian Patriotic Fund, 15 January 1916.

Canadian War Records Office. *Art and War: Canadian War Memorials.* Introduction by P.G. Konody. London: Colour, 1919.

"Canadian Women Opposed to Conscription." [editorial] *Everywoman's World,* May 1917, 19.

Chadwick, Owen. "Armistice Day." *Theology* (1976) 79: 322–30.

Chapman, Paul. 1990. *The Spirit of Canada – Uncloaked*. www.mapleleaf legacy.org/The_Spirit_Of_Canada_Uncloaked.htm (accessed 02/05/06).

Chief Electoral Officer of Canada. *A History of the Vote in Canada*. Ottawa: Public Works, 1997.

Chelkowski, Peter. "Ta'ziyeh: Indigenous Avant-Garde Theatre of Iran." In *Ta'ziyeh: Ritual and Drama in Iran*, edited by Peter Chelkowski, 1–11. New York: New York University Press, 1979.

Chown, Samuel Dwight. Pacificism at Chautauqua." *Christian Guardian*, 23 August 1916, 13.

Chubin, Shahram, and Charles Tripp. *Iran and Iraq at War*. London: I.B. Tauris and Co., 1988.

Clayton, Ann. *Chavasse – Double VC*. London: Leo Cooper, 1992.

Connor, Ralph. *The Major*. Toronto: McClelland & Stewart, 1917.

– *Sky Pilot in No Man's Land*. London: Hodder, 1919.

Coo, A.E.H. "Vimy Ceremony." *Winnipeg Free Press*, 28 July 1936, 4.

Coppard, George. *With a Machine Gun to Cambrai*. London: Imperial War Museum, 1969.

Coppin, Ronald. "Remembrance Sunday." *Theology* 68 (1965): 525–30.

Craig, Grace Morris. *But This is Our War*. Toronto: University of Toronto Press, 1981.

Craig, John. *The Years of Agony: 1910/1920*. Toronto: Natural Science of Canada, 1977.

Cunneen, Sally. *In Search of Mary: The Woman and The Symbol*. New York: Ballantine Books, 1996.

Desbarats, Peter, and Mosher, Terry. *The Hecklers: A History of Canadian Political Cartooning and a Cartoonists' History of Canada*, 1979.

Desloges, Y., L. Dick, A. Jankowski, A. Powter, D. Panton, J. Vandenberg, and A. Viel, for Parks Canada National Historic Sites. *Conservation and Presentation Plan for the Canadian National Vimy Memorial*. Ottawa: Veterans Affairs Canada, 1997.

DeYoung, Terri. "Love, Death, and the Ghost of Al-Khansa': The Modern Female Poetic Voice in Fadwa Tuqan's Elegies for Her Brother Ibrahim." In *Tradition, Modernity and Post Modernity in Arabic Literature*, edited by Kamal Abdel-Malek and Wael Hallaq, 45–77. Leiden: Brill, 2000.

"Dominion Day." *Saturday Night* (Toronto), 1 July 1916.

Doran, Robert. "The Martyr: A Synoptic View of the Mother and Her Seven Sons." In *Ideal Figures in Ancient Judaism*, edited by J. Collins, 189–221. California: Scholars Press, 1980.

– *Temple Propaganda: The Purpose and Character of 2 Maccabees*. Washington: The Catholic Biblical Association of America, Monograph Series; 12 (1981).

Dorjahn, Alfred P. *Political Forgiveness in Old Athens: The Amnesty of 403 BC*. New York: AMS Press, 1970.

Dubé, Audrey. *Biblical References Centre Block Parliament Buildings; Senate Chamber Canadian War Memorial Paintings; John Pearson's Description of the Three Windows in the Memorial Chamber*. Ottawa: Office of the Parliamentary Curator, 1997.

Eickelman, Dale F. *The Middle East: An Anthropological Approach*. New Jersey: Prentice Hall, 1989.

Eidelberg, Shlomo, trans. and ed. *The Jews and the Crusaders: The Hebrew Chronicles of the First and Second Crusades*. Madison: University of Wisconsin Press, 1977.

Elshtain, Jean Bethke. *Women and War*. New York: Basic Books, 1987.

Farmer, William Reuben. *Maccabees, Zealots, and Josephus*. New York: Columbia University Press, 1956.

Feldman, Seth (writer), and Sinclair Lewis (host). *Canada's Golgotha*. CBC *Ideas* [radio program]. Toronto: Canadian Broadcasting Corporation, 1987.

Fenech, L.E. "The Mother as Heroic Icon: Perceptions of Sikh Motherhood in the Late Nineteenth and Early Twentieth Centuries." Unpublished paper, 2001.

– *Martyrdom in the Sikh Tradition: Playing the 'Game of Love.'* Delhi: Oxford University Press, 2000.

Fernea, Elizabeth Warnock, and Basima Qattan Bezirgan. *Middle Eastern Muslim Women Speak*. Austin: University of Texas Press, 1977.

Finkel, M. "Playing War." *New York Times Magazine*, 24 December 2000, 30–7.

Folis, Tom. Review of *The Major*, by Ralph Connor. *Saturday Night* (Toronto), 5 January 1918, 7.

Freeman, Bill, and Nielsen, Richard. *Far From Home: Canadians in the First World War*. Toronto: McGraw-Hill Ryerson, 1999.

Frend, William, H.C. "Blandina and Perpetua: Two Early Christian Heroines." In *Les Martyrs de Lyons (177)*, edited by M.J. Rouge and M.R. Turcan, 167–77. Paris: Centre National de la Recherche Scientifique, 1978.

– *Martyrdom and Persecution in the Early Church*. Oxford: Basil Blackwell, 1965.

Friedl, Erika. "Ideal Womanhood in Postrevolutionary Iran." In *Mixed*

Blessings: Gender and Religious Fundamentalism Cross Culturally, edited by Judy Brink and Joan Mencher, 143–59. New York: Routledge, 1997.

Frye, Northrop. *The Secular Scripture: A Study of the Structure of Romance.* Cambridge: Harvard University Press, 1979.

Fussell, Paul. "The Fate of Chivalry, and the Assault Upon Mother." In *Thank God for the Atom Bomb and Other Essays,* 221–48. New York: Summit Books, 1988.

– *The Great War and Modern Memory.* Oxford: Oxford University Press, 2000.

Gabrieli, F. 1991. "Al-Khansa." *Encyclopaedia of Islam* 4 1991: 1027.

Geller, Gloria. "The Wartimes Elections Act of 1917 and the Canadian Women's Movement." *Atlantis* 2 (1976): 88–106.

"General Resolutions: Remembrance Day." *The Legionary,* December 1929, 25.

Gibson, Edwin, and Kingsley Ward. *Courage Remembered.* Toronto: McClelland & Stewart, 1989.

Gil'adi, Avner. "'The Child was small ... not so the grief for him': Sources, Structure, and Content of al-Sakhawi's Consolation Treatise for Bereaved Parents." *Poetics Today* 14 (1993): 367–86.

Gilbert, Sandra. "Soldier's Heart: Literary Men, Literary Women, and the Great War." In *Behind the Lines: Gender and the Two World Wars,* edited by M.R. Higgonnet, J. Jenson, S. Michel, and N.C. Weitz, 197–226. New Haven: Yale University Press, 1987.

Godwin, George. *Why Stay We Here?* London: Philip Allan & Co., 1930.

Goldstein, Jonathan A. *II Maccabees. The Anchor Bible,* vol. 41A. Garden City: Doubleday, 1983.

Gordon, Charles. *Postscript to Adventure: The Autobiography of Ralph Connor.* New York: Farrar & Rinehart, 1938.

Gosling, Harry. *Up and Down Stream.* London: Methuen, 1927.

Granatstein, J., L. Granatstein, and Douglas Lavender. *Shadows of War and Faces of Peace: Canada's Peacekeepers.* Toronto: Key Porter Books, 1992.

Gray, Charlotte. "No Idol Industry Here." In *Great Questions of Canada,* edited by Rudyard Griffiths, 81–5. Toronto: Stoddart, 2000.

Graves, Robert. *Goodbye To All That.* 1920. Reprint, London: Cassell, 1966.

Great Britain. Committee on Alleged German Outrages. *Evidence and Documents Laid Before the Committee on Alleged German Outrages.* Ottawa: Government Printing Bureau, 1916.

Gregory, Adrian. *The Silence of Memory.* Oxford: Berg, 1994.

Gullace, Nicoletta F. "White Feathers and Wounded Men: Female Patriotism and the Memory of the Great War." *Journal of British Studies* 36 (1997): 178–206.

Gwyn, Sandra. *Tapestry of War*. Toronto: Harper Collins: 1992.

Habiballah, Nahed. "Interviews with Mothers of Martyrs of the AQSA Intifada." *Arab Studies Quarterly* 26 (2004): 15–30.

Hadas, Moses. Introduction to *The Complete Plays of Aristophanes*. Toronto: Bantam Books, 1962.

Hadduck, Charles B. *Christian Education: Containing Valuable Practical Suggestions in the Training of Children for Usefulness and Heaven*. New York: American Tract Society, n.d.

Hale, Katherine. *Canada's Peace Tower and Memorial Chamber, Designed by John A. Pearson: a Record and Interpretation*. Toronto: Mundy-Goodfellow, 1935.

Halton, M.H. "His Majesty Voices Hope 'It Shall Never Happen Again,' to Mrs. Wood." *Winnipeg Free Press*, 28 July 1936, 1.

Hanna, W.J. "They Shall Not Pass," in *Everywoman's World*, October 1917, 27.

Hindle, Wilfrid. *The Morning Post, 1772–1937; Portrait of a Newspaper*. London: Routledge, 1937.

Homberger, Eric. "The Story of the Cenotaph." *Times Literary Supplement,* 12 November 1976, 1429–30.

Hopkins, J. Castell. *The Canadian Annual Review of Public Affairs, 1917*. Toronto: The Canadian Annual Review, 1918.

Horne, John, and Kramer, Alan. *German Atrocities, 1914: A History of Denial*. New Haven: Yale University Press, 2001.

Howe, Julia Ward. *Reminiscences: 1819–1899*. New York: Negro Universities Press, 1969.

Hucker, Jacqueline. "Lest We Forget: National Memorials to Canada's First World Dead." Ottawa: Parks Canada. *Journal of the Society for the Study of Architecture in Canada* 23 (1998): 3.

Hughes, E.A. "I am a Proud Mother This Christmas." *Everywoman's World*, December 1915, 11.

Hundevad, John. *Guide Book of The Pilgrimage to Vimy and the Battlefields July–August 1936*. Montreal: Legionary, 1936

Ibrahim, Youssef M. "Burning Cause: A Rush to Martyrdom Gives Iran Advantage In War Against Iraq." *Wall Street Journal*, 9 December 1983.

"If Union Government is Beaten the Joy Bells Will Ring in Berlin." *Saturday Night*, 15 December 1917, 2.

"If ye Break Faith with Us Who Die." Ottawa *Evening Journal,* 15 December 1917, 1.

Illick, Hilary. "Mother's Day 2000: Up and At 'Em, Mama!" *AlterNet*, 1 April 2000. www.alternet.org/story/13 (accessed 18/08/02).

"Interpretive Centre at the Canadian National Vimy Memorial" [information sheet]. www.vac-acc.gc.ca/general/sub.cfm?source=memorials/ww1mem/vimy/interpret (accessed 09/05/00).

Jocelyn, Arthur. *Awards of Honour: The Orders, Decorations, Medals and Awards of Great Britian and the Commonwealth From Edward III to Elizabeth II*. London" Adam and Charles Black, 1956.

Jowett, Garth S., and Victoria O'Donnell. *Propaganda and Persuasion*. Newbury Park, California: Sage Publications, 1992.

Juergensmeyer, Mark. *Terror in the Mind of God: The Global Rise of Religious Violence*. Berkeley: University of California Press, 2000.

Kawar, Amal. *Daughters of Palestine*. Albany, NY: State University of New York Press, 1996.

Kennedy, Mark. "The Crucified Canadian – A War Myth?" *Ottawa Citizen*, 12 November 1991, A1.

Ketterson, A.L. *On Active Service: Ideals of Canada's Fighting Men*. Toronto: McClelland, Stewart & Goodchild, 1918.

Kipling, Rudyard. "Recessional 1897." In *Rudyard Kipling: Compete Verse*. New York: Anchor Press, 1989.

Klausner, S. "Martyrdom." *Encyclopedia of Religion* 9 (1987): 230–8.

Knightley, Phillip. "The Disinformation Campaign." 4 October, 2001. www.guardian.co.uk/Archive/Article/0,4273,4270014,00.html (accessed 05/05/04).

Konody, P.G. *Art and War: Canadian War Memorials*. London: Colour, 1919.

Laqueur, Thomas W. "Memory and Naming in the Great War." In *Commemorations: The Politics of National Identity*, edited by John R. Gillis, 150–67. Princeton: Princeton University Press, 1994.

Lasswell, Harold Dwight. *Propaganda Technique in the World War*. New York: Garland Publishing, 1972.

Leacock, Stephen. "What of Soldiers'Pensions?" *Everywoman's World*, January 1918, 3.

Lewell, Maryanne. "My Turn at Vimy Ridge." *Maclean's*, 20 November 2000, 9.

Lincoln, Abraham. "Lincoln's Letter to Mrs. Bixby (1864)." American Historical Documents, 1000-1904. www.aol.bartleby.com/43/ (accessed 28/02/02).

Little, Margaret Jane Hillyard. *'No Car, No Radio, No Liquor Permit': The Moral Regulation of Single Mothers in Ontario, 1920–1997*. Toronto: Oxford University, 1998.

Lloyd, David W. *Battlefield Tourism: Pilgrimage and the Commemoration of the Great War in Britain, Australia and Canada, 1919–1939.* Oxford: Berg, 1998.

Longworth, Philip. *The Unending Vigil: A History of the Commonwealth War Graves Commission 1917–1967.* London: Constable, 1967.

Loraux, Nicole. *Mothers in Mourning.* Translated by Corinne Pache. Ithaca: Cornell University Press, 1998.

Lowrey, Harold. "His Unknown Mother: The Story of a Victoria Cross." *Everywoman's World*, February 1918, 6.

MacDonagh, Michael. *In London During the Great War: Diary of a Journalist.* London: Eyre and Spottiswoode, 1935.

MacDonald, Captain J.H. "The Cause of God." *Times* (London) 3 May 1916, 6.

Mahmood, Cynthia Keppley. *Fighting for Faith and Nation: Dialogues with Sikh Militants.* Philadelphia: University of Pennsylvania Press, 1996.

Marshall, David. *Secularizing the Faith: Canadian Protestant Clergy and the Crisis of Belief, 1850–1940.* Toronto: University of Toronto Press, 1992.

Mason, A.E.W. *The Four Feathers.* 1902. Reprint, London: Nash and Grayson, 1921.

McCallum, Margaret E. "Assistance to Veterans and their Dependants: Steps on the Way to the Administrative State, 1914–1929." In *Canadian Perspectives on Law and Society: Issues in Legal History*, edited by W. Wesley Pue and Barry Wright, 157–79. Ottawa: Carleton University Press, 1988.

McClung, Nellie L. *In Times Like These.* Toronto: George J. McLeod, 1917.
– *Next of Kin: Those Who Wait and Wonder.* Toronto: Thomas Allen, 1917.

McMartin, Pete. "Kin of Crucified Soldier Want Depiction Shown." *Vancouver Sun*, 14 November 1991.

Minai, Naila. *Women in Islam.* New York: Seaview Books, 1981.

Mitchell, David. *Women on the Warpath: the Story of the Women of the First World War.* London: Jonathan Cape, 1965.

Mogannam, Matiel. *The Arab Woman and the Palestine Problem.* London: Herbert Joseph, 1937.

Montgomery, L.M. *Rilla of Ingleside.* Toronto: McClelland & Stewart, 1920.

Moore, Mary Macleod. "What This Christmas Means to Canadians." *Saturday Night* (Toronto), 25 December 1915.

Morris, Philip H., ed. *The Canadian Patriotic Fund: A Record of its Activities from 1914–1919.* Ottawa?: n.p., 1919.

Morton, Desmond. *Silent Battle: Canadian Prisoners of War in Germany 1914–1919.* Toronto: Lester Publishing, 1992.

"Mother Bears her Burden Alone on Armistice Day: Mourns Loss of Two Sons." *Toronto Daily Star,* 12 November 1927.

"Mother-love." [editorial] *Everywoman's World*, February 1915, 3.

"A Mother's Answer to 'A Common Soldier.'" London *Morning Post*, 14 August 1916.

"Mrs. Wood is Dead: World War Mother Succumbs As Big Guns Roar." *Winnipeg Free Press,* 12 October 1939, 2.

Murphy, Emily, L.A. Hamilton, L. Laurier, E.A. McGillivray Knowles, L.M. Montgomery, J. Carnochan, M. Saunders, et al. "What Twelve Canadian Women Hope to See as the Outcome of the War." *Everywoman's World*, April 1915, 6, 7, 33.

Murray, W.W., ed. *The Epic of Vimy.* Ottawa: The Legionary, 1936.

Musurillo, Herbert. *The Acts of the Christian Martyrs.* Oxford: Clarendon Press, 1972.

Najar, Orayb Aref and Kitty Warnock. *Portraits of Palestinian Women.* Salt Lake City: University of Utah Press, 1992.

Nasir, Anwar. "Khomeini Faces Crunch as Gulf War Drags On." *Far Eastern Economic Review.* 30 October 1986, 36–7.

"National Committee of Patriotic Service." *Saturday Night*, 27 March 1915, 23.

Newman, Barbara. *From Virile Woman to Woman Christ.* Philadelphia: University of Pennsylvania Press, 1995.

Newman, Peter C. "We'd Rather Be Clark Kent." In *Great Questions of Canada,* edited by Rudyard Griffiths, 86–90. Toronto: Stoddart, 2000.

Nicholson, G.W.L. *Official History of the Canadian Army in the First World War: Canadian Expeditionary Force 1914–1919.* Ottawa: Ministry of National Defence, 1962.

Norman, Barbara. "The Music on the Home Front: Canadian Sheet Music of the First World War." Library and Archives Canada. www.nlc-bnc.ca/sheetmusic/m5-170-e.html (accessed 01/29/01).

Norris, Armine. *Mainly for Mother.* Toronto: Ryerson Press, 1919.

Nova Scotia. Legislature. *Official Report of Debates: Hansard.* Halifax. Resolution no. 674, 18 November 1996, 1970.

Novak, Dagmar. *Dubious Glory: The Two World Wars and the Canadian Novel.* New York: Peter Lang, 2000.

O'Connor, Mary. "The Pilgrimage to Magdalena." In *Anthropology of Religion: A Handbook,* edited by Stephen D. Glazier, 369–89. Westport, Conn.: Praeger, 1999.

"Of Sixteen Sons, Ten are Killed." *Vancouver Sun*, 12 December 1917.

Oliver, Dean, and Brandon, Laura. *Canvas of War: Painting the Canadian*

Experience 1914–1945. Vancouver: Douglas & McIntyre, 2000.

Oliver, Douglas. R. "Shrine is Dedicated to Noble Canadians by Heir to Throne." *Globe* (Toronto), 4 August 1927, 1, 3.

Omid, Homa. Islam and the Post-Revolutionary State in Iran. New York: St Martin's Press. 1995.

"One Year of Peace – Winnipeg Today Celebrates Armistice Anniversary." *Winnipeg Tribune,* 11 November 1919, 1, 2.

Ontario Election Act, 1914. Ch. 8, s. 2 (14), (15).

Orbinski, James. *Taking a Stand: The Ethics of Intervention.* CBC *Ideas* [radio program]. Toronto: Canadian Broadcasting Corporation, 2001.

Orczy, Baroness. "To the Women of England, the Answer to 'What can I do?'" London *Daily Mail* 4 September 1914.

Origen. *Prayer and Exhortation to Martyrdom.* Translated and annotated by John J. O'Meara. New York: Newman Press, 1954.

Oxenham, John. *High Altars: The Battle-fields of France and Flanders As I Saw Them.* London: Methuen & Co., 1918.

Patterson, T.A. "An Ex-Chaplain on Chaplains, Religion and War." *Saturday Night* (Toronto), 29 March 1919, 3.

Pearson, John. Personal Communication to W.L. Mackenzie King. Office of the Parliamentary Curator, file 124928. 24 June 1927.

Pearson, Lester B. *The Four Faces of Peace and the International Outlook.* Edited by Sherleigh G. Pierson. Toronto: McClelland & Stewart, 1964.

Peel, Mrs. C.S. *How We Lived Then 1914–1918.* London: John Lane, 1929.

Pelly, Lewis. *The Miracle Play of Hasan and Husain Collected from Oral Tradition.* London: Wm. H. Allen and Co., 1879.

Peteet, Julie. "Authenticity and Gender." In *Arab Women: Old Boundaries and New Frontiers,* edited by Judith Tucker, 49–62. Bloomington: Indiana University Press, 1993.

Philps, Alan. "I am not losing a son … you are going to paradise." *Ottawa Citizen,* 17 June 2002, 5.

Piehler, G. Kurt. "The War Dead and the Gold Star: American Commemoration of the First World War." In *Commemorations: The Politics of National Identity,* edited by John R. Gillis, 168–85. Princeton: Princeton University Press, 1994.

Pierce, John. "Constructing Memory: The Vimy Memorial. *Canadian Military History* 1 (1992): 5–8.

Plumptre, Mrs. "Canadian Women and the 'Peace' Congress." *Saturday Night* (Toronto), 1 May 1915, 21.

Plutarch. *Plutarch's Moralia.* Translated by P. De Lacy and B. Einarson. London: William Heinemann, 1949.

Ponsonby, Arthur. *Falsehood in War-Time*. New York: E.P. Dutton, 1928.

Potter, Constance. "World War I Gold Star Mothers Pilgrimages, Part I." *Prologue: Quarterly of the National Archives and Records Administration*, 31 (1999): 1–8. www.archives.gov/publications/prologue /1999/ summer/gold-star-mothers-1.html(accessed 04/04/06).

Prescott, John F. *In Flanders Fields: The Story of John McCrae*. Erin, Ontario: Boston Mills Press, 1985.

Punch. *Mr. Punch's History of the Great War*. London: Cassell and Company, 1919.

"Radio: A Department for Those Who Are 'Listening In.'" *Globe* (Toronto), 11 November 1931.

Raemaekers, Louis. *Raemaekers Cartoons*. London: Hodder & Stoughton, 1915.

– *Raemaekers' Cartoons with Accompanying Notes by Well-known English Writers*. 1916. Reprint, New York: Garland, 1971.

Read, Daphne, ed. *The Great War and Canadian Society: An Oral History*. Introduction by Russell Hann. Toronto: New Hogtown Press, 1978.

Remarque, Erich Maria. *All Quiet on the Western Front*. A.W. Wheen, trans. London: G.P. Putnam's Sons, 1929.

"Remembrance Day: Historical Origins." Vancouver, B.C.: Inglewood Care Centre. www.inglewoodcarecentre.com.other.remembrance day2.htm (accessed 23/03/01).

Renison, Robert John. *Canada at War; a Record of Heroism and Achievement, 1914–1918*. Toronto: Canadian Annual Review, 1919.

Richardson, Gertrude. *Canadian Forward*, 24 February 1918, 6.

– "The Cruelty of Conscription: A Letter to Women." *Canadian Forward*, 10 July 1917, 5.

– "Motherhood and War." *Canadian Forward*, 24 November 1917, 5.

Rickards, Maurice, and Moody, Michael. *The First World War: Ephemera, Mementos, Documents*. London: Jupiter Books, 1975.

Rowley, Storer H. "Soldiers in a Holy War; Children Serve in Army of Desperation." *Chicago Tribune*, 2 February 1996.

Rubio, Mary, and Elizabeth Waterston, eds. *The Selected Journals of L.M. Montgomery*, vol. 2. Toronto: Oxford University Press, 1987.

Ryder, Rowland. *Edith Cavell*. London: Hamish Hamilton, 1975.

Salisbury, Joyce E. *Perpetua's Passion*. New York: Routledge, 1997.

Sallnow, N.J. "Communitas Reconsidered: The Sociology of Andean Pilgrimage." In *Religion in Culture and Society*, edited by John R. Bowen, 182–200. Boston: Allyn and Bacon, 1998.

Schrader, Ceris. "Lady Lost Five Sons: Canada's War Mother and the Great

War." www.hellfire-corner.demon.co.uk/ceris.htm (accessed 6/29/02).

Scott, Canon Frederick George. *The Great War as I Saw It*. Toronto: F.D. Goodchild, 1922.

Shahar, Shulamith. *Childhood in the Middle Ages*. London: Routledge, 1990.

Shaw, George Bernard. *Seven Plays by Bernard Shaw with Prefaces and Notes*. 1923. Reprint, New York: Dodd, Mead, 1951.

Shipley, Robert. *To Mark Our Place: A History of Canadian War Memorials*. Toronto: NC Press, 1987.

Sifton, Mrs C. "About People You Know." *Everywoman's World*, September 1917, 17.

"Silver Cross Mother." Veterans Affairs Canada Online: www.vac-acc.gc.ca/general/sub.cfm?source=collections/books/silver (accessed: 19/01/01).

"Silver Crosses For Bereaved Mothers." *Everywoman's World*, December 1916, 3.

Singh, Amar. "Anecdotes from Sikh History, no. 4." In *Stirring Stories of the Heroism of Sikh Women and the Martyrdom of a Sikh Youth*, 3–35. Lahore: Bhai Amar Singh and the Khalsa Agency, 1906.

Singh, Bhagat Lakshman. *Sikh Martyrs*. Lahore: S. Jiwan Singh, 1923.

Singh, Jagdish. *Supreme Sacrifice of Young Souls*. Amritsar: Dharam Parchar Committee, 1997.

Singh, Satbir. *Illustrated Martyrdom Tradition*. Amritsar: S. Manjit Singh, 1983.

Stephen, A.M. *The Land of Singing Waters*. London: J.M. Dent and Sons, 1927.

Stopford, Francis. Introduction to *Raemaekers' Cartoons with Accompanying Notes by Well-Known English Writers*. 1916. Reprint, New York: Garland Publishing, 1971.

Strum, Philippa. *The Women are Marching: the Second Sex and the Palestinian Revolution*. New York: Lawrence Hill Books, 1992.

"They Know the Meaning of Sacrifice: Nine Canadian Mothers Who Have Sent Forty-Seven Sons to Fight." *Everywoman's World*, August 1917, 5.

Thomson, D. "National Sorrow, National Pride: Commemoration of War in Canada, 1918–1945." *Journal of Canadian Studies* 6 (1995): 5–27.

Thurer, Shari. *The Myths of Motherhood: How Culture Reinvents Motherhood*. Boston: Houghton Mifflin, 1994.

Tippett, Maria. *Art at the Service of War*. Toronto: University of Toronto Press, 1984.

Tuchman, Barbara. *The Guns of August*. New York: Macmillan, 1962.

Turner, Victor. *The ritual process: Structure and anti-structure*. London: Routledge & Kegan Paul, 1969.

– 1974. "Pilgrimages as Social Processes." In *Dramas, Fields and Metaphors*, edited by Victor Turner, 166–230. Ithaca: Cornell University Press, 1974.

Tertullian. Apology, ca. 200. Translated by S. Thelwall. n.d. www.grtbooks.com (accessed 11/05/06).

Tydeman, William. "An Introduction to Medieval English Theatre." In *The Cambridge Companion to Medieval English Theatre*, edited by Richard Beadle, 1–36. Cambridge: Cambridge University Press, 1994.

Tylee, Claire M. "'Maleness Run Riot' – The Great War and Women's Resistance to Militarism." *Women's Studies International Forum* 11 (1988): 199–210.

Urquhart, Jane. *The Stone Carvers*. Toronto: McClelland & Stewart, 2001.

Vaglieri, L. Veccia. 1995. "Al-Husayn." *Encyclopaedia of Islam* 4 (1995): 607–15.

– "Fatima." *Encyclopaedia of Islam* 3 (1995): 841–50.

Vance, Jonathan. *Death So Noble*. Vancouver: University of British Columbia Press, 2000.

Vaughan, Bernard. "The Very Stones Cry Out." In *Raemaekers' Cartoons with Accompanying Notes by Well-known English Writers*. 1916. Reprint, New York: Garland, 1971, 20.

Ware, Fabian. *The Immortal Heritage: An Account of the Work and Policy of The Imperial War Graves Commission during twenty years 1917–1937*. Cambridge: Cambridge University Press, 1937.

Warner, Marina. *Alone of All Her Sex: The Myth and the Cult of the Virgin Mary*. New York: Random House, 1983.

– *Monuments & Maidens: The Allegory of the Female Form*. London: Weidenfeld and Nicolson, 1985.

Wetherell, J. E., ed. *The Great War in Verse and Prose*. Toronto: A.T. Wilgress, 1919.

"When Bowed Head is Proudly Held." *Globe* (Toronto), 8 May 1916, 10.

Williams, Rev. George. "Victory Loans." *Globe* (Toronto), 10 November 1919, 1.

Wilson, Barbara M. *Ontario and the First World War 1914–1918: A Collection of Documents*. Toronto: University of Toronto Press, 1977.

Wilson, Keith. *Charles William Gordon*. Winnipeg: Peguis Publishers, 1981.

Winnington-Ingram, A.F. *Fifty Years' Work in London*. London: Longmans, Green, 1940.

– "A Word of Cheer." *Christian World Pulpit*, 8 December 1915, 353–5.

Winslow, Donald F. "The Maccabean Martyrs: Early Christian Attitudes."
  Judaism 23 (1974): 78–86.

Witt, Elizabeth A. *Contrary Marys in Medieval English and French Drama.*
  New York: Peter Lang, 1995.

Wodson, H.M. *Private Warwick: Musings of a Canuck in Khaki.* Toronto:
  The Sovereign Press, 1915.

"Women's Parliament of Canada [Prohibition]." [editorial] *Everywoman's
  World,* June 1917.

"Women's Parliament of Canada [Conscription]." [editorial] *Everywoman's
  World,* May 1917, 19.

"World War Mother Succumbs As Big Guns Roar Once More." *Winnipeg
  Free Press,* 12 October 1939, 2.

Yarshater, Ehsan. "Ta'ziyeh and Pre-Islamic Mourning Rites." In *Ta'ziyeh:
  Ritual and Drama in Iran,* edited by Peter Chelkowski, 88–94. New
  York: New York University Press, 1979.

Yerushalmi, Yosef Hayim. *Zakor Jewish History and Jewish Memory.* Seattle:
  University of Washington Press, 1982.

Young, Alan R. "'We throw the torch': Canadian Memorials of the Great
  War and the Mythology of Heroic Sacrifice." *Journal of Canadian
  Studies* 24 (1990): 5–28.

Young, Robin Darling. "The 'Woman with the Soul of Abraham': Traditions
  about the Mother of the Maccabean Martyrs." In *Women Like This:
  New Perspectives on Jewish Women in the Greco-Roman World,* edited
  by Amy-Jill Levine, 67–81. Atlanta, Ga.: Scholars Press, 1991.

INDEX